random thoughts
get real with God, others, and yourself

random thoughts

get real with God, others, and yourself

Steve Russo

a devotional for young adults

BARBOUR
PUBLISHING

Every day there are tons of random options to fill our waking hours. We can send text messages. . .eat. . .talk on the phone. . .watch TV. . .text. . .listen to music. . .eat. . .hang out with friends. . .text. . .go to school. . .do homework. . .text. . .eat. . .play Halo. . .work. . .play sports. . . .

You get the idea—there's a lot of stuff that burns up our time. And if we aren't careful to stay focused, we can let average random things—which aren't necessarily bad—keep us from getting to more important things. We all have the same number of hours in a day. The difference is how we fill the minutes that become hours that turn into days.

So what is the most important thing we should be doing each day? Here's a hint: It's more significant than eating and sleeping, going to school, or hanging out with our friends. The time we put into this "activity" will affect how we see and experience life. And it will give us wisdom for making good decisions, encouragement when we're feeling down, direction for our lives, power to face tough times, and peace in the middle of any major drama we may be experiencing. What's weird is even though there are huge benefits to completing this "important activity," a lot of us struggle with making it happen consistently.

By now you probably realize what I'm talking about. This most important activity is knowing God intimately. It should be the most important priority of our lives—chances are you probably already knew this, but is it true for you? The kind of relationship we have with God will influence every part of who we are and how we live. God knows that apart from Him we can accomplish nothing, but through Jesus we can do amazing things (see John 15:5; Philippians 4:13).

What an awesome random thought—we can know the

God of the universe personally and intimately. We can be as close to Him as we want to be. God wants to know us but won't force it to happen. It's our choice. For this to happen we have to crave God and go after Him with everything we've got. Paul, an early follower of Jesus, used these words to describe the desire that he had: "I want to know Christ and experience the mighty power that raised him from the dead" (Philippians 3:10). Not a bad idea for me and you.

Pursuing God takes time. The more you get to know Him, the more you want to know about Him. So the natural response would be to spend more time reading the Bible and praying.

This book is meant to help you get to know God personally and closely. Each day will give you an opportunity to look clearly at God, others, and yourself through the Bible as a lens or filter.

Try investing a few minutes each day for a month. See what happens when you purposefully pursue God. My guess is that you'll want more "random thoughts" to help you get real with God, others, and yourself. Then get ready to experience life as you've never known it before.

Hungry
Steve Russo

The word *appetite* usually makes us think about food. (For me, most of the time it's an Italian dish along with some kind of chocolate for dessert.) But did you know the root meaning of the word *appetite* is "to seek"? An appetite is any strong desire that drives us to go after something.

We can crave all kinds of things: food, love, attention, intimacy, power, money. . . . The appetite for these things can be good or bad—and sometimes both. What do you have an appetite for? Have you ever thought about what would happen if you had an appetite for God?

Maybe you feel discouraged because you think you have failed God in some way. Like allowing peer pressure to coerce you into sin. Or maybe you've tried so many times to overcome a sinful habit, you've given up.

Jesus has a word for you and me: Don't give up! If you truly want a life that pleases God, keep seeking after it. You'll find it!

When your driving appetite is to please God, He'll help you to live just how you desire to live. . .and to be satisfied in the process. Keep in mind what Jesus said in John 6:35: "I am the bread of life. Whoever comes to me will never be hungry again. Whoever believes in me will never be thirsty."

Just as we need "bread" every day to sustain us, we also need spiritual food.

GET REAL

What hunger is holding you back from growing spiritually? Jesus must be invited to be part of our daily lives if we are to experience the satisfaction that He planned for us to have.

What Matters Most?

Steve Russo

What means more to you than anything else in your life? Is it your family or friends? How about your grades, your achievements, or your stuff? These are all good things, and they should matter to you. But one thing should come before any of them: knowing Jesus. When you meet Jesus, everything that used to be at the top of your priority list will fall to the bottom. Once you experience Him, nothing else comes close!

Sometimes it's hard to understand, but the Bible says that compared to knowing Christ, everything else in life is junk. The apostle Paul wrote, "I once thought these things were valuable, but now I consider them worthless because of what Christ has done. Yes, everything else is worthless when compared with the infinite value of knowing Christ Jesus my Lord. For his sake I have discarded everything else, counting it all as garbage, so that I could gain Christ" (Philippians 3:7–8).

Does knowing Jesus mean this much to you? No one wants you to stop loving your family, to hate your friends, or to harm your body. But knowing Christ more intimately should be first on your priority list.

Making this happen means changing the way you think and the way you live.

GET REAL

Are you willing to rearrange your jammed schedule to spend a few minutes a day alone with God in prayer and Bible study? How about changing your goals and dreams to be consistent with what God wants for you? Whatever you have to give up is worth the sacrifice to know Jesus more closely.

God's Dream for You

Steve Russo

Did you know that God has dreams for your life? He has some amazing thoughts for your existence on this planet.

In Psalm 37:4–5 we learn the responsibility we have for God's dreams for us to become reality: "Take delight in the LORD, and he will give you your heart's desires. Commit everything you do to the LORD. Trust him, and he will help you." *Delighting in God* means experiencing amazing pleasure when we're with Him. This happens when we get to know Him more and more as we spend time with Him. Grasping how much He loves us will give us pleasure and satisfaction.

Committing ourselves to God means we entrust everything—our dreams, our relationships, and our possessions—to His control and guidance. We learn to trust in Him because we believe that He has a better plan for us than we do for ourselves.

Unfortunately, surrendering everything seems bizarre in our culture. No one wants to give up control because of the risk that things won't work out the way we want them to. But that's the deception of our self-centered culture. Things work just the opposite in the kingdom of God. Because He created us—down to the smallest detail—God knows what's best for us. So unless we surrender control of everything to Him, we risk losing out on experiencing the lasting fulfillment and satisfaction He planned for us to have.

GET REAL

What area of your life do you need to surrender to God today? Let go and allow God to give you His dreams and plans for your life.

Power Source

Steve Russo

The photographer had captured an unbelievable sight in the midst of horrible devastation caused by a Midwestern tornado. Right in the middle of the picture was a telephone pole with a drinking straw driven through it. How amazing to think that a flimsy plastic straw could be pushed through a rugged, seasoned wood telephone pole. How could this happen? The awesome power of the tornado had forced the flimsy straw right through the pole. The straw had no power of its own.

We're a lot like that straw—with no real power of our own. But we can have all the power we could ever need to get us through the confusion and trials of everyday life. Paul, a follower of Jesus, described it this way: "We now have this light shining in our hearts, but we ourselves are like fragile clay jars containing this great treasure. This makes it clear that our great power is from God, not from ourselves" (2 Corinthians 4:7).

It's mind-numbing to think that God's power is living inside us. He gives us power not only to help us live but also to do His work even though we are like breakable clay jars.

Many messages in our culture tell us we have the greatest power within us—we only have to unleash it. This isn't true unless we have a relationship with Jesus. It's living for and like Jesus that connects us to the Power Source.

GET REAL

Knowing that our power is God's and not ours should motivate us to stay connected to the Source. How's your daily contact with God?

GPS

Lesha Campbell

Today it seems like we're all headed somewhere and somewhere fast. How do we get there, what do we do along the way, and what's up when we arrive? And my personal favorite, what are we doing here?

Most of us don't use road maps anymore—is the word *road map* even in our vocabulary? Most of us have that crazy little gadget called a GPS on the dashboard or on our smartphone to lead us in the right direction. We don't even have to think, just listen and follow the verbal command. And if we get off track, no worries; the GPS recalculates our route. *Whew!* What did we do without this crazy gadget?

Well, nothing is new under the sun. God used His own GPS system earlier in human history. For example, one time the Israelites were guided through their trek in the wilderness by an "organic GPS." Check out Exodus 13:21: "The Lord guided them by a pillar of cloud during the daytime, and by a pillar of fire at night. So they could travel either by day or night" (TLB). Pretty amazing that this happened way before any of the high-tech gadgets we now have available to us.

Strange how humans invent gadgets, thinking they're so smart, and all along God already had His own supernatural guidance system in place. Weird, don't you think?

God wants to be our GPS. When we get off track, He will recalculate our route. All we need to do is listen and follow His lead.

GET REAL

Whose GPS is on your internal dashboard—yours or God's? When your internal compass gets distorted, how does it reset—by your friends or something bigger? To stay on course, check out God's GPS.

Be Quiet
Ron Merrell

I was at a park trying to do some reading. About every thirty seconds, I was interrupted by a flock of birds that would chirp loudly and then stop. Loud chirping. Total silence. Loud chirping. Total silence.

This cycle repeated for about ten minutes. Finally, I couldn't stand it any longer. I looked up to find out why they were screeching one minute and then quiet the next. It turned out they would chirp as loud as they could when they were all roosting in a tree, but as they all flew from one tree to another, they'd go silent. When they'd land, they'd resume chirping.

That's when it hit me. Sometimes to really fly, you've got to shut up. I think most of us talk too much and listen too little. God has some amazing flying for us to do, but we're too busy, too noisy, and too preoccupied with our own words.

I love 1 Kings 19, where God visits Elijah in a whisper. He doesn't show up in rushing wind, earthquake, or fire. God comes in the gentle whisper. But we can't hear His whisper unless we pay attention to the advice of Psalm 46:10, where the Lord encourages us, "Be still, and know that I am God!"

Don't let the volume of your life get so loud that you can't hear the whispers of God. It's in those whispers that some of His best plans and dreams for your life might come.

GET REAL

Go somewhere quiet and take some deep breaths. Just listen to what God has to say to you. Don't talk. Pray. Breathe. Dream. Stop. Pray. Listen.

What Lies Beneath

Chris Haidet

Have you ever had to deal with annoying, self-centered people? Maybe it's a friend, sibling, or acquaintance who needs to be the center of attention and the topic of every conversation. When they aren't, they pitch a fit and drive everyone else nuts.

How are we supposed to respond? Do we ignore them? Do we one-up them? Or do we forgive and try to understand? The Bible says, "Be kind to each other, tenderhearted, forgiving one another, just as God through Christ has forgiven you" (Ephesians 4:32).

A few years back, I was lying in the emergency room with what turned out to be an acute case of "false alarm," when across the ER I heard an annoying little girl who would *not* stop crying. I could not understand why her parents would allow this. Didn't they know she was annoying other people here—like me? Well, after a few hours, I was given a "princess" bandage and told to go home. On my way out, I witnessed something I will never forget. The tiny, crying girl was being held by her frightened parents as a doctor was slowly removing a six-inch nail that was lodged deep in her nose. My heart sank as, through the confused eyes of the little girl, I now saw the cause of the painful screams. Turns out, the annoying, self-centered person was me.

GET REAL

The next time someone annoys you, remember, there might be a painful cause just under the surface that you don't see. When exasperation hits, try taking a moment to forgive, and then reflect on Christ's forgiveness in your own life.

It's *Not* You

Patrick Dunn

No matter what time it is, you are hungry. Well, at least your ego is. We feed our egos every day just by looking around us and looking in the mirror. The problem is, some of us can get full of ourselves.

It's easy to do. Food for your ego is everywhere: You get a hot new phone, a tricked-out car; you're a member of the popular crowd. Maybe your parents are wealthy. Maybe you're a star athlete, a straight-A student, the lead in the school musical. Or you look in the mirror and see perfect abs, the body everyone wishes they had, or supermodel hair.

Maybe it's time for your ego to go on a diet.

God makes it very clear that everything comes from Him. He created it all. He created you. He put you right where you are—in your school, in your family (yes, even with your annoying little brother). He gave you your looks, your talents, your—well, everything. That's what makes it easy to go on an ego diet—it's *not* you. Habakkuk 3:19 (NIV) says, "The Sovereign LORD is my strength; he makes my feet like the feet of a deer, he enables me to tread on the heights." Nothing you have or are is because of *you*. It's because of God. Remember that and your ego stays slim.

GET REAL

The next time you get an A, score the winning goal, get on the homecoming court, or are feeling full of yourself, what will you do? Why not feed your ego a piece of humble pie and thank God for enabling you to soar?

Is Seeing Really Believing?

Mike Thune

Have you ever been on a rock-climbing trip? If not, perhaps you've heard people say how difficult it actually is to come back *down* the rock cliff. Instead of slowly climbing back down, you have to let go of the rock, lean back, and do a sort of guided fall in coordination with your belayer (the person who holds your rope at the bottom). For me, it was amazingly hard to trust that the system in place for getting me down would, in fact, get me down. And this was even after I had *seen* my belayer put on his and my safety gear, *felt* the rope's strength, and *knew* that my belayer was committed to my safe return. The passage that says, "For we live by believing and not by seeing" (2 Corinthians 5:7), suddenly became even more real to me.

Some people claim that "seeing is believing" and that they won't put their faith in a God they can't see. But since we often find it difficult to trust in things we *can* see, the demand to "see" before one believes seems more like a convenient excuse for unbelief than anything else.

We have "faith" in things we see every day—that the chair we're sitting in won't collapse, that the pilot of the plane we're flying in will get us safely to our destination, and so on. If we place our faith in all these things *in* life, how much more should we trust the character and goodness of the God who *gave us* life?

GET REAL

Take a leap of faith today. Totally believe in the God who pours His blessings on those who believe even though they do not see.

Toxic People

Ramona Richards

What a fool! That's what people thought when they heard the story of Abigail, Nabal, and David in 1 Samuel 25. In fact, that's what *Nabal* means: fool. No mistaking the lack of common sense in this man. He was rich, but he treated his servants horribly. And when David, who was traveling with four hundred armed men, asked for food, Nabal insulted him. Not a smart move.

Now imagine being married to this guy, stuck with a fool who could get you killed. But Abigail, Nabal's wife, was smart; she appealed to David's sense of justice and his relationship with God. And, in turn, she listened to his advice.

Sooner or later, we all get stuck with a "Nabal" in our lives. A toxic friend. Someone who drags us down, makes life harder than it is already, repays us "evil for good" (1 Samuel 25:21). So how do you break away from the toxicity without creating more drama?

It's never easy, but toxic friends can destroy other relationships, pull down your grades, even mess with your faith. You have to act. Sometimes following Abigail's path—seeking wise counsel and having patience about working things out—works. Sometimes you can ease out of the "friendship." Other times you just have to face it head-on, drama or not.

It may be hard, but it'll be short-term pain for a long-term gain—a peaceful life.

GET REAL

Being friends with toxic people isn't worth the trouble they create. Ask God to help you break off any toxic friendships and move on to a smoother journey.

Will It Matter Tomorrow?

Melanie Stiles

Life can move fast. Friends, school, and family pull us lots of directions every day. Sometimes it appears simpler just to go with the flow. Like when I was hanging with friends and they decided to go chill at someone's house for the evening. I knew there were other important things I needed to be doing (mainly studying for exams).

My brain did flip-flops around the decision. Go along with the crowd and they wouldn't have to sidetrack to take me home first. The decision was tougher than I wanted it to be. I was tempted to forget studying and take my chances on exams. What would you do? Take a look at Romans 14:23 (MSG): "But if you're not sure, if you notice that you are acting in ways inconsistent with what you believe—some days trying to impose your opinions on others, other days just trying to please them—then you know that you're out of line. If the way you live isn't consistent with what you believe, then it's wrong."

Sure, I wanted to be with my friends, but deep down I hoped they would understand if I did what was right for me. They might tease me a little, but there would be other nights to party. I made decent grades on my finals (yeah, probably because I studied instead of partying) and went out with my friends to celebrate afterward.

GET REAL

Even if you're feeling rushed, take the time you need to weigh your options beyond the moment. Think about what really matters, and be consistent with what you believe.

Anger Always Costs
Susie Shellenberger

I'm usually mesmerized by the athletic prowess with which Serena Williams graces the tennis court. But during the U.S. Open on September 12, 2009, I stared at the TV screen in disbelief as the pro was called on a foot fault and launched a verbal tirade of expletives at the line judge. She had already been penalized earlier for racquet abuse. Her reaction to the foot fault cost her a point penalty as well as the set, the match, and her chance at the championship title.

Was Serena justified in being angry? Probably so. The replay showed her foot was *not* over the line when she served. Her words and actions, however, *did* cross the line. She had a right to be angry. She didn't have a right to curse the line judge.

The Bible has a lot to say about anger. . .and our words. Check this out: "Your attitude should be the kind that was shown us by Jesus Christ" (Philippians 2:5 TLB).

But what about when we're justified in being angry? Jesus certainly had a right to be angry when He was falsely accused and then crucified. But He laid the anger aside for the greater purpose of paying for our sins. When we allow Christ to truly become *Lord* of our lives, we surrender everything to Him. Including our rights.

GET REAL

The next time you're angry—even though you may be justified—strive to see beyond the immediate and look instead for the greater purpose. Dealing with anger inappropriately will always cost you something. It cost Serena $10,500 and the championship. What could it cost you?

Pruning
Rusty Wright

When I was growing up in Miami, Florida, hurricanes would disrupt our lives occasionally. I kind of enjoyed them because I got to miss school.

One summer, Hurricane Donna blew through with a vengeance and knocked down an avocado tree that my younger brother had planted and cared for. A gardening specialist recommended to my father that we "cut back" the tree to allow it to grow and prosper. He offered to do the work.

The next day when I returned from school, I was astounded. What once had been a full, luxuriant tree was now just a skinny trunk with only a few barren branches. When he said he wanted to cut it back, he *really* meant cut it back!

But over time, the tree grew, flourished, and bore fruit. Cutting back or pruning the tree was the key that allowed it to thrive. Jesus said the same often is true in our lives: "I am the true grapevine, and my Father is the gardener. He cuts off every branch of mine that doesn't produce fruit, and he prunes the branches that do bear fruit so they will produce even more" (John 15:1–2).

GET REAL

Have you gone through difficulties that did not seem of your own making? Maybe God is using them to prune you to help you become more like Him. How you react to suffering makes all the difference. You can bemoan problems as obstacles or welcome them as opportunities to grow in faith and see God work.

Driven by Eternity
Zoro

Jesus wants us to tell others how they can have a relationship with Him. But it doesn't seem like very many of us take Him seriously. One tactic the devil uses to keep us ineffective in sharing our faith is fear. Another one is apathy about how others struggle through life and then what happens to them when they die. Jesus was talking about this problem in Matthew 9:37, when He told His followers that "the harvest is great, but the workers are few."

Our faith is not really complete until we have true compassion for those who don't know Jesus. God wants us to see them as He does. Remember, the one thing you and I won't be able to do in heaven is lead other people to Jesus. Earth is the only place we have this incredible privilege.

Unfortunately, many of us are more concerned with gaining the approval of friends than doing what pleases God. In order to be bold and to be obedient to God in sharing our faith, we should live with an eternal perspective. That means we don't value the things of the world too highly but recognize how important the things of God are. Someday we will answer to God alone for what we've done: "Look, I am coming soon, bringing my reward with me to repay all people according to their deeds" (Revelation 22:12).

We will be held accountable for everything—including whether or not we told others about Jesus.

GET REAL

Pray and ask God to help you be bold and courageous as you share His offer of eternal life with your family and friends.

Everyone Needs a Hero

Steve Russo

Who's your hero? I was speaking at a high school retreat and asked that question. One guy said, "Dude—my heroes are metal bands. I like going to concerts and trying to hang out backstage with the musicians. It's cool to watch the bands drinking and smoking and getting wasted. That's why I wanna be in a metal band someday." That guy needs some new heroes, don't you think?

What makes a hero? Someone who plays monster guitar or throws a football like a rocket? A celebrity whose face is on gigantic billboards or some guy who's made a bazillion bucks designing the hottest video game on the market? We have anti-heroes today, and it's tough to find real ones. Sometimes it's hard to distinguish between a hero and a celebrity. Celebrities are people who make the news; heroes are people who make history.

Heroes are admired for their achievements and demand respect. A true hero has substance and character. Heroes can motivate you to do things you otherwise might not do.

Jesus is the ultimate Hero and the One we should model our lives after. John, who walked with Jesus, reminds us why we should do this: "Those who say they live in God should live their lives as Jesus did" (1 John 2:6). Is Jesus your hero? You can admire others for their talents and abilities, but Jesus is the One we should try to be like.

GET REAL

Think about your heroes—the people you admire most and look up to.

- What do you like about them?
- Do you respect them?
- Are they people who have substance?

Stick with 'Em

Ramona Richards

Ever cheer for a losing team? How about standing by a friend when everyone thinks he's wrong? Or when things are really rough in her life?

Being loyal—remaining faithful—sounds a lot easier than it is. When life is good and everyone's happy, it's easy. But we all know that sometimes the tough stuff is just waiting to pounce on us. Parents divorce, friends lie, people close to us get really sick. That's when people can be quick to turn their backs.

In the first chapter of Ruth, Naomi's life turns ugly in a hurry. Grieving and trying to get back home to family, Naomi tries to send Ruth and Orpah back to their families as well. But Ruth decides to stick with her. Look at what she says in verses 16–17: "Don't ask me to leave you and turn back. Wherever you go, I will go; wherever you live, I will live. Your people will be my people, and your God will be my God. Wherever you die, I will die, and there I will be buried. May the Lord punish me severely if I allow anything but death to separate us!"

Ruth's words are often used in wedding vows, as two people promise to stand by each other no matter what life tosses at them. Ruth's loyalty is a picture of how God never leaves us. He's there wherever we go.

God never meant for us to be alone, and when we choose our friends wisely and stick by them, we can form bonds that last a lifetime. Like Ruth's care for Naomi, the love and support of a faithful friend makes life not just tolerable, but amazing.

GET REAL

Think about your family and close friends. Is anyone dealing with some tough life stuff, but you've abandoned them? Ask them to forgive you and then stand by them.

Opinion versus Truth

Nicole O'Dell

What's the *best* song ever written? If you asked three of your friends, would they have the same answer as you? Probably not. Would that make them wrong? Of course not! It's all about taste and opinion.

What about something more spiritual? Is Jesus Christ the only way to get to heaven? If you asked your friends *that* question, would they all have the same answer? If they didn't, would it make them wrong? This time it's more than just an opinion. It's about truth.

Having personal preferences in regard to music is one thing. But when you consider the quality of life on this planet as well as the reality of eternal life, personal opinions can only go so far. When it comes to the deep stuff that really matters, it's important for you to know the truth—in this case, biblical truth.

Today's cry for tolerance wants to extend the freedom of opinion to things like the nature of God and different paths by which we can reach Him. When eternity is at stake, we can't sit by and neglect to share with our family and friends the truth of God's Word. Jesus made it crystal clear in John 14:6 when He said, "I am the way, the truth, and the life. No one can come to the Father except through me."

Jesus left no room for discussion or opinion. Remember, you can't make someone believe. It's the responsibility of the Holy Spirit to convict people of their need for Jesus. Don't be afraid to share God's truth, but do it in love and with grace.

GET REAL

It's okay to let your friends have a different favorite song than you—even if their choice makes you cringe. But don't let them continue on a path in life that leads to an eternity spent without God. Ask God to give you courage and gentleness as you share His truth.

Standing Out in the Crowd
Dale Robert Hicks

There are people in the world who want to express their individuality by the way they dress, the color and cut of their hair, or the things they do to their bodies. The problem is that others see the unique way that we express ourselves and think it's cool, so they do it, too. Before long, what we have done to indicate that we are our own person becomes something everyone is doing. Desiring to be different isn't wrong, but we need to know why we are standing out in the crowd.

The Bible tells us how and why God wants us to be different: "But now you must be holy in everything you do, just as God who chose you is holy. For the Scriptures say, 'You must be holy because I am holy'" (1 Peter 1:15–16).

As a Christ follower, you want to be different from the world around you, just like God is different. You want the things you say and do, and the person you are, to look like God and not the world or other people. You want to be different as God is different. God is unique and without equal, and that's what His followers should strive for as well.

GET REAL

How are you different from the people around you? Do you look and act more like Jesus or like the people of this world? Be unique because He is unique. Thank God for your differences, and ask Him to help you be more like Him.

Balcony vs. Basement
Rich Thune

I heard a speaker talk about two different kinds of people in the world. One group she referred to as *balcony people*. These are the ones who are seated above us—like in a huge balcony—and they are constantly encouraging us. They're like the people described in Hebrews 11 who are great examples of faith. They've all died, but they're role models of faith to the rest of us as we struggle through life. If they could talk to us, they would say, "Hang in there! You can make it just like we did." They would try to lift us up—not drag us down!

The other group is known as *basement people*. These are ones who are critical. From their lower vantage point, they criticize everybody else and are constantly putting them down. They're negative and try to drag us down—not lift us up!

God wants us to be balcony people and to surround ourselves with other balcony people. To do so, we need to focus on the good and positive things in others, rather than focusing on the negative. We can help those around us and help ourselves by following the advice Paul gave to believers living in Thessalonica: "So encourage each other and build each other up, just as you are already doing" (1 Thessalonians 5:11).

GET REAL

What kind of person are you? How would your friends describe you? Deep down, what kind of person do you want to be? Ask God to help you do what's necessary in your life to be a "balcony person."

Mind Food

Steve Russo

What do you feed your mind? Everything you watch, read, and listen to is mind food. It shapes what you think, feel, and do. We live in a media-saturated culture that has a huge influence on our lives. Several dozen hours a month are spent occupied with media. Anything we're exposed to on this level has got to be affecting us, right?

Check the major themes in popular media: sex, violence, rebellion, suicide, alternative lifestyles, and the occult. Look around your community or on your campus and you can see the effects. Listening to music, watching a DVD, playing a game, or logging online can't make you do anything, but it can form your worldview and eventually your lifestyle.

Being a sponge—soaking up everything available into our minds—isn't healthy. God has given us an amazing filter to use. Look at Philippians 4:8: "And now, dear brothers and sisters, one final thing. Fix your thoughts on what is true, and honorable, and right, and pure, and lovely, and admirable. Think about things that are excellent and worthy of praise."

Evaluate the content of songs, games, DVDs, and websites to see how it measures up to this verse. What we put into our minds will come out in words and actions.

GET REAL

How many hours do you spend each day engaged in media (music, Internet, games, and movies/TV)? How much time daily do you spend on spiritual growth (Bible study, prayer, etc.)? What kind of food is your mind feasting on the most? Ask God to help you be more sensitive about your media diet.

Pesky People
Melanie Stiles

Have you ever been around a person who continually seems to find ways to irritate you? There's the guy who butts into conversations, saying stuff he has no business saying. Or maybe the girl who sticks her nose into your life without permission, oftentimes making difficult situations worse with her gossip.

Well, you're not alone in encountering pesky people. There's at least one in every crowd. No matter how much you try to avoid them, sooner or later it's you they are talking to or about. Retaliation is often our first plan of action. After all, it wasn't you who started this, so a few choice words to set them straight are in order. Or are they?

Peter asked Jesus what to do about pesky people in Matthew 18:21–22: "Then Peter came to him and asked, 'Lord, how often should I forgive someone who sins against me? Seven times?' 'No, not seven times,' Jesus replied, 'but seventy times seven!' "

As annoying as these situations can be, we can do ourselves a favor by considering a few things before we follow through with revenge. Will responding in a harsh way make the situation any better? We might feel great for a minute, but that feeling will pass quickly, and then what? Grace and forgiveness are two of the hardest but most important aspects of our character to develop.

GET REAL

Chances are that sometime this week you'll encounter someone who slights you. Instead of lashing out, try forgiving them. Even though it's tough, let it go and give it to God.

Superheroes
Doug Jones

Having played a few comic book characters on film, I often wonder why we are so fascinated with superheroes. Sure, they are
great fun to watch as they fly through the air and fight off bad guys
with their superpowers, but what makes us idolize them?

We need heroes in real life, people we can look up to, admire, pattern ourselves after, and feel safe with. We often find
heroes in our parents, siblings, teachers, mentors, coaches, and
best friends. I've had several such heroes throughout my life,
and there's one thing they all have in common: qualities that reflect my ultimate Superhero—Jesus Christ.

Jesus gave us a blueprint for how we are supposed to live
and care for each other. He is also that protector we long for.
Jesus said, "My prayer is not that you take them out of the world
but that you protect them from the evil one" (John 17:15 NIV). If
our real-life supervillain is the "evil one," aka Satan, then isn't it
comforting to know we have a Superhero who can defeat the
villain every time?

GET REAL

Let Jesus be seen in your behavior, as those around you
might need a Superhero today.

The Power of Words

Danny Ray

It's amazing what two little words can do to totally make someone's day. You can change the outcome of a person's entire day simply by saying two words: "Thank you."

I remember a time when I got some amazing customer service from a woman who was obviously having a horrible day. She had one customer after another who didn't like the answers she was giving them. Each customer took out their anger on her with harsh words and ugly stares. By the time I got to her, she was literally starting to tear up. She did a great job of helping me, despite how she felt; and as I shook her hand before I left, I said, "Thank you. You are doing an amazing job."

The smile on her face told me everything I needed to know: Those simple words had changed her day. All it takes is one person to show a little kindness and appreciation to make a whole day different. Consider this verse from God's Word: "And let the peace that comes from Christ rule in your hearts. For as members of one body you are called to live in peace. And always be thankful" (Colossians 3:15).

Maybe that's why God tells us more than forty times in the Bible to "give thanks."

GET REAL

Make it your goal to thank ten people today. Keep track by using the notepad on your smartphone.

Pursue the Bible

Nicole O'Dell

Have you ever noticed how a football player pursues the ball? Reckless abandon, crazy hot pursuit, and disregard for logic and personal safety. They trust in the safeguards that their coach provides for them, like shoulder pads and a helmet. They look to their teammates to offer some help and protection from the opposing team. What would happen if you went after knowing God's Word in the same way?

The writer of Psalm 42 doesn't use football as an analogy, but the language is just as vivid. Let these words sink in: "As the deer longs for streams of water, so I long for you, O God. I thirst for God, the living God. When can I go and stand before him?" (vv. 1–2).

Do you pursue studying the Bible with a strong hunger and thirst? Imagine how different your relationship with God and your life might be if you did.

Try it. Study the Bible with passion, hot pursuit, and hunger. Don't let anything or anyone stand in your way of getting to the goal of intimately knowing the living God.

Look around for others at church and on your campus who are going all-out for God's Word. They're pursuing the same prize and serving the same Coach. Lean on them for support, and look to them for guidance. Let them carry you when you're weak and encourage you when you're strong.

GET REAL

As in football, it takes discipline, time, and commitment to reach the goal of knowing God and His Word. It starts with setting aside consistent time each week to be alone with Him. Start today.

Take a Chance

Ramona Richards

What would you love to do but you just haven't had the courage? Try out for a play or for the football team? How about applying for a great job but you don't think you have the experience? Ever felt the need to stand up for something you value or a friend, but you were afraid of being trash-talked?

Ever risk your life for a cause?

Ouch. Truth is, most of us haven't. And we won't be asked to. Most of us live in a place where it's not all that risky to take a political or religious stand. Even so, we can hesitate to step out of our comfort zone. We prefer the known to the unknown.

This is human. Even Moses in the Old Testament didn't want to go talk to Pharaoh. After all, Moses stuttered. How embarrassing and potentially tragic it would be to speak for God and trip over your own tongue. But he obeyed and did it anyway. Another person in the Old Testament, Esther, stepped out of her comfort zone as well. After Esther's cousin Mordecai said to her, "Who knows if perhaps you were made queen for just such a time as this?" (Esther 4:14), she risked her life to save her people.

Stepping out of your comfort zone, even in a small way, is a good thing. It forces you to look beyond yourself and your abilities. It provides a new view of other people, places, and events. Don't be afraid to take a chance.

GET REAL

Do you need to step out of your comfort zone at home or school? Who knows? You may have been called to do something much bigger than you think.

Are All Religions Really the Same?

Steve Russo

I've lost count of how many times I've heard someone say, "All religions are basically the same. They all lead to God."

Just ask people in different faith groups if all religions are basically the same. The response will be a resounding "no." For example, Wiccans believe you can choose your favorite traits for a god and goddess. Buddhism has no god or type of final existence. The Hindu's god is impersonal, but it can be approached through countless deities. Allah, the Muslims' god, is personal. . .but there are no idols or other ways of representing him. There's no forgiveness or supernatural help in Buddhism and Hinduism, only cold-blooded karma. But the God of Christianity is personal. He completely forgives sin and offers supernatural help for life's problems.

The most significant difference among religions is how you become acceptable to God. Most religions emphasize keeping their teachings to be fulfilled or reborn. This emphasis is miles apart from the grace of Christianity. People cannot make themselves acceptable to God. The God of Christianity longs to have a relationship with us and makes this possible only through the shed blood of Jesus.

The only path to God is through a personal relationship with Jesus Christ. He made it very clear in John 14:6: "I am the way, the truth, and the life. No one can come to the Father except through me." Jesus is the only One who can bridge the gap between a holy God and sinful people.

GET REAL

Honestly compare Jesus to all other religious leaders. When you do, there will be no doubt in your mind why you should choose to follow Him.

Now What?!

Patrick Dunn

Here's a question you're going to hear at least 75,000 more times: "What are you going to do after you graduate?"

Your friends may seem to have it all together while you don't have a clue—and you're secretly worried you'll work forever at Burrito Castle.

Life will give you a lot of "I don't knows." I had mine after high school *and* college. Graduating with honors, I tucked my cap and gown away and promptly rushed off to my job at a drugstore, where I put on a green vest that loudly announced, "Hi, I feel continually humiliated!"

For another year, my college degree and I stocked pet food, pushed shopping carts, and mopped up spills. I remember crying out to God, searching for answers. Was I wasting my talents? What about my dreams? . . . Now what?!

But here's something I learned. These waiting periods are a great time to focus on other areas of your life, set goals, and then do something really crazy—trust God. Psalm 38:15 (NIV) says, "LORD, I wait for you; you will answer, Lord my God."

God used my "Green Vest Days" to change my focus from "What should I do?" to "What do *You* (God) want me to do. . .and who do You want me to be?"

Eventually God led me to a job that I had only dreamed about. But only after setting one more goal—to live for Him, even if it meant wearing a green vest for another year.

GET REAL

Your future may be filled with more questions than answers. But God promises to show us the next step if we trust Him and are willing to wait for His answer.

Transformers
Chris Haidet

Have you ever fallen victim to the "group's brain"? You know, that monstrous brain that is created whenever a group of friends gets together? It happens when we do things as a group that we would never attempt by ourselves. We get pressured and we pressure others to try, taste, drink, and look at things that we know might be bad. In the process we end up acting like someone we're not and become someone we wish we weren't. These are the times that we get into the most trouble and make the mistakes that we can't take back.

When I was in school, I fell into that trap. I would pick on others to make my friends laugh. I would drink and taste stuff that I knew was bad, all to fit in. I was weak and easily swayed by public opinion.

Look at what the Bible says: "Don't copy the behavior and customs of this world, but let God transform you into a new person by changing the way you think. Then you will learn to know God's will for you, which is good and pleasing and perfect" (Romans 12:2).

God doesn't want us to fall victim to the group's brain but wants us to transform the group with our brain and our heart. When we let God transform the way we think and act, then we influence our friends in a positive way and become the transformers God designed us to be.

GET REAL

When peers apply pressure in your life, ask God for the courage and strength to become a transformer. Look for positive ways to influence and hang with friends who will do the same for you.

Beyond 2012
Dale Robert Hicks

After the movie *2012* came out, several of my students asked me if I thought that the world was going to end in 2012. As a science teacher, my "no" brought the assurance of an expert that gave them hope. These students were looking for answers that would give them confidence that their lives weren't going to be over before they even graduated from high school.

They came to me because they knew that the predictions and publicity about the movie and year 2012 didn't worry me.

I realized that as a Christ follower, I can encourage people who are worried or having troubles in their lives. It reminded me of the following advice God has given us: "You must worship Christ as Lord of your life. And if someone asks about your Christian hope, always be ready to explain it" (1 Peter 3:15).

Even when I am going through difficult experiences, I want people to see that I have a confident hope that my life is going somewhere with God. That doesn't mean I have to like going through painful events. I just have to be able to explain to people why I believe that no matter how bad life gets, it's not the end of the world.

GET REAL

What would your explanation be to someone who asks why you have hope, even when everything in your life seems to be going wrong? Do you think others can see your optimism? What can you do to make your hope more evident?

The Trade

Ron Merrell

One year I attended a Christmas party and participated in a big gift-exchange game with a bunch of people. Everyone chose a number. The person with the number one opened the first gift. Then the next person could open a new present—taking a chance not knowing what was inside—or steal the present that had already been opened, and so on. Throughout the course of the evening, I had my hands on some pretty amazing gifts, but they kept getting stolen. The best gifts exchanged hands dozens of times.

I started the evening with an iPod in my hands and left with a pair of homemade grandma slippers. It was the worst trade ever.

I don't know if you're aware of this, but when you step into a relationship with Jesus, a trade takes place. But it's the best trade in all of human history. Second Corinthians 5:21 says, "God made Christ, who never sinned, to be the offering for our sin, so that we could be made right with God through Christ." In other words, when you accept Jesus as your Lord and Savior, here's the trade that happens: You give Jesus your sin. He gives you right standing with God. That's quite the trade.

GET REAL

When you accept Jesus, your sin has been taken care of. It's been dealt with. It's finished. And your right standing in God's sight is taken care of as well. Jesus took care of both issues in that great trade. Don't worry about doing anything today in light of that truth, except for thanking Him from the bottom of your heart.

The Problem of Me

Steve Russo

Life gets weird when we adopt the "it's all about me" attitude. Lots of people have become me-centered, not caring about other people and only worried about themselves. What we need to realize is that it's not about "me"; rather, it's about "we." This means we need to focus our eyes on others and become more aware of their needs, hopes, and ideas.

The only way the 'tude can change is when it's from the heart. It takes supernatural help. Paul, a follower of Jesus, wrote to other believers about being we-focused: "So encourage each other and build each other up, just as you are already doing" (1 Thessalonians 5:11). Everyone needs encouragement, especially when we're going through a tough time. Whether it's parent stuff at home or drama at school, it's good to have others around to encourage us. We also need to be sensitive to others who need our encouragement. A few words or actions can make a huge difference.

How different our world would be if more people were all about "we" instead of "me." The change begins with us and becomes contagious. Imagine how much more we could accomplish by encouraging each other and working together. There's a lot of stuff in our world that needs to be changed—and when we work together there's no limit to how much we can do to make a difference.

GET REAL

Think about your family and friends. Who could really use some encouragement today? Ask God to give you the right words or show you something you can do to support them.

Love and Green Beans

Melanie Stiles

What does it mean when someone tells you they love you? "I love you" can mean "I just want to take you out." Or it may mean "I have been crushing on you forever." But how do we know for sure what it means?

Check out this quick quiz. Do you love chocolate? What about cars? Your mother? How about green beans? Starting to see the problem? The English language uses one little word to describe tons of feelings and preferences.

The Bible helps us to understand the true definition of *love* with a list in 1 Corinthians 13:4–7 (CEV): "Love is kind and patient, never jealous, boastful, proud, or rude. Love isn't selfish or quick tempered. It doesn't keep a record of wrongs that others do. Love rejoices in the truth, but not in evil. Love is always supportive, loyal, hopeful, and trusting."

These guidelines are great to use in figuring out not only if someone loves us but also if and how we love them. Even with the list, love takes a lot of time to explore. Only by *not* rushing into a serious relationship do we give ourselves a chance to discover what is real. Think about it. After all, don't you owe it to yourself to see if your guy or girl loves you more than green beans?

GET REAL

Get together with your friend and compare both of your definitions of *love* to the list in 1 Corinthians 13. God's version is the best version! Make sure you're on the same page.

Who's in the Driver's Seat?

Ramona Richards

Jenny threw her backpack into the corner and sank down on her bed, mad at the world. Bad day, bad week, bad month. Problems at school just kept piling up. And to top it off, she tripped getting off the bus and ripped the heel off her favorite boot.

Jenny screamed in frustration, knowing that no one was around to hear. She wanted to stop it all—school, her job, her fights with Mom. No one listened to her, so she didn't want to listen either. Everyone else needed to just shut up.

Have you ever felt like Jenny? Most of us have, at one time or another. We dig in our heels and want to live life on our own terms.

Trouble is, the world gets in the way. Rules. Lessons. Why can't we go our own way?

Because, in the long run, none of us has the big picture. Not you, not your folks, not your teachers or your friends. Just God. He reminded Job and his friends of this truth in a bold statement that applies to us, too. "Who has given me anything that I need to pay back? Everything under heaven is mine" (Job 41:11).

Shutting down, as Job discovered, is easy. But if we remain open to what God and those He's put in our path have to teach us, amazing blessings can be ours.

GET REAL

Instead of getting frustrated with life, open yourself up to God. Listen for what He has to teach you every day. Put Him in the driver's seat, and He'll give you the ride of your life!

Red-Eye
Nicole O'Dell

The "red-eye" is an all-night flight that arrives at its destination usually close to dawn. It got that name because people who stay up that late to travel usually stumble off the plane with bloodshot eyes. Trying to stay awake, they down some caffeine and then wander through the airport in a blur searching for their luggage.

Do you "take the red-eye" by staying up too late to watch TV, go online, play video games, or do homework, and then try to make up for it the next day with energy drinks or caffeine pills? If so, do you think it's the healthiest thing to do? Maybe you don't down the caffeine, but is it healthy to go through the day like a zombie because you stayed up too late?

Most teens usually get about seven hours of sleep a night. Doctors say they really need closer to nine hours. Over time, this lack of sleep can translate into things like lower grades, bad attitudes, and stressed-out relationships. Is it worth dealing with consequences like these when all you need to do is get to bed and save the late nights for the weekend?

It might not be the most exciting option, but when you compare the results, it might be easier to make a healthy choice and a godly one. Remember the One to whom your body belongs. "Don't you realize that all of you together are the temple of God and that the Spirit of God lives in you?" (1 Corinthians 3:16).

GET REAL

Try getting a good night's sleep tonight. Notice the difference it makes tomorrow. Ask God to help you make rest a regular priority in your life.

You Can Fool Your Friends

Patrick Dunn

I stumbled across the finish line, seconds from exhaustion. Pain tore muscles apart as I gasped for air, almost falling into a crumpled heap. Yet—I triumphed! Victory was mine, and I stood tall as a ribbon decorated my chest. It was my finest moment. . . . Well, not really.

I was ten years old and my school held the "Give the Kids We Feel Sorry For a Medal" Games or something like that. I *did* get a ribbon—eleventh place.

I bragged to my friends that I won a ribbon, and they thought I was awesome. I fooled them. You can fool your friends, too. In fact, you can fool your parents, your teachers, the manager at work. Have you ever painted on a smile when you weren't really happy or told your parents you were doing homework when you were really on Facebook? What about acting tough when inside you're really hurting?

Proverbs 16:2 (NIV) says, "All a person's ways seem pure to them, but motives are weighed by the LORD." That means you've been found out. You can fool your friends, but you can't fool God. He knows the real you—deep inside. He knows your heart, your weaknesses, and your secrets. He knows you—and loves you— even when you take eleventh place, not first.

GET REAL

Talk to God about your pains, your fears, and especially your mistakes. There's no reason to live a lie when He sees the truth anyway.

Invisible
Steve Russo

Have you ever wished you were invisible? I've always wanted to be invisible so I could go into a room and play practical jokes on my friends. Just think of all the places you could go and the weird things you could do if no one could see you.

Some people have to go no further than the reality of their own lives to know what it feels like *not* to be noticed. Maybe it's their personality, the way they dress, or the "it's all about me" people around them. They are invisible to everyone. The pressure to fit in and the desire to be accepted are tough enough. Then add the pain of wondering if anyone would even notice if their life just ceased to exist. Sometimes the feelings are so strong, "invisible people" take their own lives.

No one is ever really invisible. There's One who knows who we are, no matter how unnoticed we feel. That One is Jesus. He made us and knows us better than we know ourselves. See what David wrote in Psalm 139:13: "You made all the delicate, inner parts of my body and knit me together in my mother's womb." God made each of us unique with every strand of our DNA. He gave us our looks and quirks, our gifts and talents.

You may feel invisible to everyone else, but you're not to Jesus.

GET REAL

Sometimes you have to look hard to find "invisible people." Ask God to help you notice them at school and where you hang out. When you find them, tell them about the One who created them and how to discover His awesome plan for their lives.

Laugh Track
Lesha Campbell

Have you ever heard a laugh track? It's when the TV studio wants the audience to laugh at a particular time in a performance, so they play a prerecorded laugh track to jump-start the audience. Sounds lame, but it's usually productive. Wonder where they got the idea for a laugh track? Maybe from real-life situations. Think about a time when one of your friends was laughing and you didn't know why, but once you heard their laughter, you jumped right in. Once both of you caught your breath, you asked each other, "What are we laughing at?" Truth is, neither of you knew, but you both enjoyed it.

I've been there and truly needed that "laughter for no reason" to relieve stress, keep myself from crying, or simply cope with life. Yes, I often laugh when I'm stressed. Hey, it keeps me from going insane! I suppose I get that from my dad. I fondly remember his contagious laughter and his response that more often than not accompanied it—"Sometimes you have to laugh to keep from crying."

So, after gut-wrenching, stomach-aching laughter, we ask ourselves, "Why?" Simple answer, Proverbs 17:22: "A cheerful heart is good medicine, but a broken spirit saps a person's strength."

GET REAL

Are you good medicine or do you sap strength from a friend who's already down in the dumps? If you're a sapper, try a dose of laughter next time. If you already have a cheerful heart, keep on chuckling.

Love Connection

Susie Shellenberger

Love is making a comeback.

At least that was the slogan one church decided to use in its determination to reach out to its community of twelve thousand. Church members printed business cards with the slogan, created a website that explained their desire to love people to Christ, and started passing out the cards.

The pastor, pulling out cash to pay for his meal at the taco drive-through, simply said, "I want to also pay for whoever is in the car behind me."

After learning the amount, he handed the cashier his money and gave her a card. "Please give her this card and just tell her that she's loved."

He later received a call from the cashier sharing how the recipient broke down in tears when she received the card and free meal. His church is following his example of loving its community in big and small ways to Jesus, living out 1 John 3:18 (NIV): "Let us not love with words or speech but with actions and in truth."

It doesn't take much.

A two-dollar taco. An outstretched hand. A door opened. A smile. Random acts of love go a long way toward being the hands and feet of Jesus in our world. Why? Because we're not used to kind gestures. Most of us are me-oriented. When someone deliberately places himself last and puts us first, we're immediately drawn in. Here's the bottom line: "All the special gifts and powers from God will someday come to an end, but love goes on forever" (1 Corinthians 13:8 TLB).

GET REAL

What can you do today to genuinely show Christ's love? Now. . .will you actually do it?

Saying Good-bye
Brenda Pue

It was Christmas morning. I was a teenager, the oldest of five. One of our family traditions on Christmas morning was that we weren't allowed to leave our bedrooms until we heard music playing. When we heard the music, there was a mad dash to get into the living room to see the Christmas tree lit up and piled with gifts. There was such excitement as we opened our gifts. When the last gift had been opened, my dad nervously cleared his throat and announced that he was leaving our family. As if in slow motion, he got up, walked out the door and down the sidewalk toward our family car, and drove away.

That was the day I said good-bye to a lot of things in my life. I don't remember much else about that Christmas except for my feelings of confusion, rejection, and aloneness.

That was also the year that God came to me in a new way—as my Father. My human dad left me. But God said to me, "I will never leave you nor forsake you" (Joshua 1:5 NIV). Such healing words for someone longing for a dad to talk with and get advice from. . .for someone looking for love and approval. God has been all that and more to me for many years. He is my earthly dad and my heavenly dad. He has stayed with me every step of the way—just like He promised!

GET REAL

Even the best dads are flawed. Only God the Father can be the constantly trustworthy, loving, encouraging, merciful, grace-filled dad that we all long for. Have you given Him a chance to be your loving Dad?

Loyalty
Melanie Stiles

I love my best friend. We've known each other since elementary school. Through the years we have played dodge ball, confided secrets, and cried on each other's shoulders. But somewhere along the way, we also started looking at people and places differently. I wanted to see what life looked like with Jesus, but she seemed to be drifting into another place where He was left out. We tried mixing our friend groups, but that only highlighted the differing views that were important to each of us.

Soon I came face-to-face with the fact that loyalty is one of the best traits a true friend can have. But it can also be one of the worst, especially when it comes to friends who are traveling to unhealthy places. In the end, I had to walk away.

Although my love for her hasn't lessened any, I believe God showed me the path she was going down so I could make the choice *not* to blindly follow despite our lifetime friendship. I had to choose to be loyal to God instead of being loyal to a person. Looking back, I am grateful. Consider Proverbs 20:12, which says, "Ears to hear and eyes to see—both are gifts from the LORD."

When I started paying attention, I could recognize her choices; then I figured out God had other places for me to go.

GET REAL

Is it time to open your eyes and ears to what your friends are up to? Do your priorities look similar or entirely different? To whom are you being loyal?

Still Important to God

Steve Russo

What's *sin*? Something you do or think? Is it cheating? Lying? . . . *Sin* seems like a dated word that doesn't fit into our high-tech "whatever" culture that has no right and wrong. But it's important to God.

The Bible describes *sin* as specific actions—as missing the mark, as knowing the right thing to do and then not doing it. Sin, at its core, is simply failing to let God be God in our lives.

Sin is a spiritual, terminal disease that we're all born with and that was inherited from the first man and woman, Adam and Eve. But because of God's awesome love, He provided a remedy through the death and resurrection of His Son, Jesus.

Just because we have a relationship with God doesn't mean we don't sin anymore. We're human and live in physical bodies that are still driven by natural desires for things like food, sex, and pleasure. When we give in to the wrong temptations, we sin and it gets in the way of our friendship with God.

But because He loves us, God made a way for our friendship with Him to be restored: "But if we confess our sins to him, he is faithful and just to forgive us our sins and to cleanse us from all wickedness" (1 John 1:9). If we agree with God that we have sinned, He'll remove the barrier that our sin has put between us and Him.

GET REAL

It takes humility and honesty to admit our rebellion and disobedience. Ask God to search your heart to identify any sin barriers between you and Him. Confess what He shows to you.

Word Up
Chuck Poe

Have you ever said something you immediately regretted and wished you could take back? Maybe you popped off to your parents or lost your temper on the court and played the blame game with your teammates. When this happens, friendships can be disturbed and broken.

Proverbs 18:21 (NIV) says, "The tongue has the power of life and death, and those who love it will eat its fruit." But when I was younger, I'd heard that "sticks and stones may break my bones but words can never hurt me." I would like to think this is true, but it isn't; words can wound deeply.

The brother of Jesus, James, said that our tongue, which produces our words, can bless people and curse them. He also said no one can tame the tongue—no one (James 3:7–8). Amazing!

We could say to ourselves, "Why try to watch what I say? It's useless." But there is hope. Our words not only carry weight but also carry wisdom. We can make a difference by watching what we say, how we say it, and why we say it.

GET REAL

Before spouting off with senseless words—whether spoken or written someplace for others to read (like on Facebook)—take a moment to ask yourself, "What effect will my words have?"

Hand Over the Keys

Ron Merrell

One time I let a sixteen-year-old guy borrow my little sports car to take his girlfriend to prom. As I handed the keys over to him, he smiled from ear to ear. I, on the other hand, was a little nervous. I was just hoping I'd see my car come home in one piece.

The bummer was that my young friend actually ended up crashing my car that night. He felt horrible and handed the keys back over to me in tears, head hanging low.

That's when the thought hit me that I tend to do the same thing with Jesus. I ask Jesus to hand the keys of my life back over to me to do what I want for the night. I push Him out of the driver's seat, forcing Him to ride shotgun or throwing Him out of the car altogether. When I do that, I usually end up crashing and burning.

The Bible says in Romans 10:9, "If you confess with your mouth that Jesus is Lord and believe in your heart that God raised him from the dead, you will be saved."

Jesus wants to be the boss of our lives. Lord. Ruler. King. Master over everything. In other words, He wants to sit in the driver's seat—not in the passenger seat, backseat, or trunk!

GET REAL

Where does Jesus sit in your life today? If there are any areas in which He's not driving and you have the keys, admit them to Him. Then hand the keys back over to Jesus as you admit He's the only One really suited to drive.

The Yearbook
Chris Haidet

Do you remember the moment in your life when you realized that your parents just didn't get it? That moment for me was at age fifteen. My mom did not understand my friends, my music, my issues, or anything about me. In fact, the more we argued, the more I began to think she was becoming my biggest problem. Then came the moment that changed my perception and warped my brain forever. I sat holding my mom's dusty yearbook, and what I saw shocked me.

She was in sports, in clubs, had gone to dances, and had notes written in the front and back of the yearbook from what looked like. . .*friends*. She seemed normal! Maybe even kind of cute. . . *How awkward.* So I began to ask her about her music, her friends, and her issues. I started to understand that my single, stressed-out mom might actually get it.

Ephesians 6:3 tells us, "If you honor your father and mother, 'things will go well for you, and you will have a long life on the earth.' "

I began to honor my mom when I made an effort to discover who she had been and now had become. When I realized that she'd had to deal with the same type of stuff I did, our relationship improved. I was finally able to get a much better perspective of where she was coming from.

GET REAL

When your relationship with your parents gets beyond frustrating, try this: honor them by taking time to sit down and talk with them about their past, their troubles, and their issues. Getting to know them better will improve your relationship and just might change your perspective.

Make a Difference

Ramona Richards

Massive springtime floods hit the Nashville, Tennessee, area. In some places mud smeared the homes and trees more than thirty feet high. The waters rose so fast that many people didn't even have a chance to evacuate.

As the waters receded, the call for volunteers spread quickly, for the most part virally via Facebook, Twitter, and e-mail. Teens and young adults signed up quickly, and in two days, more than seven thousand people were out sandbagging, emptying flooded houses, tearing out drywall, searching for lost pets. . . By the end of the week, the number climbed to almost ten thousand.

Churches drove a lot of this volunteer effort, with one church even making the national news for its efforts.

Youth groups by the dozen showed up to help, the experience changing students' own lives as well as the lives of those they helped. They did it out of love. God is love, so it shouldn't be a surprise that His children reflect it. Just take a look at 1 John 4:7–8: "Continue to love one another, for love comes from God. Anyone who loves is a child of God and knows God. . .for God is love."

In the end, the way people banded together made more news than the flood's destruction.

GET REAL

When the love of God lives within you, you show up wherever you're needed. To help, to love, to bring hope. You, as a single individual, can make a difference. What can you do today?

Mirror Image
Steve Russo

People do crazy things in front of mirrors. A high school student once told me he used a mirror to practice kissing. On his bathroom mirror he painted red lips with lipstick (I didn't ask where he got it). Then he closed his eyes and practiced kissing the mirror. Last time I checked, the texture of human lips is totally different from a mirror's surface. (Girls, beware of guys who kiss funny. They may be using a mirror to practice!)

Mirrors are usually used for improving or correcting things like makeup, clothes, hair, zits, or stuff stuck in our teeth. Unless we're looking into a fun-house mirror that distorts, we get a true likeness of what we're looking at.

The Bible is like a mirror. James, the brother of Jesus, described it that way. He used the illustration to show the difference between people who merely hear God's Word and those who obey it. James said if you hear it and don't do it, that's as crazy as looking at your face in a mirror and forgetting what you look like. There's a promise for those who listen and obey: "But if you look carefully into the perfect law that sets you free, and if you do what it says and don't forget what you heard, then God will bless you for doing it" (James 1:25).

The mirror of God's Word shows us a true picture of who we are and what needs to be changed. It's important to listen to what the Bible says, but even more crucial to do it.

GET REAL

Do you put into action what you have studied in the Bible? Look deep into the mirror of God's Word. What needs to be changed in the way you think, talk, or live?

Unhealthy Chat

Nicole O'Dell

Being a gossip isn't really all that bad. . .right?

- Spreading rumors and lies will make you popular.
- People will trust you more if you relate everything you hear—whether it's true or not.
- When you get excited about that latest sleaze, people will just think you're a concerned friend.

These are lies that gossips repeat to themselves on a regular basis to try to convince themselves what they're doing is okay. But God feels differently about gossip. The Bible says that gossip is destructive and wrong. Look at Proverbs 16:28: "A troublemaker plants seeds of strife; gossip separates the best of friends."

Gossiping reveals insecurity and a lack of self-worth. Think about it. If you were confident in yourself, you'd have no reason to spread rumors or bad stories about other people. You'd just rest in your own self-worth.

And how about the harm to your reputation? "Word is sure to get around, and no one will trust you" (Proverbs 25:10 MSG). Once you become known as a gossip, you'll have a difficult time erasing the impression others have of you.

GET REAL

Choose the kind of friend you want to be before you fall into the trap of gossip, slander, and lies. Ask God to help you develop a reputation of telling and living the truth.

Fame
Dale Robert Hicks

I often hear students talking about what they want to be when they get older. Many dream of being an athlete, actor, or rock star. Their reasoning is they want to be rich and famous and take the best routes they can to get there. When I ask them what they want to do when the fame runs out, most students are surprised and simply respond by asking, "What do you mean?"

Consider these words from Ecclesiastes 4:15–16 (MSG): "I saw a youth. . .start with nothing and go from rags to riches, and I saw everyone rally to the rule of this young successor to the king. Even so, the excitement died quickly, the throngs of people soon lost interest. Can't you see it's only smoke? And spitting into the wind?"

There's nothing wrong with being famous, but if that's your goal in life, you might find it to be an empty one. The quest for fame tends to be a self-centered pursuit, and often leaves people empty and unhappy in the end. The Bible says that satisfaction with life is found when one follows God and lives for His eternity. After all, the fame we get from people only lasts until the next "hip" thing comes along—but the blessings of God are forever.

GET REAL

Are you living your life for the fame and glory that will be here today and gone tomorrow, or do you want to make your life count, not for a generation, but for eternity?

Words as a Weapon

Ron Merrell

One dad always told his son that he should "stop acting like a little girl." If the son got emotional about something, the dad would grab him and yell at him, saying, "Just stop being a little girl. That's all you are, a little girl—and that's all you'll ever be!"

It got worse. The boy went on a camping trip with a church youth group. During a hike, the boy slipped. The other boys hiking with him started laughing and making fun of him. "Just get up and keep moving. . . . You're such a little girl!"

The other kids didn't know how hurtful those words would be to that boy. They didn't know what was going on in that boy's family. But the damage was done.

James gives us pretty strong instructions about our words: "The tongue also is a fire, a world of evil among the parts of the body. It corrupts the whole person, sets the whole course of one's life on fire, and is itself set on fire by hell" (James 3:6 NIV). This insight is probably what motivated Paul to encourage Timothy to watch his speech. James and Paul both understood that our words are able to inflict deep, lasting harm on others.

GET REAL

Consider your words recently. How many of your words would you consider to be ones that build people up? How many are just neutral with no real impact one way or the other? How many rip people apart? Try speaking words today that are only encouraging. See what happens.

Never Alone

Melanie Stiles

Your friends are all around you. Could be nothing is wrong, or maybe it's everything. Either way, you feel alone. All alone. Most everyone has been there. Something just isn't quite right, and we don't connect with anyone around us.

When I feel this way, I try to think of Jesus, just before He was crucified. That day Jesus felt the same distance from those around Him that we sometimes experience. So He headed to an olive grove called Gethsemane to talk to the only One He was sure would hear Him. Holding nothing back, He admitted He wasn't happy with what was going on in His life. He recognized that God—and not His friends—could change everything. He also knew His Father had a plan for His life. I like reading His prayer in Mark 14:35–36 (MSG): "Going a little ahead, he fell to the ground and prayed for a way out: 'Papa, Father, you can—can't you?—get me out of this. Take this cup away from me. But please, not what I want—what do you want?' "

Dealing with the rough stuff in our lives is never easy. Feeling completely alone can be very difficult. But recognizing that there is Someone who wants to hear what you have to say, no matter what it is, helps.

GET REAL

If life really stinks right now, find your own olive grove and spend time with the One who always listens. Tell Him everything on your mind.

The Island

Steve Russo

Lincoln Six Echo is a resident of a utopian but contained facility in the mid-twenty-first century. Like all the inhabitants of this carefully controlled environment, Lincoln hopes to be chosen to go to "The Island"—supposedly the last uncontaminated spot on the planet. It's the utopians' only motivation for living.

While the story is fictional, the search for "The Island" is real. Everyone wants a place to go that's safe—a paradise where problems seem to disappear. We want a place where we can find hope and help. "The Island," the refuge we're looking for, can only be found in the living God. It's a common theme in the Bible, one that's important for us to remember. The writer of Psalm 91:2 put it this way: "This I declare about the LORD: He alone is my refuge, my place of safety; he is my God, and I trust him."

When we're afraid or feeling overwhelmed by the problems of life, God is our shelter. Our faith in the living God will carry us through all the fears and dangers of life. But we must learn to trade all of our fears—no matter how intense they might be—for confident faith in the Lord. That means we must live and rest in Him each day. The promise is powerful: if we trust ourselves to God, we will be kept safe.

GET REAL

God eagerly waits for us to surrender not just our fears and concerns to Him, but our entire lives as well. So, have you escaped to the Island? If not, what are you waiting for?

Everyone Will Know
Brenda Pue

Sometimes life gets a little crazy! Most of us go through seasons of life when we are close to burning out. There is nothing wrong with seasons of hard work as long as certain disciplines are in place.

A friend of mine told me about a wise mentor who gave him the best piece of advice he has ever received: spend time alone with God, nurturing your relationship with Him every day. For twenty years no one will know that you did this, but after twenty years everyone will know if you didn't.

Imagine your twenty-year high school reunion. Picture what your life might be like. Envision what some of your classmates will be like in twenty years. I guarantee you this: there will be many surprises!

If you follow this one discipline—spending time with God every day—your life will be transformed from the inside out. The secret to true happiness is a close relationship with God. Spend time alone with Him, reading His Word and talking with Him through prayer. There are no substitutes or shortcuts.

Jesus said, "It is written: 'Man shall not live on bread alone, but on every word that comes from the mouth of God' " (Matthew 4:4 NIV). I personally can't imagine life without bread! That's how important the Bible should be to us.

GET REAL

How would you rate your personal time with God? Nonexistent? Occasional? Average? Fantastic? If it's anything less than fantastic, take whatever steps are necessary to make God your number-one priority in life. It will be the best decision you ever make. Every day.

The Ride of a Lifetime

Chris Haidet

There I was, sitting with my friend on what felt like the top of the world. As I looked over the edge, my heart pounding with anticipation, I realized that the only thing between certain death and me was my faith in this perfectly engineered, full-bodied safety bar. I held my breath, raised my hands up high, and then it happened—a 216-foot drop on the world's newest, fastest, $46 million roller coaster. Over the next two minutes, I was hurled into a world of ups, downs, twists, and turns on a ride into the unknown. I was totally out of control and loving every breathtaking second of it. Afterward, I turned to my friend: "Why can't everyday life be this exciting?"

Sometimes life feels like a fast-paced roller coaster, spinning down the tracks of uncertainty. We scream, but where's the excitement? Why is there so much pain? Plus, where is that perfectly engineered safety bar?

Look at Hebrews 11:1: "Faith is the confidence that what we hope for will actually happen; it gives us assurance about things we cannot see."

Faith is a trip into the unknown. The ups, downs, twists, and turns of life can be frightening if we are unsure of our destination. But when our faith rests in Christ, we can be confident that no matter what life hurls at us, our destination is secure.

GET REAL

When life speeds you into the unknown, pray for God to show you the way. When the ride becomes terrifying, ask Jesus to hold you secure and give you faith that *He* is the perfect safety bar in your life.

I'm Bored
Patrick Dunn

I'm not doing anything right now—and that's okay.

Some people have to stay busy, or they crave the thrill of adventure. Normal life makes them cringe. But should it?

Adventure can build our faith and lead us to overcome fear or self-doubt—like I did when I went rock climbing, despite a fear of heights. But seeking adventure also increases our risk of making bad choices.

A few years ago I went skiing with friends who were better skiers. They decided to hit a trail on the top of the mountain. I went along when I should have said no. I won't get into the details, but it was ugly.

There are TV shows filled with guys trying something new and seeking another thrill (and it usually involves duct tape, fire, and probable electric shock). Sometimes this leads to nothing but laughs. But are we laughing at someone else who may be a victim? Have we crossed the line into doing stuff we shouldn't?

God has wired many of us for adventure. But He also calls us to be wise, to watch how we act, and to watch how we treat others. He also desires us to be at peace. In Philippians 4:12, one of His followers talks about learning the secret of being content in any and every situation. That includes normal everyday life, without multitasking, adventure, or an adrenaline rush.

GET REAL

The next time you feel restless or bored, talk to God. Ask Him to show you peace and contentment. Look to Him first, before you look to people, things, activities, and another adventure.

Satisfied

Steve Russo

Have you learned to be content with a lot or a little? It's not easy.

If we really want to be satisfied, we have to learn to recognize the difference between what we need and what we want. First, we have to stop comparing ourselves to others and listening to the empty philosophies of consumerism. No matter how much bling and bank we have, we won't be satisfied.

We also have to appreciate the things we do have. We take a lot of things for granted because we forget to be grateful for what we do possess. It's amazing how I stopped taking basic things in life for granted after I started traveling to less fortunate parts of the world.

There's a deeper secret in learning to be satisfied. It's simple—taking God and His Word seriously. Paul, an early Jesus follower, had some great insight: "Not that I was ever in need, for I have learned how to be content with whatever I have. I know how to live on almost nothing or with everything. I have learned the secret of living in every situation, whether it is with a full stomach or empty, with plenty or little. For I can do everything through Christ, who gives me strength" (Philippians 4:11–13).

Our ability to be satisfied is connected to the depth of our relationship with Jesus and our ability to rely on Him. There's no shortcut to lasting satisfaction.

GET REAL

Have you learned the difference between need and want? Ask God to help you. Once you discover this secret for yourself, don't be shy. Share it with those you love and care about.

Prepare to Live or Die

Steve Russo

Deciding how to live is a choice we all make; to die is not. What are you willing to live and die for? As followers of Jesus, we ought to ask, "Am I willing to die for my God and His purposes? Faced with the challenges of life and the possibility of death, can I let go of my life for the sake of Jesus?" Following Jesus means we stop worrying about ourselves and start becoming more concerned about obeying God.

This is the kind of attitude Paul wanted the believers at Philippi to have: "For I fully expect and hope that I will never be ashamed, but that I will continue to be bold for Christ, as I have been in the past. And I trust that my life will bring honor to Christ, whether I live or die. For to me, living means living for Christ, and dying is even better" (Philippians 1:20–21). Paul is challenging the Philippians *and us* to develop an eternal perspective.

Millions need answers to the daunting questions: How should I live today, and how can I be ready to die? Where is God in all the human tragedies and natural disasters we see happening around the world? It's time for us to get serious about telling others how they can experience God's love, peace, and hope.

GET REAL

Are you prepared to give an answer for the living and dying hope within you? If you don't have anything worth dying for, you don't have anything worth living for. The only thing worth living and dying for is Jesus. Ask Him for courage to tell others.

An Open Heart
Ramona Richards

How do you know when you can trust a friend? Is it because they keep your secrets? Or do you share the same dreams? Are they always there when you need them? Do they keep on loving you even when they know *way* too much about you?

Have you ever trusted someone even before they proved you could rely on them?

Most of us have, at one time or another. You meet someone, and without going through any sort of trouble, you just know—they have your back.

God is like that. Some of us call on Him every day, and He stands by us. In Psalm 3:5 David knew God had been there, even if it was just to get him through the night: "I lay down and slept, yet I woke up in safety, for the LORD was watching over me." Others of us may never cry out for Him, but we trust Him anyway because He knows every thought we have, good and bad. He knows everything we do, good and bad.

And He loves us anyway.

Life isn't easy; it's not supposed to be. Tough times will come no matter what. But if we keep our hearts open to God, we'll be able to see how and when He helps get us through.

GET REAL

What are you trusting God for today? You may not always be able to see God's work in your life, but He's always there. He has your back, every day. Thank God for watching over you.

Uncontaminated

Kati Russo

My sister and I attended an in-studio concert at a radio station with the Jonas Brothers. After they performed, we got to talk to them. I asked Kevin, "Is that a purity ring you're wearing?" He lit up, and Joe and Nick turned to smile at me. Kevin replied, "Yes." He said he was glad I noticed the ring and he loves it when their fans ask about them. I told him I thought it was really awesome that they wore purity rings. Then I showed him mine.

So what is purity, and why is it such a big deal? Imagine a glass of water. When first poured, it's clean and pure; but if you add a lemon slice, your water is now contaminated. Even a tiny grain of sand in the water makes it impure.

The Bible talks about more than just sexual purity; it also talks about purity of our hearts and lives. Take lying, for example: when you lie to a friend or family member, you're contaminating not only that relationship but yourself as well.

Psalm 119:9 provides a simple answer to how we can remain pure: "How can a young person stay pure? By obeying your word." The only way to obey God's Word is to know it. Try memorizing some verses on purity. Then when faced with a difficult situation, you can lean on the Bible to help you make right decisions.

GET REAL

Living a pure life involves everything about us—our thoughts, actions, relationships— everything we are and do. Where do you struggle the most when it comes to purity? What does God's Word have to say about this area? Have you asked Him for help?

Overcoming Anxiety

Rusty Wright

What makes you feel anxious? Schoolwork? Finances? Maybe conflict with your friends, family, or neighbors?

Anxiety is everywhere. An unpredictable economy can affect bank balances, education, and your future plans. Wars, storms, and floods can make stomachs churn.

As a teenager, I was anxious about lots of things. The prospect of meeting new people could make me worry. So could taking exams, asking a girl out, and participating in challenging athletic events. I was a high jumper on our track team. When my name was called, I often took several minutes to just stand and nervously stare at the bar before I would jump. The judges didn't like it.

But after I came to know Jesus in college, I found a new, inner peace that did not depend on circumstances. As I learned to trust Him, I became more patient and peaceful. One of His followers wrote, "Don't worry about anything; instead, pray about everything. Tell God what you need, and thank him for all he has done. Then you will experience God's peace, which exceeds anything we can understand. His peace will guard your hearts and minds as you live in Christ Jesus" (Philippians 4:6–7).

Life will not become perfect, but the Problem Solver helps put things in perspective and calms us down as we put our problems in His hands.

GET REAL

Is something worrying you right now? Tell God about it. He already knows your concern, of course, but being honest with Him can open your heart for Him to heal you with His love, peace, and power.

Yes Moments
Melanie Stiles

Parents. Why is it that some days it feels like they are doing everything they can to frustrate us? Surely they see how much you want to go to your BFF's house. Or to buy that new video game—no matter what it costs. Or even to upgrade a cell phone. So what's up with no, no, no?

In a "no" situation, parents look like bad guys. Part of the deal may be that we have a problem with the "just do as I say" presentation. Unfortunately, the reasons for a particular "no" are not always explained. It's frustrating. But God wants us to obey our parents. Check out Ephesians 6:1: "Children, obey your parents as believers in the Lord. Obey them because it's the right thing to do" (NIrV).

So maybe there is more than one way to look at the situation. First, this might be a good time to count up recent "yes" moments that you've forgotten. One no inside a series of yeses can lessen our opinion of parents if we let it. Another thing to consider—could accepting a no with a good attitude move us closer to a more important yes coming up? Having a decent attitude after hearing a no shows a mature spirit that builds trust. And trust opens the door to yes in the future. It just might be worth it.

GET REAL

Complain to God and not a parent when your emotions are running too high to think sanely. That gives you the opportunity to say later what you really want your parents to hear.

How Much Is Your Life Worth?

Steve Russo

Ever thought about putting yourself up for sale? How much would you get on the "open human market"? There's a website that attempts to place a value on your life, using things like athletic ability, education level, income, amount of exercise, weight, and sense of humor. Nearly twenty million people are listed for sale on this site.

Looking at our culture today, you'd think we put a small value on human life. Consider things like abortion, drunk driving, violence at school and at home. Life seems pretty cheap and expendable.

But humans have immeasurable worth in God's eyes. Moses talked about this in the first book of the Bible: "So God created human beings in his own image. In the image of God he created them; male and female he created them" (Genesis 1:27). We are made in the likeness of God. This is huge!

We're of such awesome worth to God that He gave the life of His only Son to pay our sin debt. Romans 5:8 says, "But God showed his great love for us by sending Christ to die for us while we were still sinners." What an unbelievable concept to grasp!

From God's perspective, no amount of money could ever come close to measuring the true value of your life. Never forget that you're a priceless treasure of the living God!

GET REAL

Do you value your life in the way you live and in your relationships? Or do you allow yourself to be misused and abused? Ask God to show you what needs to be changed and for the power to do it.

Hating Life
Dale Robert Hicks

Maybe you've never uttered "I hate life" out loud, but I bet those words have crossed your mind. The thought is pretty common. There's even a guy in the Bible named Solomon who said, "So I came to hate life because everything done here under the sun is so troubling. Everything is meaningless—like chasing the wind" (Ecclesiastes 2:17).

All of us have those moments when life seems to be a waste. Perhaps you worked really hard on something at school only to get a bad grade. Maybe you've had a close friendship fall apart. Things at home aren't how you'd like them to be. If you think you've tried everything under the sun, and there is still something missing from your life, you're not alone.

Solomon had it all—wealth, fame, women, and power. He made a list of all the ways he tried to find meaning in life. He tried being smart, partying hard, and buying anything and everything he thought might make him happy. Over and over again he found that these things were meaningless. In the end it was something bigger than himself that gave meaning to his life—God.

GET REAL

What has you hating life? Maybe you need to focus on something bigger than yourself. What gives your life meaning? If it's not God, maybe it's time for a change. If God is the source of your meaning and purpose, take a minute to give thanks for the good things He's blessed you with.

Eagles, Honda Pilots, and Oranges
Carson Pue

A friend, Courtney, was visiting my family, and she wanted desperately to see a bald eagle. We looked but never found one while she was with us. Of course, the day after she left, one landed in the tree right outside the window. So I took a photo and sent it to her with a note saying, "Every time I see an eagle I am going to say a little prayer for you"—and it worked! It helped me to remember to pray every time I see an eagle, so I started to create more "prayer prompts."

Today when I see an eagle, I pray for Courtney. A Honda Pilot prompts me to pray for Steve. Oranges prompt me to pray for children living in poverty (World Vision's logo is orange). I have lots more—a mom walking with a boy prompts me to pray for Kristin; cows prompt me to pray for Shari (she was in 4-H); guitars are prompts for Jeremy; home hardware stores for Jason; police cars for police, firefighters, and our armed forces personnel; coffee beans for Christian pastors in Russia; opera for Anne Marie; bagpipes prompt me to pray for Bill; a church for pastors; car keys for Jamey; AAA batteries for Sharon; comics for Jon; BMWs for Rob and Claudia; one-way traffic signs for Mark and Larry; and a fountain pen for John.

All these reminders help me to "pray without ceasing" (1 Thessalonians 5:17 NKJV), and I do it joyfully.

GET REAL

Think of someone to pray for and use your imagination to match them with a creative reminder or prayer prompt. You may be surprised how often you may see an eagle just when your friend needs prayer.

Giving. . .What?

Nathan Finfrock

Why do you give? Do you even give? Think about it. We live in a culture that emphasizes me, me, me first; you second. Our culture says this is the way to live a happy life. What do you think? Does this resonate with you?

Whatever happened to loving your neighbor and all that good stuff the Bible says? Gone, right? No way! The problem is that Satan always distorts truth. In this area he strives to deceive you by saying somehow you are more important or better than the next person is. Reality check—you're not! The truth is, God put a compass in our hearts, something that can prompt us to help others and allows us to feel rewarded when giving of our time, goods, talents, or love. We need to give because we want to benefit other people.

So what have you done for someone else lately? "You should remember the words of the Lord Jesus: 'It is more blessed to give than to receive' " (Acts 20:35). Simply put, God will bless us if we give.

GET REAL

This week, find a way to give. Realize, however, that you need to give consistently to make an impact. This is not a onetime deal. So find a church or an organization and start giving your money. If you only have a little money, then find a way to give of your time. Try mowing your grandma's lawn or helping that weird neighbor everyone avoids. It's time to get involved and give. This week live in God's truth, not yours!

The Metal in Me

Chris Haidet

Do you know that person at your school? You know, the one who usually dresses in black, listens to ear-piercing music, and doesn't care what you think? That's my brother, my sister. . . You see, I'm a metal head, and we stick together through thick and thin. We long for each and every concert, as our favorite band melts our faces off with the crash of the cymbal, the riff of a guitar, and the ear-splitting vocals—our bodies being crushed together at the front of the stage, hands raised in unison, and songs being shouted at the top of our lungs. There is something about music that stirs the soul and something about heavy metal that bonds together its followers. What about your group of friends? What are they like? Are you better because of them, and they because of you?

The Bible says, "As iron sharpens iron, so a friend sharpens a friend" (Proverbs 27:17).

Authentic friends speak the truth to each other, even when it hurts. They hold each other accountable and lift each other up. Friends are willing to band together and take on all comers. They will stand for the truth and not allow division to enter the ranks. Friends make each other better.

True friendship is based on faith in each other and in God. With God in the middle, the closer you each grow to Him, the closer you'll grow together, and the better your friendship with each other will become.

GET REAL

Work on sharpening your friendships. Place God in the middle of all your friendships, and pray that He will make them stronger.

Know-It-All

Steve Russo

You think you know everything. Did you know any of the following?

There are more chickens than people in the world.
A crocodile can't stick its tongue out.
It's impossible to lick your elbow.
The shark's the only fish that can blink with both eyes.
Like fingerprints, everyone's tongue print is different.

Now, you do know a lot of things, but only God knows everything!

God's not a "know-it-all," but His knowledge is complete and perfect—past, present, and future. King David describes how much God knows about us in Psalm 139:1–6:

O LORD, you have examined my heart and know everything about me. You know when I sit down or stand up. You know my thoughts even when I'm far away. You see me when I travel and when I rest at home. You know everything I do. You know what I am going to say even before I say it, LORD. You go before me and follow me. You place your hand of blessing on my head. Such knowledge is too wonderful for me, too great for me to understand!

No detail of our lives escapes God's attention. Nothing happens to us that takes Him by surprise. He knows everything about our past and present. God also knows our future. He has answers to all the questions we'll ever have. He's more than able to help us through any difficulty we face.

GET REAL

Since God is all-knowing, do you trust Him with everything that you should? What's your biggest concern today that you need to release to Him?

Sin Is Killing You

Ron Merrell

I have a friend who has a pretty big scar on his face that came as a result of a bad car accident he had while drinking and driving. For the rest of his life, he's stuck with this visible reminder of his poor choice. It's an outward sign of a moment of sin that affected not only his life but many other people's lives as well.

This got me thinking. What if every time we did something wrong, we could see its visible effects on our body in the form of a physical scar, disfigurement, or injury? If this actually happened to us when we sinned, we'd probably start to realize that sin really is as harmful as the Bible says it is.

Romans 6:23 says, "The wages of sin is death, but the free gift of God is eternal life." Sin pays death. That's where our sin is leading us. While we can't always feel the immediate effects, it is always damaging to us. It's separating us from God and from others. Left unchecked, it will separate us forever from God. It can become a permanent scar.

GET REAL

Don't let your heart get hard about sin in your life. Don't get used to it. Be honest before God right now. Admit to Him that you are scarred by sin, even though you may not be able to see it. Then get ready for God to begin the healing process. As you confess, He forgives and heals!

It's Not Fair
Ramona Richards

Penny couldn't believe it. David had forgotten her. Again! He'd promised, more than once, to help her train for the half-marathon. He knew how much this meant to her, that she was running in memory of her mother who'd died from breast cancer just a few months ago. David knew she needed him! How could he do this to her?

Penny fumed as she stretched, her eyes clouding with tears. Why were people always leaving her?

Penny learned the hard way a nasty fact of life: it's not fair. No one ever promised it would be. Being a good person, even being a Christian, doesn't make problems go away. Psalm 34:19 reminds us that God's children will always have a lot of trouble: "The righteous person faces many troubles, but the LORD comes to the rescue each time."

Loving God, and experiencing His love, doesn't mean we get to avoid difficulties. But we can depend on God to help us.

Penny still ran, despite her disappointment with David and her broken heart over her mother. God reminded her how much her mother loved helping others. Now Penny trained so she could raise money for those who suffered like her mom had. She prayed to God for strength. . .and found it.

People might let her down; God never would.

GET REAL

Do you feel like life isn't fair right now? Ask God to help you deal with the situation and move on.

Valuable Instructions

Steve Russo

Have you ever wondered if you can trust the Bible? How do we know someone didn't just make it up? What sets it apart from other religious books?

The Bible is the most unique "book" ever written. It's the Word of God. The Bible was written over a fifteen-hundred-year span of time by forty-four different authors—all living in different places—in three different languages (Hebrew, Aramaic, and Greek) and on three different continents (Asia, Africa, and Europe).

Paul, a follower of Jesus, described it this way: "All Scripture is inspired by God and is useful to teach us what is true and to make us realize what is wrong in our lives. It corrects us when we are wrong and teaches us to do what is right" (2 Timothy 3:16).

God supernaturally supervised what the authors wrote, allowing them to use their own vocabulary and style. The Bible has one main message: humanity's problem is sin, and the remedy is found in Jesus.

When we read the Bible, it helps us to know and understand God and how He works. It also helps us to know ourselves and provides answers for life.

The Bible is our ultimate source of truth. It doesn't make any sense for people to base their eternal destiny—and life on the planet—on someone's opinion when we have God's Word available to guide us.

Our growth and success in life are determined by what we do with the Bible.

GET REAL

You will get out of Bible study what you put into it. Have you decided to make studying the Bible a priority yet?

Own Up
Melanie Stiles

Everybody messes up, but not everybody will admit it. It's pretty hard to own up to a mistake. We don't want anyone to think less of us. Truth is, we really don't want to think less of ourselves. Even though it feels bad enough keeping it all inside, the idea of owning up to it is even worse.

I experienced this in a big way when I said some rude stuff to my mother. There was no reason other than I was having a bad day that gave me a bad attitude. The second the words left my mouth, I prepared for her to correct me. To my surprise, she let it slide. But that didn't make it better. Even though there wasn't any fallout, I still felt bad. The next day I decided I would try to forget what happened with my mom, but I finally realized these feelings weren't going away until I made the situation right.

As soon as I apologized to my mother, I felt much better. I was living out Proverbs 28:13: "You can't whitewash your sins and get by with it; you find mercy by admitting and leaving them" (MSG).

It felt great to move on to better thoughts—ones of doing the right thing for God, myself, and the people around me.

GET REAL

How long does it take before you get tired of the mess you've made and get up the courage to agree with God that what you did was wrong? If any situation is gnawing at you today, talk with God about owning up to your blunder and making it right.

Credit to the Creator

Steve Russo

Visiting the San Antonio Zoo was amazing. I watched lions, tigers, bears, and monkeys resting or frolicking in areas resembling their natural habitats. I walked through an aquarium filled with fish in different shapes, sizes, and colors, then visited a reptile building housing almost every kind of snake and lizard.

I even walked through cages among birds and butterflies. How cool to have different kinds of butterflies flying around me! And I can't leave out the big guys—giraffes, rhinos, and elephants. They're awesome animals with fascinating capabilities.

While walking through the zoo, I wondered how anyone could accept evolution. How can you observe these creatures and truly believe they're all a result of random mutations over millions of years? I guess I don't get it.

The Bible's story of creation makes far more sense than evolution. Look at what Moses wrote about the creatures I saw at the zoo: "Then God said, 'Let the waters swarm with fish and other life. Let the skies be filled with birds of every kind.' So God created great sea creatures and every living thing that scurries and swarms in the water, and every sort of bird—each producing offspring of the same kind. . . . Then God said, 'Let the earth produce every sort of animal, each producing offspring of the same kind—livestock, small animals that scurry along the ground, and wild animals.' And that is what happened" (Genesis 1:20–21, 24).

It makes the most sense to enjoy creation and give the credit to the Creator. But you have to believe.

GET REAL

Have you made up your mind about creation versus evolution? Examine, think, and pray about this issue. Don't leave out the faith component.

Puppet Play

Lesha Campbell

How long has it been since you played with a puppet? As a ventriloquist, I play with puppets every day. Weird, yes, but I do. And I've found that, more often than not, people have at least one memory of a puppet in their childhood—fond or fearful. Remember the birthday party puppet show that made your day, or the puppet horror movie that made your nightmares seem so real? I've heard all the memories—good and bad.

More often than not, adult audience members get more out of one of my shows than the child they brought along for the ride. At least, that's what they tell me. Maybe it's because my approach to using puppets is like that of the original Puppet Master, God.

God was the original puppeteer/ventriloquist. He once used a donkey as a puppet. God has a crazy sense of humor when He wants to get our attention. Check out Numbers 22:28: "Then the Lord gave the donkey the ability to speak. 'What have I done to you that deserves your beating me three times?' " Whoa. . .a talking donkey?

God even used a talking bush to get a man's attention in Exodus 3:4. "When the Lord saw Moses coming to take a closer look, God called to him from the middle of the bush, 'Moses! Moses!' " I'll bet Moses listened up very carefully after that. Wouldn't you?

GET REAL

If God speaks through objects and animals, maybe He could use you! We just need to be alert, willing, and submissive. Pay attention to what's happening around you and what God may want to say through you.

Living in the Mystery
Dale Robert Hicks

I am one of those people who likes to figure things out before others. I'll watch a TV show where the main characters are trying to solve a murder and guess who committed the crime before the guilty party is revealed. Sometimes it's obvious, and other times I'm stumped. I've learned to look for the clues that the writers of the show leave to point to the guilty person. These clues help me figure out where they are taking the story long before the action ever gets there.

There are times I approach my understanding of life in the same way. Rather than trusting in God to lead me through situations, I try to guess what He's up to and act accordingly. Sometimes I get it right, and sometimes I get it wrong. I've come to understand that the following words from Isaiah 55:8 mean I can't outguess God: " 'My thoughts are nothing like your thoughts,' says the LORD. 'And my ways are far beyond anything you could imagine.' "

TV writers know where to take the story and how to end the show. There are times when I can guess their direction and plot twists. There are other times that I cannot. Knowing that God is so far beyond my understanding means that rather than anticipate His moves in my life, I need to trust Him.

GET REAL

Do you trust God with your life? If you do, then stop trying to anticipate His every move, and simply enjoy the ride. If you don't trust Him, why not? Ask God to help you boost your confidence in Him.

Lasting Fruit
Rusty Wright

Have you ever communicated your faith with someone you never expected to see again? Maybe you wondered how—if at all—God would use your brief encounter. This story might encourage you.

One day I spoke about Jesus with Bert in his Georgia Tech dormitory room. He didn't seem sure of his relationship with God. I tried to tactfully explain that he could know he was linked with God for eternity.

At that point, Bert escorted me to the door, thanked me, and said good-bye. I didn't see him again and had no idea what happened after our meeting. . .until thirty years later when Bert found me on the Internet.

It turns out that Bert had thought about our conversation all that day. That night, while lying in his dorm bed, he realized he needed to trust Jesus as his personal Savior. He read the booklet I'd left him and placed his faith in Christ.

Eventually Bert served in Africa and helped thousands of high school students come to faith. Today he spearheads Christian leadership development efforts across the African continent. Bert feels these words of Jesus describe his life: "You didn't choose me. I chose you. I appointed you to go and produce lasting fruit" (John 15:16).

My brief encounter with Bert germinated into a vast harvest of lasting fruit.

GET REAL

In God's plans, seeing results sometimes takes time. You may never know, until years later, the results of the seeds you plant. Take the long view of serving Jesus. You are sowing seeds for decades in the future and for eternity.

Rescued from the Wrong Voice

Brian Sumner

As I travel across the country doing skate demos and speaking at events, I continually see that the world has an evil influence on a lot of people. Think about some of the messages we hear day in and day out online, on TV, and on the radio. Many different voices are trying to shape us by getting our attention. Whose voice is shaping your thinking? Is it for good or evil?

This all started back in the beginning of human history with the first man and woman—Adam and Eve—in the Garden of Eden. The devil, disguised as a serpent, tempted Eve with the fruit of a tree. God had told her to stay away from this tree, but Eve gave in to the wrong voice. Before long, Adam gave in to the wrong voice—Eve, who had been influenced by the devil. Then the trouble *really* began.

The devil has never given up trying to tempt people to disobey God. He did this with Jesus in the desert and continues to do it with me and you. We, too, have a choice as to which voice we will listen to and obey. And God has given us everything we need to know and understand His voice. Check out Galatians 1:4–5: "Jesus gave his life for our sins, just as God our Father planned, in order to rescue us from this evil world in which we live. All glory to God forever and ever!" God wants to rescue us from listening to the wrong voices. He wants to change the way we think. "Instead, let the Spirit renew your thoughts and attitudes" (Ephesians 4:23).

Each and every day God offers you a new opportunity to step out of the everyday world and fix your eyes on Him. Doing so will transform you from the inside out. How cool is that!

GET REAL

Make the choice today to follow God's voice, which will guide you the right way. Strive to be more selective about what you allow inside your head to influence your thinking. Be careful of what you read, watch, and listen to.

When in Rome
Tracy Klehn

On our last day in Rome after close to three weeks abroad, our family walked around checking out the sights one last time. We ate gelato, bought souvenirs, and took pictures of amazing historic buildings and statues that surprised us around almost every corner. Finally we returned to one of our favorite destinations, the Trevi Fountain. After a few minutes of taking pictures, I realized that my daughter Grace had become very quiet. When I put my camera down, I saw her eyes were filled with tears. I asked her what had upset her, and she shrugged her shoulders. . .but something told me she was homesick. "Do you miss your friends?" I asked quietly, and that was all it took for the tears to start rolling down her cheeks.

At that moment I was reminded of what Philippians 3:20 says: "But we are citizens of heaven, where the Lord Jesus Christ lives. And we are eagerly waiting for him to return as our Savior."

The truth is, while we walk this earth and see wonderful sights around every corner, there will always be a longing deep within us that is never satisfied and perhaps makes us feel a little sad sometimes. The reason is that we were created for another world. We are like Americans walking in Rome, waiting for our chance to return home and be reunited with the ones we love.

GET REAL

The next time you feel a little sad or empty, remind yourself, "I'm not home yet, but one day—because of my faith in Jesus—I will be."

Bungee Cords
Brenda Pue

I've noticed that sin has a way of tugging at us. *All* of us. Those who give in to sin once find it a little easier to choose it again. And again. So how does the sin cycle stop?

There are two answers to that question. For those who don't know God personally, the only way to stop the sin cycle is through the cross of Jesus. There is no other way to fix our sinful nature. God provided the way to forgiveness by allowing His Son to take all our sin on Himself by dying on the cross. The result? Freedom. Peace. Joy. Laughter.

The second answer is for those who know, love, and serve God. Even though Christ followers have made the commitment to live for God, sometimes sin still seems to have a grip on us. That's because Satan uses sin like a bungee cord in our lives. We can take a few steps, but then the bungee cord gets taut, and we can't seem to move forward.

When that happens, all we need to do is confess (humble ourselves and *name* the sin) to God—every time it happens. Confess over and over again, because "if we confess our sins, he is faithful and just and will forgive us our sins and purify us from all unrighteousness" (1 John 1:9 NIV).

GET REAL

As you confess your sins today, you will notice that Satan loses his grip on the bungee cord. Sin will no longer have power over you. That's because "the one who is in you [God] is greater than the one who is in the world [Satan]" (1 John 4:4 NIV).

I Can't, but He Can

Steve Russo

How do you respond when facing a huge life obstacle that's beyond your capabilities? Often we let the obstacles grow in our minds as we let feelings of fear take over. Then we run from the challenge to where we think it's safe. But running actually leads to failure by causing us to chain ourselves to an "I can't do it" attitude, which can shape our choices in the future.

Feeling inadequate is normal. But there's another option besides running—trusting God. This struggle is nothing new. When the Israelites were on the brink of entering the Promised Land, they were consumed by fear. They were comparing themselves to a powerful enemy and freaked out. Moses tried to encourage them by reminding them that God was more than adequate in this situation: "Look! He has placed the land in front of you. Go and occupy it as the Lord, the God of your ancestors, has promised you. Don't be afraid! Don't be discouraged!" (Deuteronomy 1:21).

Unfortunately, the Israelites didn't listen to Moses and trust God. They ended up wandering in the desert for forty years and never entered the land God had given them. We can lose out if we let fear chip away at our faith.

When you're facing a task far beyond your abilities, don't run. Rely on God and the promises of His Word.

GET REAL

The courage to trust God and move forward when you're feeling inadequate is based on past experience with Him. Think about the obstacle you are facing today and how God has fulfilled His promises to you in the past. He won't let you down if you trust Him.

Capable of More
Melanie Stiles

Rachel Guzy was a sixteen-year-old working as a camp counselor in New York. One day she climbed aboard the camp bus with nine other kids—all between the ages of seven and fourteen. As they cruised down the street, their bus driver suddenly collapsed and literally fell out of the bus, leaving Rachel and the other kids driverless. As they headed for a busy intersection, Rachel realized she had to do something. She quickly jumped into the driver's seat and found and pulled the emergency brake. The bus slowed a great deal before skidding into a minivan. Amazingly, there were no injuries to anyone in the bus or van.

Rachel didn't even have her learner's permit. She had certainly never thought about how to stop a bus. Later Rachel said she'd been a nervous wreck. She was shaking and crying the entire time and so scared she could hardly breathe. Yet, without any previous knowledge or skill, Rachel saved at least ten lives. She ended up a hero.

Hearing Rachel's story reminded me that we are capable of far more than we give ourselves credit for on most days. *Hopeless* and *helpless* should never be in our vocabulary. Rachel's story is a great example of Philippians 4:13: "For I can do everything through Christ, who gives me strength."

Rachel wasn't an expert. She didn't even know how to drive, yet God used Rachel in ways she never could have imagined.

GET REAL

Today, think about the fact that God can use anyone. . .anywhere. . .anytime. Be ready, because you never know when God will use you in a special way.

You Matter

Ramona Richards

It seems like most everybody wants to be famous. Everyone wants their time in the spotlight—their fifteen minutes of fame.

Why? Do we really believe that having a lot of people pay attention to us is the only way we'll feel significant in this world? Or that having cameras focused on us is the only way we'll have meaning and purpose?

The truth is, you already have significance! Think about it. Go out some night, look up at the sky, and remind yourself that in all the vastness of this amazing universe, God chose you to be you. He knew you and what His plan for your life would be before you were born. Only you can live that life. Only you can be you. If you don't take the path God intended for you, who will?

Even David, one of the most famous men in the Bible, felt overwhelmed by God's attention to humans on this planet. In Psalm 8:4 he asks God, "What are mere mortals that you should think about them, human beings that you should care for them?"

Eventually most of us will ask, Why me? Why do I matter?

We do matter, we do have significance, because we matter to God. His plans for us are unique. And only you can achieve what God has in store for you.

GET REAL

Thank God for making you who you are. Ask Him to help you live today like the significant person He made you to be.

Unseen Monsters

Chuck Poe

We all have things that we consider "monsters"—obstacles or problems we need to overcome. Yet many times when we face these kinds of issues, people around us try to stop or hinder us from dealing with these "monsters."

When King David in the Bible did what his father asked him to do, his brothers tried to discourage him. However, David had a personal passion to defend the nation of Israel and realized the power of God for his people. David went to King Saul and said that he would take care of a Philistine giant named Goliath. Saul tried to help David by giving him his armor, but David couldn't use it because it was too big and heavy. Instead, he took his staff, his slingshot, and five smooth stones from the creek. Then "as the Philistine [Goliath] moved closer to attack him, David ran quickly toward the battle line to meet him. Reaching into his bag and taking out a stone, he slung it and struck the Philistine on the forehead. The stone sank into his forehead, and he fell facedown on the ground" (1 Samuel 17:48–49 NIV).

Notice that when David was faced with a monster, he ran *toward* the problem. We need to face our issues and run to them with God's power. Trusting God instead of listening to other people can make all the difference we need to overcome.

GET REAL

Identify the "monsters"—seen and unseen—in your life. Then determine an action plan to conquer them. Instead of listening to the crowd, depend on God's power within you, trusting Him to help you overcome.

Advice
Steve Russo

Where do you go when you need advice? There are lots of places we can look besides Dr. Phil and Oprah. Websites, blogs, and social networking sites offer endless resources for guidance. Some of this guidance is beneficial; some of it is crazy and potentially harmful.

Family and friends are always available to give their opinions about what we should and shouldn't do. But, again, their advice can be helpful or harmful. It all depends on whether they're using insight from the world or from God.

The best and most reliable source for answers to the questions we have about life is God and His Word. Both are always true, right, and trustworthy. It's sad, but God—via the Bible and prayer—is usually the last place we go for direction. Most of the time we go to someone who will tell us what we *want* to hear rather than what we *need* to hear. The truth isn't always easy to swallow.

If we really want solid advice and solutions, the Bible is the greatest resource we have: "For the word of God is alive and powerful. It is sharper than the sharpest two-edged sword, cutting between soul and spirit, between joint and marrow. It exposes our innermost thoughts and desires" (Hebrews 4:12). If we're willing to take the time to search the Bible, and then pray, listen, and obey, we will find the answers we need.

GET REAL

Is God your first resource or your last resort for advice? Do your actions match your words about your trust in God? Pray, search His Word first for direction, and then follow His advice.

The Great Expectation

Chris Haidet

We all live by certain expectations. We might be expected to clean our room, get good grades, do the chores, and be nice to our siblings. Most of the time these expectations are important and easy to achieve. But sometimes expectations can be hard. We are expected to live up to a never-ending list of "never do this" and "always do that," "Why aren't you more like this person?" and "Can you be less like that one?" The frustration builds with each expectation not met. We let guilt and stress creep in as our mind focuses on our failures, and we lose sight of what's important in life.

The Bible says, "Therefore, since we have been made right in God's sight by faith, we have peace with God because of what Jesus Christ our Lord has done for us. Because of our faith, Christ has brought us into this place of undeserved privilege where we now stand" (Romans 5:1–2).

Did you know that Jesus failed people's expectations as well? The crowds and leaders of the people were expecting a king to give them peace on earth, but God had planned something far greater, a Savior who would bring us peace for eternity.

When you put your faith in Jesus, you have already met the greatest expectation: God's. Then, by living your life for Him, you are freed from the frustration that weighs you down, and you become confident in what lies ahead.

GET REAL

When life's expectations get hard, remember Jesus had them, too. He knows what you're dealing with. Turn to Him for guidance. When life is going well, thank God for what He has done.

Three Bones
Rich Thune

Former Michigan State football coach Duffy Dougherty believed that a player needed to have three bones in order to be successful at football. The first bone is backbone. Duffy wanted all of his players to have courage and strength of character. *Backbone* is another word for toughness. The second bone in Duffy's formula is a wishbone. A wishbone suggests something to hope for, something to believe in, something to aspire to. Duffy helped his players set goals to see their dreams become reality. He helped them turn their wishes into wins. The third bone the coach talked about is the funny bone. He didn't want his team to take life too seriously. They needed to find humor in everyday things.

There's a parallel to everyday life in the coach's three bones. To be successful we need to have backbone. God's Word says we should be "strong and courageous" (Joshua 1:6). We also need a sense of hopefulness and dreams to live for—a wishbone. In Romans 15:4 we read, "Such things were written in the Scriptures long ago to teach us. And the Scriptures give us hope and encouragement as we wait patiently for God's promises to be fulfilled." And we need a funny bone. The Bible reminds us that "a cheerful heart is good medicine" (Proverbs 17:22). Laughter cuts through the stress of life and enables us to smile even in the most difficult times.

GET REAL

Life can be a jungle of temptations, so how's your backbone? Are you standing strong in your faith? Where are you placing your hopes and wishes? How about your funny bone? Do you find relief in laughter?

Run the Race
Dale Robert Hicks

The 1968 Olympic Games were a long time ago, but a story from those weeks of athletic competition reminds us that God has called us to run the race of life so that we might win.

A marathon runner named Akhwari fell during a race and injured his leg, but he kept running. When he entered the stadium, many of the fans had left, for the medalist had completed the race, and Akhwari, representing Tanzania, was the last man to finish. The remaining spectators looked on in amazement as this man, in obvious agony, reached the finish line. When he was asked why he didn't just quit the race, Akhwari replied, "My country did not send me 5,000 miles to Mexico City to start the race. They sent me 5,000 miles to finish the race."

Consider this verse from Hebrews 12:1: "Therefore, since we are surrounded by such a huge crowd of witnesses to the life of faith, let us strip off every weight that slows us down, especially the sin that so easily trips us up. And let us run with endurance the race God has set before us."

GET REAL

If you want to run the believer's life the best that you can, think about the things that slow you down and what you're going to do about them. Akhwari ran the race because of his country. Jesus ran the race for the joy waiting for Him. The questions you must answer are these: Why do you run the race? How do you run it? For whom do you run?

Shark-Victim Surfer Girl's Faith

Rusty Wright

If I ever get discouraged, I just need to remember Bethany Hamilton.

Bethany looks like any fun-loving young American—bright-eyed, smiling, excited about life. She's athletic, attractive, trim, tanned, and blond. But she faces a special challenge. She's missing her left arm just below the shoulder, lost to a shark attack while she was surfing in Hawaii at age thirteen. She's fortunate to be alive.

Bethany was Hawaii's top-ranked female amateur surfer before the attack. Merely three months after the mishap, she was surfing competitively again. She even won an amateur national championship and a junior professional competition.

Rather than hiding her left arm under clothing, she displayed it in tank tops and called it "Stumpy." When her prosthetic turned out to be too light in color to match her suntan, she nicknamed it "*Haole* Girl," slang for a non-Hawaiian. She peeled tangerines by holding them between her feet and using her right hand.

Why the bright outlook on life? Bethany says it's because of God. On her website she says that Jesus gave her peace when the shark attacked and that God gives her continued courage: "This is my command—be strong and courageous! Do not be afraid or discouraged. For the Lord your God is with you wherever you go" (Joshua 1:9).

GET REAL

Are you facing disappointment? God loves you and wants your best. Read Bethany's story and be inspired. Then read the Bible and ask your heavenly Father to help strengthen your faith.

Limitless Power
Steve Russo

A lot of people are looking for power. They want power to change their lives, power to feel special, and sometimes power to get vengeance on those who have hurt them.

Are you looking for power in your life? Have you found it yet?

Some claim they've found power in Wicca or the inner-self philosophies of eastern religions. This kind of power is limited and doesn't last. Still others think that power comes from wealth or position. This kind of power is also limited and eventually fails.

But there is a source of power that is supernatural and un-limited. Anyone can get it, but there are conditions. This power is found in the person of Jesus and His resurrection. Paul, an early follower of Jesus, wrote how he wanted this power to be real in his life, too: "I want to know Christ and experience the mighty power that raised him from the dead" (Philippians 3:10).

Think about it. The same power that brought Jesus back to life after He'd been in the grave for three days is available to help us overcome all our life challenges. But in order for us to experi-ence this resurrection power in our daily lives, we first have to die to ourselves and to sin. It means surrendering our lives to Jesus so we can live for and like Him by His power.

GET REAL

Where could you use supernatural, unlimited power in your life today? Whatever the problem is, surrender it to God and rely on Him to give you the power you need. Then wait for Him to deal with it in His way and time.

What If I Doubt?

Melanie Stiles

Can you honestly say you have total faith that God is with you all the time? I wish I had total faith. But more than one time I've cried out loud, "God? Jesus? Are You here with me now?" My faith had dipped pretty low at those times. In other situations, I've been absolutely certain He was right in the middle of what I was doing.

The Bible relates several incidents involving a guy named Thomas. He wanted to believe in Jesus, but he struggled with doubts. But Thomas still hung out with Jesus while he was sorting out his beliefs. I like that about him. He chose not to walk away until he knew what Jesus was all about. He even stuck around after He died.

After Jesus was resurrected, He visited the disciples. When He came into the room to greet them, Jesus bypassed all the other disciples who *didn't* doubt to speak to Thomas first. In John 20:27 Jesus said to Thomas, "Put your finger here, and look at my hands. Put your hand into the wound in my side. Don't be faithless any longer. Believe!"

Jesus wanted Thomas to know He was for real. He wants us to ultimately get over our doubts, too. In the meantime, He's patient with us while we figure them out.

GET REAL

When you struggle with doubt, do you stick it out like Thomas? Doubt can be okay if you honestly are in search of answers.

Endurance
Nicole O'Dell

It's not easy to be a long-distance runner. It takes a lot of hard work to build up the strength and endurance needed to compete. Runners need to be faithful to finish the race. They must make sure nothing will slow them down—from their shoes to their jersey to their body weight.

We have to think and prepare in a similar way if we want to finish the race of life that God has prepared for us. Paul gave Timothy some advice about the race of life, reminding him it wasn't going to be easy. "I have fought the good fight, I have finished the race, and I have remained faithful" (2 Timothy 4:7).

We can't complete the race of life if we lack endurance or if any people or things are holding us back. And often these are not necessarily bad; even good things and people can hinder us from finishing the race the way God planned for us to. Maybe for you it is the amount of time you spend hanging out with friends. Or it could be a sport or video game that's consuming you and getting in your way in the long-distance race of life.

GET REAL

A lot of your weight may be the friends you hang with. Or maybe you carry secret weights that aren't readily visible to others. Ask God to help you deal with the people and things that are holding you back in your race.

Asking the Right Question

Susie Shellenberger

Have you noticed that we often hide our real questions behind facade questions? For instance, when we ask, "Why did *she* get that award?" what we're really asking is, "Why didn't I get it? What does she have that I don't?"

But we're not alone in asking the wrong questions. The disciples often did the same thing. In John 6 we read about a storm. The disciples were in a boat; Jesus hadn't joined them yet. Verse 19 gives us a closer view: "They had rowed three or four miles when suddenly they saw Jesus walking on the water toward the boat. They were terrified."

Jesus told them not to be afraid. He got into the boat, and *suddenly* they were on the shore! When they reached the shore, the crowds who had been following Jesus couldn't believe He was there. They knew He hadn't rowed there. They wanted to know *how* and *when* He had arrived.

Jesus told them they weren't asking the right questions. You see, their question really revealed the question behind it! They weren't actually interested in what Jesus was doing on the shore. Rather, they were into the spectacular. They wanted to know about the "magic" of *how* He got there and *when* it happened.

Later in the chapter, Jesus tries to realign their focus and urges them to spend their energy going after things with eternal value.

GET REAL

Will you allow God to realign *your* focus? Jesus loves your questions! But He wants you to be asking the right ones. Consider the questions you ask. Is there another question behind what you're asking?

More Important Than Candy

Steve Russo

Easter is one of my favorite times of the year. Part of it has to do with chocolate bunnies and eggs. I love chocolate! But the idea behind Easter is far more important than candy. The first Easter morning Jesus came back to life after being dead in a grave for three days. The world would never be the same after His resurrection. Everything else about the Christian faith becomes meaningless without this event. The empty tomb guarantees us that everything Jesus taught is true.

Jesus' resurrection is the most unique moment in history. No other religious leader in human history has even hinted at the possibility of conquering death. Paul wrote about how important the Resurrection was to early Jesus followers living in a corrupt society: "I passed on to you what was most important and what had also been passed on to me. Christ died for our sins, just as the Scriptures said. He was buried, and he was raised from the dead on the third day, just as the Scriptures said" (1 Corinthians 15:3–4).

The resurrection described in these verses is physical, not spiritual. The word *resurrection* literally means "the standing up of a corpse." Think about how important this is to you and me today. One day our dead bodies are going to "stand up" from the grave! The amazing thing about the Christian faith is that we never see death as the end. Instead, we look into eternity and see the hope that is offered through the resurrected life of Jesus.

GET REAL

Who or what have you put your hope in for today and the future? Make sure it is securely anchored in Jesus.

No Limit
Nicole O'Dell

Forgiving others is hard to do—especially when we've really been hurt by someone. It doesn't always feel right to let somebody off the hook for what they've done. And it's particularly tough when we need to keep forgiving someone repeatedly. If we aren't careful, we can become bitter, and this attitude can have a destructive impact on our relationships with God and others.

This topic came up when Jesus was teaching the disciples one day. "Then Peter came to him and asked, 'Lord, how often should I forgive someone who sins against me? Seven times?' 'No, not seven times,' Jesus replied, 'but seventy times seven!' " (Matthew 18:21–22).

In biblical times religious teachers would tell people that they needed to forgive someone three times. Peter probably thought he was being pretty generous by upping it to seven times. Can you can imagine how Peter and the other disciples felt when they heard Jesus say they needed to keep forgiving someone over and over again? The lesson: there's no limit on the number of times we're to forgive others.

God wants us to always forgive those who come to us who are truly sorry. We also need to be ready to forgive someone even if they express no regret for what they've done.

GET REAL

Is there someone who has hurt you or someone you care about whom you need to forgive? Ask God to give you the ability to forgive them—even if you need to keep doing it. Pray that you won't keep track of how many times you have to forgive them.

Stepping Off the Edge
Dale Robert Hicks

When I was learning how to rappel down a cliff, I learned what the word *encouragement* really means. I had gone with a group of students to learn the art of climbing down the face of a mountain. The instructor asked who would like to be the first to rappel down this thirty-foot cliff. None of the other students stepped up, so I, being their leader, volunteered to go first. I hooked up to the rope, got to the edge of the cliff, and froze. The instructor finally tied off another rope next to mine and said, "I'll go down beside you, one step at a time." He talked to me the whole way down—encouraging me with his words and his presence. He literally shared his courage with me.

Think about God's directions concerning encouragement found in Hebrews 10:25: "And let us not neglect our meeting together, as some people do, but encourage one another, especially now that the day of his return is drawing near."

I have found the same thing to be true in my relationship with Christ. There are times in my life when I am afraid, and something keeps me from doing what He wants me to do. That's when I need other Christians to come alongside me, talk me through my fear, and just be there with me—to *share* their courage.

GET REAL

How can other Christ followers be an encouragement to you? How can you be an encouragement to others?

The Gift That Keeps Giving

Chris Haidet

I grew up playing a sport not known for its athletic prowess or the popularity of those who participated. I was a bowler. That's right—a bowler. I was pretty good, too. In fact, I could beat most people by throwing the ball between my legs. Bowling was my love, and I planned on making it my life's career. God, however, had other plans, so bowling became something of my past as I focused on what God called and gifted me to do.

The Bible says, "God has given each of you a gift from his great variety of spiritual gifts. Use them well to serve one another" (1 Peter 4:10).

God has gifted us in many areas of life, and we are called to use these gifts to serve others. But what about those talents and abilities that we love but can't quite figure out how to use?

Two years after I gave up the bowling career idea, I got my answer. I was doing a project to raise funds for an orphanage, and I couldn't figure out what to do. Finally I thought, *What about bowling?* As weird as it may sound, I was able to raise thousands of dollars by setting a record, bowling between my legs.

If God can use something as weird as that, He can use *anything*. What are you good at? What can you do that few other people can do? Even if it's weird, are you using it for God?

GET REAL

List the gifts you have, even if they're weird. Pray for God to give you creative ideas for using them for Him and others.

Ask, Look, and Listen
Ramona Richards

The questions we have about life are constant. It seems like there's a new one every day. About things like relationships, sex, faith, achievements, the future, goals. The *whys* and *whats* seem to go on and on. Why should I go to college? What job should I apply for? Why did they act like that? Why did I mess this up? Why didn't God answer my prayer?

Finding answers isn't always quick and easy. And sometimes it seems like God isn't listening. Most of us don't hear the audible voice of God giving us answers. So where do we turn?

The best and most reliable place to start is the Bible. Look at Psalm 119:105: "Your word is a lamp to guide my feet and a light for my path." Everything we need to know about life is found in the Word of God.

But sometimes it's good to have someone to talk with about the questions we have. That's why God puts people in our lives who can help. Proverbs 11:14 says, "There is safety in having many advisers." God surrounds us with wise people who can help guide us through the issues in life. He can speak through counselors at school, pastors, and even our parents to give us the answers or insight we need. Sometimes God even provides answers through the most unlikely people.

All we have to do is listen. But it's good to remember that we should test any advice with the filter of the Bible. If we keep an open heart and mind, we'll get God's answers to all our questions sooner or later.

GET REAL

What questions do you have today? Have you looked in the Bible for an answer? Is there someone you respect whom you can talk with? God always answers if we ask, look, and listen.

Can God Hear Me?

Ron Merrell

I had the unique privilege of driving a deaf woman and her assistance dog from a public-speaking engagement back to the airport. Even though she could speak well, I was nervous about the hour-long ride I was about to take with her. I didn't think she was going to be able to understand me, and I was also pretty sure her dog was going to eat me.

We drove and chatted for about thirty minutes as she read my lips from the side. I actually started to doubt that she was really deaf and began to think of ways to test her hearing! Late in the ride, she closed her eyes for a moment. I screamed as loudly as I could in her ear! Unfortunately, I had forgotten about her dog. Within seconds it leaped over the seat and woke her up, snarling and spitting. I nearly wet my pants.

Do you ever doubt that God can hear you? Psalm 34:17 (NIV) reminds us, "The righteous cry out, and the LORD hears them; he delivers them from all their troubles." And 2 Chronicles 16:9 (NIV) says, "The eyes of the LORD range throughout the earth to strengthen those whose hearts are fully committed to him."

Just because God isn't answering prayers in your timing or according to your plan doesn't mean He's not listening.

GET REAL

God is bigger than your doubts. If you're having trouble believing that He hears you today, be patient. Keep praying. Focus more on fully committing yourself to Him than on the issues you're facing. See what He does.

Gaining Control

Steve Russo

An inbox overflowing with texts. . .too much drama at home. . .
unrealistic expectations from the opposite sex. . .teachers who
forget I have a life outside of school. . .life responsibilities. . .a
crazy schedule. . .pain. . .pressure from friends. . .

My life is out of control! Can you relate?

How do you stop life from spinning out of control? The answer may surprise you: to gain control, you have to give it up.

Jesus said, "Come to me, all of you who are weary and carry
heavy burdens, and I will give you rest. Take my yoke upon you.
Let me teach you, because I am humble and gentle at heart, and
you will find rest for your souls. For my yoke is easy to bear, and
the burden I give you is light" (Matthew 11:28–30).

A *yoke* is a heavy wooden harness that fits over the shoulders of oxen. It's attached to a piece of equipment the oxen are
pulling. What are you trying to pull and carry?

Jesus doesn't always remove the things that weigh us down,
but He frees us from them. The yoke Jesus gives us is a partner-
ship—He carries us and works alongside us. The weight of life
now falls on His shoulders. Someone with unlimited power is now
up front, pulling us through the struggles and challenges of life.

GET REAL

Are you afraid to give up control—even if it would
lighten your load? What are you trying to carry today
that's weighing you down? Surrender it to God and let
Him pull you through and free you.

Dirty Laundry
Melanie Stiles

Everybody has a favorite pair of jeans. You know the ones. They're worn in and fit just right. Because they're so comfortable, you'd wear them all the time if you could. Don't lie—you usually wear them several times before you toss them in the laundry. Still, sooner or later, you have to break down and wash them, because if you didn't, everyone would start to notice. Most of all, you!

Sometimes we can treat sinful behaviors just like we treat our comfortable pair of jeans. It's easy to just slip into them without really thinking about what we're doing. And when we don't do anything to stop them, they can start to feel like they fit just right. Let's say we tell a few lies. Then, before we know it, lying becomes a habit hidden deep in our heart. After the first one, what's one more? That's exactly why we shouldn't go too long before taking the time to clean up the "dirty laundry" in our lives. But how do we deal with sin? Follow the advice in 1 John 1:9: "If we confess our sins to him, he is faithful and just to forgive us our sins and to cleanse us from all wickedness."

Remember, you need God's help to change. You can't do it without His power. Start by agreeing with God that what you're doing is wrong. Decide not to repeat the behavior. Start over again. Once that's done, your heart is clean, just like your jeans after you wash them. But with sin, it takes daily spiritual cleaning to keep your heart unstained.

GET REAL

....

Have you checked your spiritual laundry today? Use the Bible as a filter; then ask God for help.

A Revealing Question

Susie Shellenberger

One day the disciples asked Jesus a question: "Who then is greatest in the kingdom of heaven?" (Matthew 18:1 NKJV).

They were assuming the greatest spot would go to one of them. It's dangerous to assume things in our relationship with Christ. But that's exactly what the disciples did.

After all, the position of prestige in His kingdom will surely go to one us, they must have thought. *We're the Big Twelve. We're the ones who have left all to follow Him. We're the disciples. We're the ones He chose. We've been with Him for three years. We've walked with Him. Listened to Him. Watched the miracles. We've healed in His name and in His power.*

Surely when Jesus sets up His kingdom, one of us will be His vice president. But which one of us will it be?

Peter probably assumed it would be him. After all, he was a natural-born leader. He was always the first to speak and the first to act. He was bold. Outspoken. An extrovert in every sense of the word. And Jesus *did* say, "On you I will build My church. You're the *rock*, Peter."

And Peter *did* walk on water. Surely, underneath Jesus, Peter would be the greatest in God's kingdom. But Jesus revealed that the "greatest" position would go to whoever humbled himself like a little child.

GET REAL

Can you remember a time when your assumptions were proven to be wrong? Even embarrassing? Follow Christ's example of humility. He came to earth as a servant. Spiritual growth never happens through assumptions of greatness; it always happens through humility and brokenness.

Facing Death

Rusty Wright

We could tell right away that something was wrong. The spring of my sophomore year at my university, my roommate and I returned to our fraternity house one evening after a double date. The first person we encountered was Ed, trudging gloomily down the stairway, looking like he had just lost his best friend. He had.

Mike, the student living in the room next to me, had been playing golf that afternoon. When a thunderstorm came up, he sought shelter under a tree. Lightning struck, killing him instantly.

For some time after Mike's death, our fraternity was in a state of shock. What should have been a happy time at semester's end became filled with mourning and confusion. My friends were asking questions like, "What does it mean if life can be snuffed out in an instant? Is there a life after death? How can we experience it?"

My roommate and I mourned Mike's loss with our friends. And we explained that Jesus, through His sacrificial death and resurrection, paid the price for our sin so that we—and they— could be forgiven and spend eternity with Him. Jesus said, "I am the resurrection and the life. Anyone who believes in me will live, even after dying" (John 11:25).

GET REAL

Are you sure you'll spend eternity with God? You can be sure. Simply ask Jesus to use His death as the means of your forgiveness, to enter your life, and to become your friend forever. He'll never leave you.

Help! I'm Alone!
Patrick Dunn

Remember the shock and terror of your first pimple?

You did almost anything to hide it: way too much makeup; the "bandage trick," where you told everyone your dog scratched you; the fake beard. Anytime you looked in the mirror or talked to someone, you thought about *the pimple*.

Well, that's how being single can feel sometimes. You try to ignore it, cover it up, make excuses. . .but it's always there, lurking.

The pressure to be with someone can be intense. Everyone around you seems to be dating. Your friends start pointing out people you'd be "perfect" with. And you may be tempted to think, *What is wrong with me?*

Being single can be frustrating. It's like that pimple—it's *so hard* to avoid. If it's not the outside pressure, then there are the days you honestly wish you were with someone.

You may be tempted to harden yourself and decide you don't need anyone. Or you may think, *I have plenty of friends. . .in my online world.* That really doesn't count.

The good news is we are truly never alone. In Matthew 28:20 (NIV) God promises, "Surely I am with you always, to the very end of the age." That may sound like spiritual gibberish during those times you feel lonely, but it's true. Take God's hand by reaching out to Him in prayer. You don't need a fake beard or makeup to do it.

GET REAL

Talk to God about your desire to be with someone. He can fill you with peace, strength, and contentment, giving you the patience to wait for Ms. or Mr. Right.

It's All Relative, Isn't It?

Mike Thune

In our culture today, it is very easy to "go along to get along." The popular belief that each of us has our own truth and that "what is true for you may not be true for me" is called *relativism*.

Surveys indicate that a majority of Christ followers in our culture—including teenage believers—have accepted relativism. But relativism runs contrary to scripture and, if we think about it just a little bit, is obviously false. For example, *if* relativism were true, we would have to say that the views of any given culture are just as valid as those of any other—including the racist views of the KKK, the genocidal views of the Nazis, the absurd views of the "flat earth society," and so on. But we know that these views are all false and in *no way* valid. Therefore, it follows logically that relativism is false.

Have your friends or perhaps even some of your teachers encouraged you to think that everything is relative? Let's be real: Jesus *didn't* say, "If it's true for you that I'm the only way you can get to heaven, that's great; but other people have their own truths for how to get to heaven, and all of these work just as well." Instead, He said, "I am the way, the truth, and the life. No one can come to the Father except through me" (John 14:6). And that, my friends, is God's honest truth.

GET REAL

In what ways does society pressure you to accept relativism? Choose today to stand firm for what's right and true, even if it goes against the cultural or popular grain.

Too Much Drama

Steve Russo

Every time I speak at an assembly on a school campus, I'm amazed at how many students' lives are ruled by drama. It can be about anything and everything—friends, parents, teachers and grades, boyfriend/girlfriend stuff. . . Sometimes stuff just happens. Other times something that's not very important gets blown up.

Sometimes life is just tough. Like baby-mama/baby-daddy drama when a classmate gets pregnant. Or a friend takes his or her own life.

If the drama's real, that's okay. But when it comes to acting overly dramatic about things just for the thrill of it, life is too short for that kind of stage show. James, the brother of Jesus, gives us a reality check to consider: "How do you know what your life will be like tomorrow? Your life is like the morning fog—it's here a little while, then it's gone" (James 4:14).

Life is short no matter how long we live. It's easy to be deceived into thinking we have a lot of time left to enjoy family members and friends or to get our lives together and do what we know we should. A lot of people live like there's always going to be a tomorrow. The reality of how short life is slams us hard when a friend our age dies.

Why not live for Jesus today? Then no matter when your life ends, you can have the satisfaction of knowing that you accomplished what God wanted you to do.

GET REAL

What life drama is getting in the way of your living for God? Is it because of the friends you hang with? Is it something that you can change? Remember, life's too brief to let drama rule.

Damage Control
Ramona Richards

God, why did I say that? Insults. . .put-downs. . .criticism . . .hate. . . Have you noticed how easy it is for a thought to be in your head and out your mouth before you can stop it?

Do you sometimes have a problem controlling your words? Most of us do at one time or another. Our ego gets in the way of our wisdom, or our emotions override our intellect. We can be really smart but forget that not all words are worth saying. We let our desire to be clever or to show off defeat any sense of compassion we may have for others.

It's definitely not a new problem. Check out Proverbs 21:23: "Watch your tongue and keep your mouth shut, and you will stay out of trouble."

Words can—and do—hurt. They damage relationships and create pain that lasts for years. And you can't just blow it off by saying, "I didn't really mean that." Once the words leave your mouth, it's impossible to take them back.

Changing this kind of behavior involves more than just thinking before you speak. It also means loving those around you and wanting the best for them. It means keeping their hearts safe by keeping your tongue in check.

GET REAL

It's okay to be clever and show off sometimes. It's not okay to hurt others in the process. Today make a real effort to say only positive and encouraging words to others. You'll be amazed at the results!

Stuff
Dale Robert Hicks

I had to take a cell phone away from a student one day, and as I did she began to cry. By the end of the class period, she proceeded to tell me that I had ruined her life because I had kept her cell phone from her for fifty minutes. It became very apparent to me that her phone was the most important thing in her life—more important than her grades, her work in class, and probably a whole lot of other things.

That experience got me to thinking: What would cause me the greatest grief if I lost it? That's when this verse came to mind: "Yes, everything else is worthless when compared with the infinite value of knowing Christ Jesus my Lord. For his sake I have discarded everything else, counting it all as garbage, so that I could gain Christ" (Philippians 3:8).

All the "stuff" you have in the world, when you compare it to knowing Jesus, is garbage. But how much of our stuff gets in the way of developing our relationship with Him? Do our cell phones, PS3s, Xboxes, iPods, computers, and cars keep us from the infinite value of getting close to Jesus? In simpler terms, is the stuff in our lives more important to us than knowing our Lord?

GET REAL

Ask yourself what is the one thing that would cause you to feel the saddest if you lost it. Is it more important to you than knowing Christ?

New Shoes

Lesha Campbell

Do you love mall crawling and looking for the latest shoes on the shelf? I certainly do! As a matter of fact, one of my favorite places to "visit" is an online footwear page. Yes, I know I don't need so many shoes—hey, I only have one pair of feet, and I can only wear one pair at a time—but they must go with the right outfit or at least not be out of style.

When I went to the mall just before school started, lots of kids were trying to find the perfect pairs of shoes. Notice I said "pairs," not "pair." And the same for clothing. Everyone wanted the latest style of jeans and the perfect T-shirts to accent the "look" so they'd feel confident on the first day of school and fit right in with everyone "important."

No doubt parents and kids certainly don't see the same things as "cool" or "perfect." Parents look at the cost, the need, and whether the clothes and shoes are appropriate for the school's dress code—unless, of course, the students wear uniforms.

Wouldn't it be amazing if we never had to buy new shoes or clothing? That happened in the Bible once. "For forty years you sustained them in the wilderness; they lacked nothing in all that time. Their clothes didn't wear out and their feet didn't swell!" (Nehemiah 9:21 TLB). God supplies our needs, too. Pretty cool, huh?

GET REAL

Next time you're checking out the latest styles in shoes and clothes, run them by your "need or want" meter. Go with the need.

Basic Needs

Steve Russo

Although each of us has specific talents and desires, there are a few basic needs we all share. Everyone has the need to fit in somewhere. And we all need to be confident that we can succeed. Also, although lots of people struggle with a poor self-image, we all need to be able to say, "I matter."

We matter because Jesus paid a huge price so we could be forgiven and have new life. Sometimes we forget God cares about us as individuals. A great reminder is Jesus' story about a lost sheep:

> "If a man has a hundred sheep and one of them gets lost, what will he do? Won't he leave the ninety-nine others in the wilderness and go to search for the one that is lost until he finds it? And when he has found it, he will joyfully carry it home on his shoulders. When he arrives, he will call together his friends and neighbors, saying, 'Rejoice with me because I have found my lost sheep.' In the same way, there is more joy in heaven over one lost sinner who repents and returns to God than over ninety-nine others who are righteous and haven't strayed away!" (Luke 15:4–7)

God's love for every person is so great that He seeks out each one of us and celebrates when we're found! And He wants to provide every one of us with everything we need. Now that's something to celebrate!

GET REAL

Only God can provide for our basic needs. What is missing in your life? Ask God to meet this need today. Then live confident of God's power in your life.

No Noise

Melanie Stiles

Smartphones. Facebook. Twitter. Staying connected is easy. But when I have big decisions to make, it can seem like there's too much noise—everybody has too much to say. I ask for opinions and listen for answers that I really need. But if I ask ten people, I get twenty different answers. In the end my head is spinning, and I have very little confidence in anything I've heard. Ever been there? About this time I realize what I really need is an absence of noise—it's time to look for silence.

I've learned that quiet is the place where I can hear God give me answers for my life. But it usually takes awhile because the absence of noise is uncomfortable for me at first. I'm used to being hammered by sound of some sort all the time. I get restless when doing nothing but sitting quietly.

If I can resist bringing back the noise—even for a little while—I can hear from God. Think about the words of Psalm 46:10: "Be still, and know that I am God! I will be honored by every nation. I will be honored throughout the world."

An amazing thing happens in this moment of stillness. I am able to see that no matter what is going on in my life, God has answers and will be there to see me through. Then I can walk back into the noise with peace and direction.

GET REAL

Have you experienced being still lately? Try setting aside two minutes every day with no noise. You'll be surprised what happens.

Recognized
Steve Russo

Have you ever run into a celebrity at a mall or a restaurant? What happened when you recognized them? Some people are afraid to go up and say something or to ask for an autograph. For those living in Southern California, there are frequent "celeb watch" opportunities to run into them—especially in Hollywood or at L.A. Live, where there are several places they like to hang out. If you pay attention when you're in these areas, it's usually easy to recognize them even if they're wearing a hat or sunglasses. Most of them are pretty friendly and will take time to talk once they are recognized.

There's an interesting parallel to being recognized in the book of Acts. Peter and John had been arrested and brought before a group of religious leaders for questioning. "The members of the council were amazed when they saw the boldness of Peter and John, for they could see that they were ordinary men with no special training in the Scriptures. They also recognized them as men who had been with Jesus" (4:13).

The council knew that Peter and John had no training and recognized what being with Jesus had done to them. A changed life can be very convincing.

Have you been changed by being with Jesus? Do others in your family and school recognize that something is different about your life?

GET REAL

Being with Jesus should change our attitudes, the way we talk, the way we treat others, and the things we do. Are you spending time with Jesus consistently enough that others will know you've been with Him? Make the time—you'll be surprised how different your life will be.

Anchored
Carson Pue

I live by the ocean and love to go sailing. I've gone exploring in some incredible little bays where I'd anchor for the night. What always amazes me is how small the anchor is in relation to the size of the boat; and yet, when it locks into the bottom of the ocean, it is able to hold us in place. The sailboat swings on the anchor with the current and tide, but we stay basically in our same position, unable to make any forward progress.

In life we can actually get anchored to things that are not helpful. Being closely tied in friendship with one who is not following Jesus or with a bad habit can cause us to be stuck in our growth. It has happened to me before—how about you?

We cannot avoid being around people who are not Christ followers. In fact, Jesus doesn't even want us to steer clear of them. He wants you and me to be like lights in a dark world without getting locked into their lifestyles or thinking. A Christian leader named Martin Luther once said that we cannot prevent the birds from flying about our heads—but we can prevent them from building nests in our hair.

If you are going to anchor yourself to anyone or anything, let it be Jesus. Hebrews 6:19 (NKJV) describes our hope in Him as an "anchor of the soul, both sure and steadfast." Don't let an anchor set elsewhere hold you back.

GET REAL

Are any of your friends or habits causing you to be stuck? Sail away from their influence and anchor yourself with Jesus.

The Finest Form of Flattery

Chris Haidet

Have you ever seen someone who could impersonate a celebrity so well that you thought to yourself, *Wow, that's so close to the original that I can barely see the difference*? I have. In fact, I worked with a comedian once who was so good at it, he ended up on national TV, side by side with the president, doing his routine in front of millions. I remember asking him one day, "How can your words, facial expressions, and actions be so identical?"

He said he simply begins to study the person. He watches carefully and observes the subtleties of their movements and expressions and sees how they react in different situations and then begins to implement his research into his own life. Then he practices in front of the mirror until the reflection he sees is as close to the original as possible. What if we applied this strategy with God?

The Bible says, "Imitate God, therefore, in everything you do, because you are his dear children. Live a life filled with love, following the example of Christ" (Ephesians 5:1–2).

When we study and learn from Jesus, we discover how to live our lives for and like Jesus. We see His actions, thoughts, and teachings, and we learn how to apply them in our everyday lives. So when people see us, they see the reflection of Jesus in all we do.

GET REAL

Take time each week to study Jesus. Read His words, observe His actions, and begin to apply them daily. Pray to God every day for help, and watch yourself become more like Him.

Keep Your Word

Steve Russo

My grandfather worked for the mob—gambling and collecting money. He was known as Big Ernie.

Keeping your word was an important lesson my grandfather taught his grandkids in different ways. The message was always the same: Keep your word, no matter what the cost. "There will be times," he'd say, "when you will shake hands, make a commitment to someone, and the situation won't turn out like you planned. But you keep your word—even if it's more than you had bargained for. A man always keeps his word." It's a principle most of us grandkids continue to practice to this day.

My grandfather was concerned about living out his word, not acting for convenience. He'd say, "A man is no better than his word. If he doesn't keep his word, he isn't much of a man."

Jesus was big on keeping His word. There was no room for empty promises. Vows were all too common in His day, but He taught His followers that their word alone should be enough. In Matthew 5:37 He says, "Just say a simple 'Yes, I will,' or 'No, I won't.' Anything beyond this is from the evil one." It's interesting that my grandfather was introducing biblical truth into our lives but didn't realize it. Even more amazing: six weeks before he died, he committed his life to Jesus.

GET REAL

Are you known as a person of your word? Can others depend on you to keep your commitments—written or verbal, convenient or not? Even when it comes to the little things, do you keep your word? Today and every day, make your yes, yes, and your no, no.

Parents
Doug Jones

Respecting Mom and Dad. Yeah, yeah, we know we are sup-posed to, but what if they aren't respectful of us? What if they are living lives that are full of stupid decisions, sinful choices, addic-tions, or abuse? Yep, we still have to respect them. Our very lives depend on how we treat them, according to Exodus 20:12 (NIV): "Honor your father and your mother, *so that you may live long in the land the LORD your God is giving you*" (emphasis added).

This doesn't mean we have to agree with them when they are wrong, any more than we have to agree with the president when he makes a decision we find questionable. But we still honor the office of the president with respect. Same thing with Mom and Dad.

Parents come in all packages—the kind who totally get us and are supportive, and the kind who are completely out of touch with our needs and dreams. Then there are the ones who are just plain absent because of either divorce or abandonment. In all cases, good and bad, they are human beings doing the best they know with the flaws that accompany being human. Let's learn from their successes and their failures so that when we grow out from under their roof and their rules, we can have the honor and respect due to us from our own children.

GET REAL

Next time you see Mom and Dad, hug them and say, "I love you." Then start living that long life God promises.

Did You Hear. . .?

Ramona Richards

Cindy loves secrets, the sleazier the better. She especially likes the kind she can share with her best friend. And her sister. And the guy sitting next to her in Algebra. And the girl. . .

You get the idea. Cindy likes to gossip and enjoys spreading rumors. Most of all, she loves being the first to know—and tell—any sleazy tidbits.

No matter who the gossip hurts. The important thing is that *she* gets to tell it.

Most of us have a Cindy in our lives. Someone who wants to be trusted, but you know you can't. Anything you say to them will end up circulating around the school and maybe even go viral before the sun sets.

Maybe you're a Cindy. Check out Proverbs 26:20: "Fire goes out without wood, and quarrels disappear when gossip stops." Gossip is never positive for anyone who falls into its trap. Look at the company it keeps in Romans 1:29: "Their lives became full of every kind of wickedness, sin, greed, hate, envy, murder, quarreling, deception, malicious behavior, and gossip."

Ouch!

Avoiding a gossip can be much easier than avoiding *being* a gossip. Remember that words hurt much more deeply than a physical wound. Refraining from gossip is about pleasing God and valuing others.

GET REAL

Don't be a gossip. If you know a secret, keep it, no matter how juicy. Ask the Lord to help you overcome the temptation to spread rumors.

Care for the Needy

Ron Merrell

I have a really big Adam's apple. One time I was were working down at an orphanage in Mexico, and dozens of little orphan kids came running up, trying to grab my throat and saying, *"Que es esto?!"* (What is this?!) They'd never seen an Adam's apple this big in their country before. I told them I had an apple stuck in my throat, and they all gasped in amazement!

With twenty orphans pawing at my throat, one of my friends slipped a real apple in my hand, and I began to make noises like I was ready to throw up. At the perfect moment, I threw the real apple on the ground and all the kids screamed, thinking my throat had exploded.

This was all in good fun, but scaring little orphan kids is not exactly what God had in mind when He inspired James to write, "Pure and genuine religion in the sight of God the Father means caring for orphans and widows in their distress and refusing to let the world corrupt you" (James 1:27).

God has a huge heart for the broken and needy. His heart beats for those who are fatherless. He wants those who need help and hope to find it!

GET REAL

No matter how young you are, God can use you to play a part in the type of religion that He loves best. How can you help a single mom or a hurting kid or someone in need this week? Think of some ways you and your friends can bring the hope of Jesus to these people!

Red Light, Green Light
Melanie Stiles

Taking driver's education was a great reminder that God's answers to prayers are a lot like traffic lights. Red light—stop—God says "no." "No" may not be what I want to hear, but it's easy to follow. It's time to put on the brakes. Green light—go—God says "yes." It means I can put my foot on the gas.

It's the yellow light that gives me trouble. I have to decide whether to risk running through a yellow light into an intersection full of cars. If I'm not cautious, the situation could have bad consequences. Not slowing down and waiting on God can produce some tough consequences as well.

God's yellow light is "wait." It took a while for me to understand that "wait" is just as important as His "yes" or "no." "Wait" means being patient in spite of how I feel. It's never easy waiting on God. But it's always the best thing to do.

Check out what David wrote in Psalm 27:14: "Wait patiently for the LORD. Be brave and courageous. Yes, wait patiently for the LORD."

It's easy to mess up what God has planned for your life. . .things you may not even know about yet. Waiting is easier to manage if we keep in mind that He wants the best for us.

GET REAL

What are you waiting on God for today? Think of a time in the past when you had to wait for an answer from Him. Thank God for what He did then and what He's going to do in your current situation.

Vampire Nibbles

Steve Russo

Vampires are everywhere—websites, movies, TV shows, games, dolls, books, even underwear.

Some people have bought into this way of life and developed a morbid taste for blood. They're deceived into believing they now possess immortality and supernatural powers.

Vampire beliefs are about achieving power from a source other than God. It's important to guard against the blurring of fantasy and reality.

Vampires aren't mentioned in the Bible, but blood and power are mentioned frequently. Blood is sacred to God, and the devil is perverting its meaning, deceiving people into thinking that by drinking blood they can gain power. Peter, a follower of Jesus, talked about the blood: "For you know that God paid a ransom to save you from the empty life you inherited from your ancestors. And the ransom he paid was not mere gold or silver. It was the precious blood of Christ, the sinless, spotless Lamb of God" (1 Peter 1:18–19).

Blood is a symbol of life, because without it, we're physically dead. And without the blood of a perfect sacrifice to pay for our sins, we're spiritually dead. Jesus was the perfect sacrifice. Because of Christ's death on the cross, we can be forgiven and have spiritual life through His blood. When we accept His shed blood for our sins by faith, our empty lives are filled with meaning and purpose.

GET REAL

Are vampires nibbling away at your time, energy, and passion? What about your relationship with Jesus? Has it taken a backseat to pop culture vampires?

A Hug from the Coach

Rusty Wright

In the 1982 NCAA basketball championship game, freshman Michael Jordan hit a jump shot with only seconds left to give North Carolina the lead. Then Georgetown guard Fred Brown dribbled down court to set up one last shot for the national title. In a horrible miscue, he passed the ball to a North Carolina player, thinking from his peripheral vision that the unguarded player was his own teammate. North Carolina rejoiced in the victory.

With the nation watching, Georgetown coach John Thompson, a tall, burly man who loved his players, embraced the crestfallen Brown in a bear hug. It was as if he was warmly assuring his dejected player that it was okay, helping him feel safe from the pain and sorrow of his public humiliation. Two years later, as Fred Brown came off the court at the end of Georgetown's 1984 NCAA championship victory, he got another warm hug from his coach.

I'm glad I have some John Thompsons in my life, people who give glimpses of God's love for me when I've dropped the ball at a crucial moment. But more important, when I blow it and come off the court, I know that the open arms of my heavenly Father wait to console me. I'm reminded of Jesus's words, "Come to me, all of you who are weary and carry heavy burdens, and I will give you rest" (Matthew 11:28).

GET REAL

Do you and your friends console each other when you fail? Ask God to give you wisdom and strength to develop bonds like that.

From Brokenness to Peace
Brenda Pue

Let's face it. Life is messy! Life can be painful! If you come from a broken or abusive family or are dealing with unhealthy friend issues, you know this is true.

Once trust has been broken, the road back to wholeness can be very long. Having navigated the painful journey of my parents' separation and divorce, I can attest to how uncomfortable it feels to live in the wake of divorce. It's a journey of confusion, frustration, and anger.

I have learned, and am still learning, that God wants to journey with me in and through the messiness of life, whether it's divorce or something else. This is the very place that God desires to meet us. He wants you and me to know that when others fail us, He is trustworthy. He is faithful. He is there for me. He is there for you. He thinks about and plans for you and for me: " 'For I know the plans I have for you,' declares the LORD, 'plans to prosper you and not to harm you, plans to give you hope and a future' " (Jeremiah 29:11 NIV).

It is possible to feel loved, to feel joy and goodness, to be at peace, to be hopeful, to be fulfilled. God can free you from all the pain and messiness surrounding brokenness.

GET REAL

Are you dealing with pain and confusion in your life right now? Take the verse above to heart. God has big plans for you. He desires you to grow beyond your current circumstances to a place of peace and contentment that is beyond your wildest dreams!

Role Models
Danny Ray

Who's your role model? Maybe you have more than one. If you're into sports, it could be a pro athlete. If music is your passion, it could be a well-known singer or musician. What kind of role model are they? Besides being a great musician or athlete, what kind of person are they? I hear a lot of celebs say they aren't good role models and shouldn't have to be careful how they live and what they do. Those who say this are usually people you don't want to imitate.

How about you? Are you a positive role model? What kind of example are you when it comes to living out your faith? God wants us to be good role models as we try to live like Jesus. It's not an easy thing to do, and we can't do it without help. The valuable advice that Paul wrote to a young leader named Timothy is also good for us: "Don't let anyone think less of you because you are young. Be an example to all believers in what you say, in the way you live, in your love, your faith, and your purity" (1 Timothy 4:12).

God wants each of us to try every day to be the best role models possible. He is not looking for perfect people, but He is looking for people who want to live like His Son, Jesus. He wants examples who live life totally sold out for Him no matter what the cost or the circumstances.

GET REAL

One of the best ways to stay on the path of being a godly role model is to memorize God's Word! Pick one of the following passages and try to memorize it today: Psalm 119:9–11; 1 Thessalonians 1:6–7; Colossians 3:12; or Philippians 2:3.

The Amazing Race

Chris Haidet

I have a lot of great memories from growing up in Southern California, but one of my favorites is of going to the 1984 Summer Olympics as a young boy. I remember sitting in the historic Los Angeles Memorial Coliseum and witnessing the moment many people had waited for—the start of the 100-meter dash. The crowd was hushed with anticipation; then, with the loud bang of the starter's gun, the silence was broken. The massive crowd rose, screaming in unison, beckoning our sprinter to win the race and become the fastest human in the world. In 9.99 frantic seconds, Carl Lewis won the gold, electrifying the crowd. Chants of "USA-USA-USA" were filling the 90,000-seat stadium. I used to dream that someday the person they cheered for would be me. Have you ever wondered what it would be like to have everyone cheering for you?

The Bible says, "Therefore, since we are surrounded by such a huge crowd of witnesses to the life of faith, let us strip off every weight that slows us down, especially the sin that so easily trips us up. And let us run with endurance the race God has set before us" (Hebrews 12:1).

Wow! How awesome is that! As we follow God, a heaven-sized crowd is cheering us on, screaming for us by name. We are engaged in a lifelong race, running for God, and we are called to give it everything we have.

GET REAL

When life is going well, thank God for the race. When life gets rough, focus on God and ask Him for strength to make it through. Remember, no matter what, you are being cheered for each step of the way.

The Unanswered Question

Susie Shellenberger

Peter, a first-century follower of Jesus, likely assumed that he would have a high position in Christ's kingdom; John, another follower of Jesus, may have assumed the position would go to *him*. Though Jesus had twelve disciples, He was closest to three: James, John, and Peter. And of those three, He was even closer to one—John.

Who sat next to Jesus at the Last Supper? John.

John was so comfortable in His presence, he leaned over and rested his head on the shoulder of Jesus. So surely if Christ was going to install someone as His "vice president," it would be John—the one to whom He was closest.

But James must have felt pretty important as well. He was one of the "inner three" closest to Jesus. The Bible mentions him in the Mount of Transfiguration incident: Jesus, James, John, and Peter went up on a mountain and were visited by Elijah and Moses.

James hadn't forgotten that incident. He felt privileged to have been a part of such an experience. Obviously, Jesus trusted him. So perhaps James was thinking, *I'm in the running.* It's easy from our vantage point to say that the disciples needed a "heart check" like we read about in Psalm 139:23–24: "Search me, O God, and know my heart; test me and know my anxious thoughts. Point out anything in me that offends you, and lead me along the path of everlasting life."

Are you assuming things about your relationship with Christ? What kinds of questions are *you* asking? Your questions will reveal what's inside your heart.

GET REAL

Go ahead and ask Christ to search your heart. Ask Him to reveal anything that's not pleasing to Him. And when He does? . . . Give it up.

Daily Conflict

Steve Russo

Every day we're involved in a conflict with the world's way of thinking. This struggle with worldliness is intense in our "whatever" culture.

The Bible warns us not to love the world's ways. Why? Check out 1 John 2:16: "For the world offers only a craving for physical pleasure, a craving for everything we see, and pride in our achievements and possessions."

We live in a sex-crazed world where gratifying physical desires has become a top priority for a lot of people. Our culture also encourages us to bow to the god of materialism. It's all about bank and bling—get all the stuff you possibly can. The third unhealthy attitude in this struggle is an obsession with status and importance. That's one reason we see so many people trying to get their "fifteen minutes of fame."

If these attitudes are left unchecked, patterns develop that can be toxic to our spiritual growth. Satan used these same areas of attack in the beginning of human history with Eve in the Garden of Eden (see Genesis 3:6). Amazingly, he used the same strategy with Jesus in the wilderness (see Matthew 4:1–11). One lost the struggle, and one had victory.

When you're tempted with these attitudes, remember what God values: self-control, a spirit of generosity, and humbleness to serve others. The constant struggle for us is to maintain our commitment to biblical values while still connecting with and loving those in the world who do not know Jesus.

GET REAL

Which attitudes and values are most important to you? God's way may not be easy, but it's worth it. Ask for His help.

Belief versus Conviction

Steve Russo

What's your price? How much would it take to get you to compromise your values or do something totally disgusting? Living with integrity seems to be getting increasingly more difficult in our culture—especially if we are trying to live in a way that pleases God.

The Bible gives us some good examples of people who stuck to their convictions even when everything in their culture opposed their faith. One of my favorites is Daniel.

He and his friends had been taken from their home country and forced to live in captivity in Babylon. Even though Daniel lived in a foreign nation and his future was in doubt, he refused to disobey God and give in to the culture. "But Daniel was determined not to defile himself by eating the food and wine given to them by the king. He asked the chief of staff for permission not to eat these unacceptable foods" (Daniel 1:8).

Daniel was able to deny himself and obey God because he had developed convictions to live by. A conviction is different than a belief. A belief is something you will argue for, while a conviction is something you would die for because you value it so much.

Because of his relationship with God, Daniel was able to resist the culture around him. He made a conscious decision to obey God and develop convictions in his life.

Do you live by convictions or beliefs? To survive in a culture that contradicts our faith, we have to become Daniels.

GET REAL

Start developing a set of biblically based convictions to help you obey God—even in the tough situations of life.

Hanging Out
Ramona Richards

God is big on us being with other people. He never meant for us to be alone. God tells us to love one another and affirms that two are better than one. In Proverbs 27:17 we read about how important friends can be: "As iron sharpens iron, so a friend sharpens a friend."

Jesus pointed out that when two or more are together, He's there—which must mean He likes hanging out with our friends as much as we do.

Being with our friends is more than just fun. We learn from each other, and sharing good times and laughter with those we care about makes those moments all the more memorable. Good times with friends linger in our hearts and minds, making memories that can get us through some pretty tough times.

Kids hanging in groups sometimes get a bad rap because, yeah, there are a few troublemakers out there. But it's usually more about belonging, having a good time, and making lasting friendships. So keep hanging with the right people, and you'll be taking part in something much bigger than yourself.

GET REAL

You need to hang out. Make some plans to do something cool with your friends sometime this week. And make it a point to care about each other—through good times and bad.

What You Cannot See

Melanie Stiles

It takes courage and faith to believe in something you cannot see but trust is possible. Think about the men who traveled to and walked on the moon. How about people like Bill Gates who transformed the world through technology—and continue to do so? Go back further in history to the men who invented trains, cars, and planes. Can you imagine being friends with the Wright brothers when they were getting ready for their first flight? How amazing it would have been to see it all happening.

All of these developments came out of a belief in what had not yet been seen. The people involved had faith to keep going. It seems to me that these people may not have been any braver or smarter than me.

Are you stepping out in faith for something you believe could be a reality? There's a great example of this in Matthew 14, which tells how Jesus walked on water out to a boat carrying the disciples. "But Jesus spoke to them at once. 'Don't be afraid,' he said. 'Take courage. I am here!' Then Peter called to him, 'Lord, if it's really you, tell me to come to you, walking on the water.' 'Yes, come,' Jesus said" (vv. 27–29).

When I first read about Peter climbing out of a boat and walking on water, I thought no way could I do that.

Because Peter had faith in Jesus, he was able to do what seemed impossible. God can help us walk on water in our lives if we have a faith-filled attitude.

GET REAL

Is it time to step out of your boat? Believe that God can help you do the impossible.

Time to Declutter

Kati Russo

Ever walked into someone's house and nearly suffered a concussion because of falling boxes? Or opened a closet door and had an avalanche of anything and everything topple you? When I went to a friend's house, I had to search for the floor because there was so much clutter everywhere. This experience got me wondering if we do the same thing with our minds. Do we carry around junk that takes away space from more important thoughts? Do we need to do a complete makeover to get rid of the clutter?

If someone asked you about the latest celebrity gossip, would you be able to tell them every juicy detail? What if someone asked you what the Bible said about relationships—would you be able to answer them?

Philippians 4:8 talks about decluttering: "Fix your thoughts on what is true, and honorable, and right, and pure, and lovely, and admirable. Think about things that are excellent and worthy of praise."

That verse is an excellent filter for what we allow into our minds. Anything we buy, watch, or read should be put to the test with this verse. Is it true and pure or full of bad words and sex? If it's full of things that do not pass the filter test, then we should not fill our minds with it.

GET REAL

Think about the CDs you listen to, the books you read, the websites you visit, and the TV shows you watch. Would they pass the filter test? If not, try initiating a mind makeover. You'll be amazed at how much better you'll think and feel!

Ask Why

Steve Russo

Students in the college classroom listened intently to the elderly woman speak. Edith Franke, a Hungarian Jew who survived the Holocaust in World War II, was talking about how she and her family members were sent to concentration camps in various locations in Europe during the war.

She spoke of being humiliated by her captors and forced to go without water or toilet facilities for days. While in one concentration camp, she lost all of her family—except for a sister—before being freed. Edith softly added, "All because of hatred for a religion."

Edith's words were not bitter. She was quick to remind students never to hate anyone. "You're the future," Edith said. "Let's make this world a better place. Don't ever hate. You can accomplish so much more with kind words. When you're told to hate someone, ask, 'Why?'"

Paul gives us wise advice about hatred: "We were full of evil. We wanted what belongs to others. People hated us, and we hated one another. But the kindness and love of God our Savior appeared" (Titus 3:3–4 NIrV). Instead of hating others, God wants us to demonstrate the kindness and love that we've experienced from Him. There's no reason to hate another person because of his or her religion or skin color. Just imagine how different our world would be if everyone followed Edith's—and God's—advice.

GET REAL

Hate is a heart problem. Are there people you can't stand because of what they've done to you or others close to you? Ask God to free you from hatred and help you to be kind and loving.

Unlocking the Combination
Dale Robert Hicks

I went with my son to register for school, and while we were there, we went to his locker so he could practice opening it. I showed him how to dial the combination and open the locker. He tried it a few times and thought he had it. Later, as we were getting ready to leave, he asked me if he could go try his locker one more time. Not wanting to look foolish on his first day at school, he wanted to practice to make sure he got it right.

My son's desire to work at his combination until he was confident reminded me of the following Bible verse: "Work hard so you can present yourself to God and receive his approval. Be a good worker, one who does not need to be ashamed and who correctly explains the word of truth" (2 Timothy 2:15).

We need to work hard at understanding what God has said. First, we work at it because it pleases God. Then we work at the Bible so that we can explain or share with others what God has said. We need to study the Bible and practice applying it to our lives. Then, as our confidence in it grows, we don't have to worry about looking foolish.

GET REAL

Each time you read the Bible, ask God to show you how to put into practice what you just read. Keep track of your reading and your practice, and see if your confidence grows. If you still have fear, don't worry; just let the Holy Spirit guide you.

Teamwork

Nicole O'Dell

Teams and group projects can be hard for some of us. We'd rather do things ourselves than work with others. For some sports, that's fine. Singles tennis. Swimming. Golf. But for sports like volleyball, basketball, or soccer, it would be a disaster if people didn't team up.

What would happen if our body parts didn't work together? That would be disastrous, too. Paul compares the human body to the church—the body of Christ—in 1 Corinthians 12: "The human body has many parts, but the many parts make up one whole body. So it is with the body of Christ. . . . Yes, the body has many different parts, not just one part. If the foot says, " 'I am not a part of the body because I am not a hand,' " that does not make it any less a part of the body. And if the ear says, " 'I am not part of the body because I am not an eye,' " would that make it any less a part of the body? If the whole body were an eye, how would you hear? Or if your whole body were an ear, how would you smell anything? But our bodies have many parts, and God has put each part just where he wants it" (vv. 12, 14–18).

Just like the many parts that make up the human body, each one of us has a specific and important purpose in the body of Christ. God made us to function as a team.

GET REAL

Be careful you don't get proud about your abilities or, on the other hand, think you don't have anything to offer the body of Christ. Ask God to clarify your purpose and to help you fulfill it.

Comforter
Brian Sumner

As a teenager from England who took off to America to live out my dream, I thought I had all the comforts of life. Touring the world on a piece of wood with wheels attached can seem pretty cool at first. I felt like I had nothing to worry about. It was all about me. . .my skill. . .my courage. . .my strength. As time went on and life changed, I saw that my comfort—my security in life—could be taken away at any time. How about yours?

I began to realize that if I got injured, or if I failed to live up to the standards and expectations of others, or if something went totally wrong somewhere, somehow, I would lose everything!

All that changed when I encountered Jesus. He provided security and help. Jesus told His followers, "I will ask the Father, and he will give you another Advocate, who will never leave you" (John 14:16). By giving us the Holy Spirit, God ensured that we would have a helper and comforter who would always be with us.

Because of our relationship with Jesus, we can be encouraged and helped in everything—no matter what we face. In your problems and challenges, remember you have a secure source of hope and comfort.

GET REAL

In what have you put your security and comfort today? If it's something that can be taken away at any time, regroup and turn your eyes and heart to the living God. Put your trust in Him.

Remember His Hand
Tracy Klehn

What would it mean to you if you found out someone had saved a thirty-year-old letter that you had written to them? After my grandma passed away, I was going through some of her things when I came across a letter I had written to her when I was eight years old. It was even in the original Holly Hobbie envelope, complete with the address scrawled at a diagonal in my little-kid handwriting! It made me feel pretty special and very loved to know that I mattered so much to her that she treasured that note until the day she died.

What would it mean to you if I told you that God has your name written on the very palm of His hand and that He has been treasuring it for way more than thirty years? Check out Isaiah 49:15–16: "Can a mother forget her nursing child? Can she feel no love for the child she has borne? But even if that were possible, I would not forget you! See, I have written your name on the palms of my hands."

GET REAL

Next time you are feeling worthless or forgotten, ask God to help you remember His hand and your name written there. . .for eternity.

It's Always Too Soon to Quit

Steve Russo

When my friend and mentor Dr. Ted Engstrom went home to be with the Lord, I felt like I lost my dad for the second time.

For more than a dozen years, Dr. Ted was a constant source of encouragement and wisdom. He had a passion for telling others about Jesus and always challenged me to find new methods to reach young adults.

Dr. Ted was also there for me during the darkest time of my life. He would faithfully tell me, "It's always too soon to quit." And these were the last words he said to me before he died. It seemed like he wanted to remind me one last time to continue to live for Jesus—no matter what.

I've had some other tough times since he died. Sometimes I wish he never would've told me, "It's always too soon to quit," because that's exactly what I've wanted to do—especially when it felt like I was facing an impossible situation or challenge. But Dr. Ted's advice was solid and not original. God tells us the same thing in Hebrews 10:36: "Patient endurance is what you need now, so that you will continue to do God's will. Then you will receive all that he has promised."

When life gets ugly, God wants us to stick with Him, even though we may be tempted to give up. When we persevere, we get all He has promised us.

GET REAL

Think about it: What other option do you have if you abandon God? Rely on yourself? And what about all you give up if you walk away from Him? When tough times hit, keep living for Jesus.

Practicing "No"
Melanie Stiles

Have you ever said yes when you didn't want to? We all have at one time or another. I used to be a person who did more stuff I *didn't* want to do than stuff I *did* want to do because I was so uncomfortable saying no.

One day I decided to stop always responding with a yes. It happened when the guy sitting next to me in class motioned for me to let him look at the answers on my test. I had studied far more than I wanted to the night before, and he picked the wrong moment. I was tired and irritable. I just wanted to take the test and be done with it. I hunched over my paper, shaking my head vigorously—*no*!

I realized then the reason my no was so infrequent. I had trouble explaining why I couldn't do something. It was really a struggle for me to figure out just the right thing to say so I wouldn't step on any toes or hurt any feelings. I found strength and encouragement in Matthew 5:37: "Just say a simple, 'Yes, I will,' or 'No, I won't.' Anything beyond this is from the evil one."

I really didn't need to make any excuse for saying no. My one-syllable answer was already complete. The more I did it, the easier it became, and along with that ease came a new confidence.

GET REAL

Start today by saying no in small ways, and then work your way up to more significant things.

Banana Boy
Nathan Finfrock

I was a comedian in high school, or at least I thought so. Everything was fodder for a joke or prank. One day in the quad, I saw an opportunity to make everyone laugh. A guy was bending over a bench only a few steps in front of me. I had a banana left over from lunch and, well, I hatched a brilliant, idiotic idea. Unfortunately for this guy, the banana became lodged in his buttocks, and it was not a pretty sight! It took a few seconds for people to realize what had happened, and then everyone in the quad began laughing hysterically. Yes, it was funny, but at what cost? Almost instantly I felt terrible for the guy, and I am probably still on his people-to-kill list. Until that point in my life, I never realized mocking people was wrong. Everybody makes fun of others. It's just human nature, right?

God has a lot to say about mocking. Check out Job 12:5: "People who are at ease mock those in trouble. They give a push to people who are stumbling." The author of Proverbs expands that thought: "Fools mock at making amends for sin, but goodwill is found among the upright" (14:9 NIV).

It's easy to put others down because they are different, they just flat out deserve it, or it makes you feel better about yourself. God calls us to a higher standard.

GET REAL

Start today by encouraging people, and avoid making friends who turn life into a Comedy Central roast.

Looking over Your Shoulder

Ramona Richards

One too many hurts. One too many fights. One too many betrayals. One too many put-downs.

One too many. . . You start to flinch when someone speaks, or you spend way too much time looking over your shoulder, expecting trouble. Fear begins to take over, like a poison, messing up the way you think and live. In Proverbs 29:25 Solomon describes fear as being a snare, a trap, one that captures your heart and soul. A trap that is unbelievably easy to fall into.

One reason fear takes over is that we think we should be able to control what happens to us. If we're good, smart, or strong, we should be able to take care of our problems. If we have enough money or power, nothing should bother us.

But that's a lie. Problems are a part of life. The only sure thing in our world is that God wants us to feel safe in Him, in knowing that no matter what happens, He can help us through it.

He doesn't want us to live with a spirit of fear. He wants us to feel strong, but not because of anything we can do or control. Our power comes from Him. "For God has not given us a spirit of fear and timidity, but of power, love, and self-discipline" (2 Timothy 1:7).

GET REAL

Fear can be a natural response to problems. Try remembering that God's strength and support are supernatural. It'll help get you through.

Has Jesus Made a Difference?

Steve Russo

The Passion Play is performed every ten years in Oberammergau, Germany. Hundreds of years ago a plague swept across Europe, and the citizens of this Bavarian village attempted to seal themselves off. When a homesick young man sneaked into the village, bringing the disease with him, people started dying. In desperation, the town council made a vow that if God would stop the plague, they'd present a play depicting the life and suffering of Jesus as long as the village existed.

Miraculously it stopped. True to their word, the villagers performed their first play in 1634 and have continued ever since. It's an amazing display of pageantry, costumes, and music. Hundreds of actors and live animals participate in the play, which lasts from morning until late afternoon for a couple of days.

Selecting the man to play Jesus starts five years in advance of the first performance. Several people are chosen, and one is selected as first choice. He is presented to the village, and everyone is encouraged to watch him carefully over the coming months—his behavior, his language, everything about his life. The goal is to see if he lives a life worthy of playing Jesus. If he doesn't measure up, he's disqualified, and the process, starts over. This continues until one man is found worthy of playing Jesus.

According to Ephesians 4:1, we should all be able to pass the test. "Therefore I, a prisoner for serving the Lord, beg you to lead a life worthy of your calling, for you have been called by God."

GET REAL

If people followed you around every day carefully examining your life, what would they find? Are you living a life "worthy of your calling"?

Expiration Date
Steve Russo

Sometimes I have these random thoughts that invade my mind. Here's one: Do croutons ever go bad? It seems like they would get better with age. Or how come sour cream has an expiration date? Isn't it already sour when you buy it?

Lots of things have expiration dates. Food and medicines must be sold or removed from the shelf by a certain date because they're no good past that point. Things like licenses and warranties also have expiration dates, after which they're no longer valid.

What about grudges—do they have an expiration date? It seems like there should be a time when they run out. But sometimes when someone hurts us or we suffer a big disappointment, we keep our feelings of resentment on the top shelf of our lives. These feelings lead us to become bitter. And when bitterness is left unchecked in our lives, it becomes toxic. . .like a cancer slowly eating away at our hearts. We can even be tempted to rebel against God for allowing these things to happen. Bitterness can affect our relationships as well.

The early Christians were struggling with the same thing, so God gave them some advice through the author of the book of Hebrews: "Look after each other so that none of you fails to receive the grace of God. Watch out that no poisonous root of bitterness grows up to trouble you, corrupting many" (12:15).

Let the Holy Spirit heal the hurts in your life.

GET REAL

What grudges are you still carrying past the expiration date? Ask God to help you forgive; then let them go.

Never Alone

Ramona Richards

Nicki hates being alone. She thrives in the company of her friends. She feels more energized, more alive when she's with them.

Mark, on the other hand, is perfectly content on his own. He has friends he cares about, but when he was twelve, he discovered he loved history. He really enjoys surfing history websites on his own. Yeah, it's geeky, but he's okay with that. After some time alone, he heads out to see his friends in a lighter mood than if he'd spent all day in a crowd.

Left alone, Mark experiences a sense of contentment and growth. Nicki just feels lonely and abandoned.

Times of solitude can be good. If we are content, being alone can help us grow and depend on God. Even Jesus sought out times of isolation to pray and think.

But God never intended for us to be lonely, to feel the pain of abandonment. Ecclesiastes 4:9–12 reminds us it's good for people to be together: "Two people are better off than one, for they can help each other succeed. If one person falls, the other can reach out and help. . . . Likewise, two people lying close together can keep each other warm. But how can one be warm alone? A person standing alone can be attacked and defeated, but two can stand back-to-back and conquer. Three are even better, for a triple-braided cord is not easily broken."

Even if people leave us, God never does. With Him in our lives, we're never really alone.

GET REAL

If you're feeling lonely, look up as well as around. Check in with a friend and talk with God.

Ants

Lesha Campbell

I love to watch ants. Weird, but it's very interesting how they are constantly moving in a line, getting the job done, and not tripping up any of the ants before or after. They form a steady line of progress and are always headed toward the goal before them. They carry more than their little bodies seem equipped for, and still they march toward the objective of the colony of ants as a whole.

The ant mound is huge and has tons of tunnels. It is awesome in its construction and amazing in how quickly it can be rebuilt after destruction. That's because the ants always work together, without dissension or discouragement. It reminds me of a children's song, "High Hopes," about an ant moving a rubber tree plant. The ant never loses hope and continues his quest, even though everybody thinks the ant is a fool.

The first time I ever heard the "High Hopes" song was on TV. It's a catchy little tune and sticks in your mind. Many times when I started feeling down, I'd remember those little phrases to pick me up along my way. Later I realized the song's message was actually in the Bible, right there in Proverbs 6:6: "Take a lesson from the ants, you lazybones. Learn from their ways and become wise!" Now that's pretty awesome—life lessons from the tiniest of creatures.

GET REAL

Next time you're scratching and clawing your way through a struggle, don't give up. Remember the ant— keep your hopes high and aim toward the prize!

The Value of Tears

Melanie Stiles

I hate to cry. I don't want others to think I'm a crybaby. It makes me feel weak. But like it or hate it, I've experienced times in my life when I couldn't do anything else. My sorrow was so intense it had to escape somehow. So the tears would flow. I have to admit crying often causes me to take the time to think long and deeply about why I'm upset. It gives me space to examine all of my motives—good and bad. I can also check out the actions of others from a different perspective. Sometimes I even discover my sadness is my own fault.

Everyone cries sooner or later—even great men in the Bible like David and Jesus. I can't help but believe that God's heart aches when we cry because of the special way He handles our sorrows and tears, as expressed by David in Psalm 56:8 (MSG): "You've kept track of my every toss and turn through the sleepless nights, each tear entered in your ledger, each ache written in your book."

Although crying may not be my favorite thing to do, I am comforted knowing that God is not only with me during my sorrow but also counting my tears. That could be why, after a good cry, I always seem to feel better whether my problem is solved or not.

GET REAL

The next time you have a good cry, take comfort in the fact that God is there collecting your tears.

Take a Chill Pill

Chris Haidet

I remember being in charge of a major concert once, with thousands of dollars on the line. Everything was going wrong, and the stress and fear were weighing me down. I was panicked, and then somebody walked by and said, "Take a chill pill. God's in control." He was right, yet to be totally honest, I wanted to punch him in the throat. But when I took a moment to pray and give it to God, all my stress slowly disappeared.

What about you? Do you like to be afraid? It's fun when it's not real. When I was younger, I loved horror movies, haunted houses, extreme rides, and adventures. But what happens when our fear of people, things, and events becomes very real? We feel trapped with no place to run. We cry out, but no one listens. Life becomes frightening, causing us daily stress and panic.

Life can be scary if we don't have anywhere to run. But God's Word gives us an answer: "Don't be afraid, for I am with you. Don't be discouraged, for I am your God. I will strengthen you and help you. I will hold you up with my victorious right hand" (Isaiah 41:10).

It's natural to be scared, but with God, we have hope for the future and a friend in all circumstances. He is all-knowing, all-powerful, and all-loving. Nothing is greater than Him. He is with us every day, ready and willing to give us strength.

GET REAL

List five things that cause you fear. Pray about each one, asking God to give you the strength and wisdom to journey through it.

Come Back Home
Steve Russo

Are you living away from home right now? Not physically, but spiritually? Home is with the God who made you; and if you're trying to live without Him, you're probably experiencing loneliness, frustration, depression, anger, and lack of purpose in your life.

Sin cuts us off from God. Wrong thoughts, words, and actions are all sin. At its core, sin is trying to live without God. Sin offends our heavenly Father.

God's desire for us is to live in an intimate relationship with Him on earth and forever in heaven. He's waiting for us to recognize our need for forgiveness because of sin and to come back to Him. Jesus told a story about a son who took his share of his inheritance and left home. He moved to a distant place and wasted all of his money. He finally woke up to what he was experiencing and decided to go back home. Recording Jesus' words, Luke, a doctor, writes what happened next in the story: "So he returned home to his father. And while he was still a long way off, his father saw him coming. Filled with love and compassion, he ran to his son, embraced him, and kissed him" (Luke 15:20).

The son confessed his sin, all was forgiven, and a huge celebration took place.

This is a picture of how God feels about us when we are living away from home and what happens when we decide to come back.

GET REAL

If you're trying to live without God, turn your life around. Don't wait. Do it now and start experiencing His love, forgiveness, and power.

Head-Butting God
Ron Merrell

I was in line at a Starbucks, standing behind a young mom holding her baby boy in her arms. The little boy had the hugest head I've ever seen! There were planets orbiting around his enormous cranium! What made it worse was that the boy was trying to head-butt his mom in the face. Over and over again she dodged his attacks. Then, as she turned her attention to place her order, he leaned back, shot forward, and caught his mom square in the jaw!

The whole crowd gasped. The mom's expression totally changed. Fire shooting from her eye sockets, she screamed, "No head-butting Mommy! *Don't do that again!*"

The little boy crinkled up his face and started to cry. He responded through tears, "Okay, Mama. . .no. . .more. . .head-butting." The mom turned to finish placing her order, and the boy leaned back and head-butted her one more time!

I'm a lot like that kid, constantly "head-butting" God by disobeying Him. I'm so thankful that no matter how many times I fail, He's there to forgive. I'm glad that when I do things that hurt others and Him, He doesn't drop me. Second Peter 3:9 (NIV) reminds us, "The Lord is not slow in keeping his promise, as some understand slowness. Instead he is patient with you, not wanting anyone to perish, but everyone to come to repentance."

GET REAL

Today, thank God for His patience. Ask forgiveness for things that you may have done to hurt others or Him lately. Then soak up His love and lean back into His strong hands, which will never let you go.

The Same Question

Susie Shellenberger

All of the disciples were interested in vying for the position of prominence in Christ's kingdom. It wasn't just Peter. Or John. Or James. Matthew, a pretty important guy as well, was jockeying for the position. He had walked away from a lucrative business to follow Jesus. Surely Christ saw a lot worth admiring in Matthew or He wouldn't have chosen him.

And the other disciples? Actually, they were assuming the same thing: *The position of greatness in His kingdom will probably go to me.*

How do we know? Because right after Mrs. Zebedee (James and John's mom) asked Christ if her sons could have the two most important positions in His kingdom (the right and left seats next to His throne), the other disciples heard about it. And scripture tells us "they were *indignant*" (Matthew 20:24, emphasis added). They were furious! Each one of them wanted the position of greatness in Christ's kingdom.

So it looks like we have twelve amazing disciples who have left all to follow Christ. But twelve amazing disciples who are full of themselves.

Me. That's what it's all about. I deserve. . . I have a right to. . .

And how does Jesus handle the question of greatness? Matthew 18:2–3 (NKJV) gives us His solemn answer. "Then Jesus called a little child to Him, set him in the midst of them, and said, 'Assuredly, I say to you, unless you are converted and become as little children, you will by no means enter the kingdom of heaven.' "

GET REAL

How are you responding to the answer Jesus gave in the verses above? Are you starting to learn that it's not about you, but all about God?

What's Important?

Dale Robert Hicks

Throughout history, humankind has accomplished a lot of significant things. You've probably done a lot of things that you consider important, too. Think about an event that you think is the most meaningful thing that has ever happened. Now give some thought to how essential the following statement is to you: "So the Word became human and made his home among us. He was full of unfailing love and faithfulness. And we have seen his glory, the glory of the Father's one and only Son" (John 1:14).

Jim Irwin was one of the few people in history to walk on the moon. No matter how you slice it, man walking on the moon is a distinguished event. But as Jim Irwin stood there on the lunar surface, looking back at the earth, he thought about nations fighting nations, poverty, hunger, and all the wickedness in the world, and he realized: "What is more important than man walking on the moon is that God should walk on earth."

When you understand who Jesus is and what He has accomplished, it doesn't make what you've done any less important, but it does help you understand why what you've done can be crucial. The fact that God came in the flesh and walked among us gives our lives and actions value.

GET REAL

When you accomplish something significant, remember that God's walking with people makes what you've done even more important. Even if you never do something you consider a big deal, remember you are important to God.

Eager to Hear
Rusty Wright

As a junior in college, I wrote a paper for my Abnormal Psychology class, discussing a biblical therapy for anxiety. I mailed a copy to the author of our textbook, a prominent UCLA psychologist. His warm response surprised me. He liked it and asked permission to quote from it in his textbook revision.

That summer, we met at his lovely Malibu home overlooking the Pacific Ocean. He confided, "I don't have this peace of mind that you do. I don't have this relationship with Christ." I showed him a short presentation of Jesus' message.

After a few questions, this professor invited Christ to forgive him and enter his life. He had heard this message many times—his father was a minister—but he had never understood how to place his faith in God. We discussed spiritual growth; he took some literature to share with his students.

The next edition of his text contained a short portion entitled "Religion and Psychotherapy" and included part of my faith story. I began telling psychology professors I was a case in their abnormal psychology textbook. Many invited me to speak in their classes. This helped launch a speaking career that has taken me around the world, allowing me to present biblical perspectives in academia and the media.

People everywhere are interested in Jesus. As He said, "Wake up and look around. The fields are already ripe for harvest" (John 4:35).

GET REAL

Ask God to give you wisdom and strength to talk about Him with someone today. That person's response might surprise you!

Help Someone Cry
Steve Russo

A four-year-old child lived next door to an elderly man who recently lost his wife. Seeing the man cry, the little boy went into the old man's yard, climbed onto his lap, and just sat there. His mom asked what he said. The boy replied, "Nothing. I just helped him cry."

When was the last time you helped someone cry? There are a lot of hurting people who would love to have someone understand and cry with them. How well do you listen? Hurting people need someone who will listen with their ears and their heart. When you hurt, the last thing you need is a mini-devotional or someone shoving a "Bible pill" down your throat. You want someone to experience your pain through listening, hugs, a gentle touch, and even tears.

I visited a friend whose wife was dying of cancer. After talking with his wife, he and I sat in another part of the house. For more than an hour I sat with him as he wept. I probably said less than a dozen words the entire time. But there were plenty of tears rolling down my cheeks.

In Philippians 2:1 Paul asks, "Are your hearts tender and compassionate?" This can happen only when we love one another, caring for the problems of others as if they were our own. When we do this, we demonstrate Christ's example of putting others first.

GET REAL

Ask God to help you become sensitive to hurting people who intersect your path each day. Pray that He will use you in the lives of others through your smiles and your tears. Go help someone cry.

Storms
Brenda Pue

Several years ago I was invited to go on a boat trip with some good friends. I packed my gear, my contributions of food for the week, and my sense of adventure.

The last thing we expected was a storm. It came upon us suddenly with gale force winds, crashing waves, torrential rain, thunder, and lightning strikes everywhere we looked. One of the worst places to be in a lightning storm is on the water. The U.S. Coast Guard went into action, ordering boats into nearby harbors to wait out the storm. We set our bearings accordingly and eventually made it safely to a harbor. We have never experienced a storm like that before or since and are grateful to have survived it.

That experience was a great backdrop to another storm described in the Bible. Luke 8:23–25 says that a squall came on the lake so that the disciples' boat was being swamped and they were in great danger. Then Jesus, who had been sleeping in the boat, got up and rebuked the wind and the raging waters, and the storm subsided and all was calm—from raging to calm in a matter of seconds. Mark 4:41 (NIV) says the disciples asked each other, "Who is this? Even the wind and the waves obey him!"

GET REAL

When you face storms in your life, be encouraged that there is a God who can calm your fears and your storms. God is all-powerful. He wants to bring you through the great storms of life to a place of peace and calm. All you have to do is ask for His help. Do so today.

Feeling Abandoned?

Carson Pue

I met a man at the leisure center of a hotel. Although we were total strangers, he began to complain to me that his business colleagues purposely abandoned him at the hotel without a car while they went into the city to "party it up."

They were all attending a business conference together and had told him to meet them in the lobby at 6:00 p.m. He arrived on time and waited and waited for his "friends" to appear. Finally, asking the desk manager to call their rooms, he was told, "Oh, they left at 5:00 p.m."

Sensitively, I commented on how much abandonment hurts and asked if he had ever experienced it before.

"Yes, my father abandoned our family when I was seven years old, but he emotionally abandoned our family years before that." Then he asked me if I ever felt abandoned.

"I used to, but not anymore. But you may not like the reason why I can say that now," I responded gently.

"Tell me," he said.

This conversation led us to a deep talk about Jesus and how as a Christian I now live with God's promise, "I will never leave you nor forsake you" (Hebrews 13:5 NKJV). In other words, God is saying to us in a loud voice, "I am here! I will never abandon you!"

GET REAL

Try living today with the awareness that God surrounds you. You are not alone. God will never abandon you. Jesus is with you always. He loves you—adores you, even!

Love Is Always Risky

Steve Russo

Love makes you vulnerable. Sometimes its consequences can be painful. Just ask Superman, who took kryptonite, or Samson, who let his hair be cut. Have you ever risked loving someone only to have them stomp on your heart? It can hurt for a long time.

But there was another man who risked it all for love, and he changed the course of human history. Jesus left heaven to live on earth and die for humankind.

It's a story of vulnerability that you frequently see in history and most often in fantasy. Someone with supernatural powers gives up those powers to become human for one reason: love. The difference with Jesus is that when He gave up His power, He also handed over His life to hang on a cross. It was a risk Jesus took for me and you.

Love was God's motivation: "God showed his great love for us by sending Christ to die for us while we were still sinners" (Romans 5:8).

This is amazing news! God sent His only Son to pay the debt for our sin—not because we were good enough—but because He loved us so much.

Love is always risky. There's no way you can express love and not give up something. You automatically put yourself in jeopardy when you choose to love another. Sometimes this risk can be painful. But most of the time it's worth it.

GET REAL

Take the risk. Surrender to God's love. Giving up control of your life makes you extremely vulnerable, but you can trust Him to guide and protect you. You'll never be sorry, because love is worth the risk now—and for eternity.

Wait It Out

Melanie Stiles

I prayed. I waited. I prayed some more. God still hadn't answered my prayer. Why not? Have you ever experienced this same thing? I used to get really frustrated about moments like this until I realized the true definition of *God's timing*. I trust God to get me through anything, but that doesn't mean He will do something exactly when or how I think He should. God's timing does not mean that when I beg, plead, or cry, He will jump in to save the day. It means when He thinks it's best to deliver me from a situation, He will do it.

Trusting God's timing means I might have to navigate some not-so-fun stuff until that happens. Check out Psalm 91:14–15 (NIV): " 'Because he loves me,' says the LORD, 'I will rescue him; I will protect him, for he acknowledges my name. He will call on me, and I will answer him; I will be with him in trouble, I will deliver him and honor him.' "

If God will "rescue" us and be with us in "trouble," then that tells me no one escapes rough places in life. This passage also has a great ending that I like to focus on—the promise that He will come in His timing and honor us in the end.

My prayers now include asking to be content with His timing instead of my own. I know that waiting it out won't always be easy, but God will be there.

GET REAL

Thank God for the last time He rescued you, and ask Him to help you wait out the current situation.

I Can't Believe

Steve Russo

Do you have doubts about God and your faith? You're not alone—lots of people do. Satan wants us to doubt God's character, His credibility, and the promises of His Word. Unfortunately, some people think doubt is a sin. They're confusing doubt with unbelief. Some people have to doubt before they believe.

Doubt is "I can't believe"; unbelief is "I won't believe." Doubt is a healthy sign that you're thinking, sincerely searching. One of Jesus' followers struggled with doubt right after Jesus rose from the grave. Thomas wasn't with the other disciples when they saw Jesus, so when they told him they'd seen Jesus, he replied, "I won't believe it unless I see the nail wounds in his hands, put my fingers into them, and place my hand into the wound in his side" (John 20:25). Eight days later Thomas did these things. His doubt was gone.

Chances are you won't see Jesus face-to-face until you get to heaven. But you can overcome doubt. And you will be blessed if you do! So instead of letting doubt morph into stubbornness and become a lifestyle that weakens your faith, let it *deepen* your faith as you look for truth and answers.

GET REAL

Studying the Bible is crucial in overcoming doubt. As you read it, God's Spirit will confirm that you can trust Him. Talk with God about your doubts. Ask Him for answers, and act on them.

What Are You Looking For?

Mike Thune

Have you ever wondered why you are alive now, in the twenty-first century, rather than in some century long ago? Is this just coincidence? Should we just feel lucky that we live in the modern world with all of our medical advancements and technological conveniences? Or is there a reason, a plan behind our existence?

I was reading Acts 17:24–31 and realized more than ever before that God has a purpose for each of our lives. The passage tells us that God determined in advance the exact times and places where people should live. What is really awesome is the reason God did this: "His purpose was for the nations to seek after God and perhaps feel their way toward him and find him—though he is not far from any one of us" (v. 27). Before we were born, God was already pursuing us and looking out for our ultimate well-being!

God is near to us, and He has created each of us at this time and in this place so that we would have the opportunity not only to seek after God but also to find Him! He wants a real relationship with us, and real relationships are not one-sided. We have to freely choose to get to know God better and to become more like Him as we live our lives each day.

GET REAL

In what specific ways are you responding to God's desire for a relationship with you? Do you regularly take time to pray, read God's Word, and draw near to Him?

R U Pursuing Your Dream?

Kati Russo

Bill Gates's name is known throughout the world for thinking big and pursuing his dream to get computers in every home. Like many dream chasers, he faced obstacles, but he believed in himself and persevered until his dream became a reality.

What is your dream? To be a doctor, a Halo video game champion, a billionaire? Mine is to become successful in Hollywood and to use my platform to help others.

Most of us do not pursue our dreams like we could. One of the biggest obstacles is us. Are you holding yourself back? Is it fear that you will not be good enough to attain your dream? Is it people telling you that you'll fail before you even begin? Is it you not believing in yourself? Is it fear of success, of how your life will change once you've achieved your dream?

We will face a lot of obstacles in our pursuit, along with failure. We need to learn from these and keep pushing on. Remember this verse: "For I can do everything through Christ, who gives me strength" (Philippians 4:13). Did you catch that? *We can do anything through Christ because He gives us strength.* He wants us to be successful in accomplishing our dreams.

Christ created you to do big things. He believes in you; now you need to start believing in yourself and reach for your dream.

GET REAL

Don't give up; keep pushing toward your goal daily by doing something that will bring you one step closer to living your dream. Memorize Philippians 4:13, and draw on it whenever you feel like you're hitting obstacles amid your pursuit.

School Daze

Chris Haidet

There are two types of people in the world—those who love school and those who don't. I was the latter. I loved the sports, activities, and social aspects of school but hated homework with a passion. I simply didn't care, and my grades reflected that. As I grew older, I began to realize that my lack of effort in school was costing me big-time in other areas of my life.

The simple fact is that school helps prepare us for every aspect of life. Remember, it's not about the grades you get, but the effort you show. God wants you to do your best in everything—nothing more, nothing less. A wise man once said, "Getting wisdom is the wisest thing you can do! And whatever else you do, develop good judgment" (Proverbs 4:7).

God asks us to be wise and develop good judgment—above everything else—and never let it go! The Bible is our primary source for wisdom, but being knowledgeable in math, language, history, and the sciences helps prepare us for life. School trains our minds, develops strong habits, and allows us to become the leaders God wants us to be. It's that important.

GET REAL

Set aside time each day to study in a place with no distractions. Ask God to give you the wisdom and strength to use this time in your life wisely and give it your all.

Heel, Sit, Stay!
Chuck Poe

When I hear the word *obedience*, the first thing I think about is obedience school for dogs. I know it sounds crazy, but have you ever seen a dog that has been trained? It's amazing to watch how a trained dog responds to its master's voice and obeys its master's commands. The dog and its owner have to spend hours together. The problem with many dog owners is that they want and expect their dog to obey them without undergoing any training.

Let's look at this concept in the spiritual realm. God wants us to be obedient. Our difficulty is that, like King Saul, we want to do things our way rather than God's way. Saul thought he would be obedient by making a sacrifice instead of following direct orders from God, prompting Samuel to ask him, "Does the LORD delight in burnt offerings and sacrifices as much as in obeying the LORD? To obey is better than sacrifice, and to heed is better than the fat of rams" (1 Samuel 15:22 NIV).

You and I might not fail as badly as Saul did; nonetheless, we may not always be obedient. Or we do what God asks but only when it's convenient for us. Delayed obedience is disobedience. We need to strive to be obedient to God daily and in His timing.

GET REAL

Through prayer and Bible reading, keep your ears and eyes open to what God wants you to do today. Remember that ultimate obedience to God is submitting your will to His, whether or not you understand His reasoning.

The Darkness Inside

Steve Russo

Dealing with the darkness inside is a struggle for everyone. God calls it our sinful nature. We all have evil desires that we cannot ignore. Check out Galatians 5:19–21: "When you follow the desires of your sinful nature, the results are very clear: sexual immorality, impurity, lustful pleasures, idolatry, sorcery, hostility, quarreling, jealousy, outbursts of anger, selfish ambition, dissension, division, envy, drunkenness, wild parties, and other sins like these. Let me tell you again, as I have before, that anyone living that sort of life will not inherit the Kingdom of God."

That's one ugly list! It includes some of the obvious well-known sins. But it also inventories some less clear things that can be just as destructive to our spiritual growth. Things like hostility, jealousy, and selfish ambition. All of these things can affect our relationships with Jesus and others.

People who ignore these sins and refuse to deal with them are basically admitting that the Holy Spirit is not living within them and transforming their lives.

We have to deal with the darkness inside us properly and decisively so we can follow the guidance of God's Spirit to live as we were designed to live from the inside out. We must be honest with ourselves and with God if we're going to experience victory. Just remember—you can't do it on your own—you need the power of the living God.

GET REAL

What are you struggling with today? You can have victory over the darkness within if you daily surrender these desires to God and rely on His power to bring them under control.

Quick and Slow
Melanie Stiles

I was trying to help my friend with algebra—she didn't know how to factor polynomials. She just wasn't getting it. After repeating the instructions three or four times, I started to get impatient. Math comes easy for me, so I really didn't see what her problem was. We both could have been doing a lot of other things. Why couldn't she just get the hang of these math problems so we could move on to something else? My mood was swiftly changing, and I was about to lose control of my mouth. Fortunately, I caught myself just before saying something I would have regretted.

My friend and I are very close. I thought about how God gave us a relationship that complemented both of us. She struggled with math, and I needed her skills for my English papers. How many hours had she spent editing for me? Time to refocus.

I asked her to explain once more what it was that she didn't understand. This time I kept thinking about James 1:19: "Understand this, my dear brothers and sisters: You must all be quick to listen, slow to speak, and slow to get angry."

I figured out the step she was missing, and she finally got the hang of factoring. I had come very close to damaging our relationship, but by listening instead of getting angry and saying something dumb, I found a way to work it out.

GET REAL

Ask God to help you have patience with others and listen to them before reacting—at school and at home.

Narrow by Definition
Steve Russo

You don't have to go very far to find people who need to know Jesus. They're everywhere—at home, on your campus, and in your city.

It's important to respect a friend's beliefs, even though they may be different from your own. Just don't fall into the "cultural toleration trap." There's a lot of talk about "being tolerant," but I'm not sure there's an understanding of what it really means. It means you allow someone to have beliefs that differ from or conflict with your own. Unfortunately, in our "whatever" culture, we're led to believe that we must embrace and support all different beliefs. Not true. When we share our faith with someone who is not a Christian, we need to respect their beliefs but share the truth with them. The real issue is not one of tolerance but of truth. Jesus said, "I am the way, the truth, and the life. No one can come to the Father except through me" (John 14:6).

The best way to start sharing your faith with someone from another religion is to find out "what's in it for them." Try to determine what need or needs your friend is getting met in their life by practicing their religion. You can accomplish this by asking questions about their beliefs and listening carefully.

Ultimately, sharing the truth with your friend means explaining what you believe, why you believe it, and who gives you power for daily living—Jesus.

GET REAL

As you share with your friends that Jesus is "the only way to God," don't worry about sounding too narrow. Remember, truth by its very definition is narrow.

Whose Body?

Steve Russo

We live in a sex-crazed society. It sells everything from vitamins to cars. If you're online, you don't have to go looking for porn—it'll pop up when you least expect it. In the media, sex outside of marriage appears to be a "desirable part of life." Unfortunately, a lot of your friends have probably given in to this temptation.

God is not some cosmic killjoy being difficult and wanting us to miss out on the fun everyone seems to be having sexually. Pressure to have sex is huge! God knows the power sex has to destroy us spiritually and physically. Look around at the countless lives it has destroyed. God wants to protect us from hurting others and ourselves. "Run from sexual sin! No other sin so clearly affects the body as this one does. For sexual immorality is a sin against your own body. Don't you realize that your body is the temple of the Holy Spirit, who lives in you and was given to you by God? You do not belong to yourself, for God bought you with a high price. So you must honor God with your body" (1 Corinthians 6:18–20).

God created sex to be an awesome part of marriage—but when sex is pursued outside of marriage, someone always gets hurt. Sex without the commitment of marriage hurts people emotionally, and then there's also the possibility of sexually transmitted diseases. Ultimately, it harms us spiritually. It damages our relationship with God because it demonstrates that we'd rather follow our own desires instead of trusting Him to know what's best.

GET REAL

Are you honoring God with your body? It's not too late to change. Run to God for help.

Accepted

Rich Thune

When I was in college, I remember wanting to fit in with all the right people. It was about wearing the right clothes, saying the right stuff, and doing awesome things—like being a star on the basketball team. But I always felt nervous because I never knew if I'd done enough to measure up to other people's expectations.

I found out that I wasn't alone in this. Everybody wants to feel significant and to be accepted, especially by family and friends. But attaining the approval and acceptance of others can be difficult. It is too often based on performance. If we perform to expected levels, we're all right. If we don't, we're not.

That's why being accepted by God is so important for us to understand. Fortunately, He accepts us unconditionally, just as we are. Ephesians 1:4–5 tells us, "Even before he made the world, God loved us and chose us in Christ to be holy and without fault in his eyes. God decided in advance to adopt us into his own family by bringing us to himself through Jesus Christ. This is what he wanted to do, and it gave him great pleasure." How cool is that! If the Creator of the universe accepts us, we don't need to worry about the opinions of other people. We can relax and just be ourselves.

GET REAL

You don't have to impress anybody or do anything for approval. You've been declared "okay" by the God of the universe. When you get a grip on this concept, it will change your life forever. Today, set yourself free from the struggle for acceptance.

School Jitters

Steve Russo

Violence on school campuses is on the rise. Principals are being physically assaulted in school hallways, teachers are being attacked in the classrooms, and students are tired of being threatened and bullied. The fear factor is escalating as schools have become battlefields—physically, emotionally, and morally. Truth is relative, and lots of people don't know how to handle their anger. Families are broken, and there are no moral absolutes. So what's the answer?

King David had a similar question centuries ago and found an answer: "The foundations of law and order have collapsed. What can the righteous do? But the LORD is in his holy Temple; the LORD still rules from heaven. He watches everyone closely, examining every person on earth" (Psalm 11:3–4). The solution starts with a choice to turn back to God and a desire to take seriously the Bible's practical wisdom for living. As followers of Jesus, we must set the example for how to live with a biblical worldview—and be at peace with one another. Ultimately, we will only have peace when Jesus, the Prince of Peace, lives in our hearts. When we have peace with God, then we can experience it with each other—on our campuses, at home, at work, and in our world.

GET REAL

Let's model how to be peacemakers and respect one another. Make yourself available to your friends. Walk with them through their fears, and help them to make sense out of their confusion. Ask God to use you to influence others to choose to live their lives for and like Jesus.

Nuggets of Gold
Doug Jones

The old saying "Don't judge a book by its cover" holds much truth. It means that if you see someone who looks a certain way, it's easy to assume what they are like just by their outward appearance. But just as a book has hundreds of pages whose content the cover could never tell you at one glance, people are even more complicated. They are layered with an exterior that could never tell their whole story with one look.

Just like my character Billy in *Hocus Pocus*. Billy is a zombie who looks frightening, but by the end of the movie, viewers find out he's really a good guy who wants to help the kids defeat the bad witches. Billy is glad those kids give him a second chance to prove himself. Can you remember the many times you've been given a second chance?

No matter the flaws we might wear on our faces, it's what (and who) lives in our hearts that truly defines us. Here is a proverb that tells it like it is: "As a face is reflected in water, so the heart reflects the real person" (Proverbs 27:19). Let's make it a habit to search for the nugget of gold in every person we meet. While we're at it, let's look within ourselves. If Jesus is living in our own hearts, that's a pretty big nugget.

GET REAL

Today, look within your own heart. Is Jesus there? If not, give Him room to reside. Then, as you go through your day, look for the good within everyone you meet.

Fleeing Bad Spots

Ron Merrell

One time I had to stay the night in a really bad motel. The blanket on the bed looked like it had been run over by a greasy truck. Instead of paintings on the walls, someone had wiped boogers all over them. The inside of the shower was covered in hair. Hair on the curtain. Hair on the walls. Even hair on the ceiling of the shower. Was Chewbacca showering in here? Did a dog explode? What happened?!

I left immediately, but a few days later I remember wishing I had the same reaction to sinful situations in my life. I wished I saw how dangerous my sinful choices were and chose to run from them. The Bible has it right in 2 Timothy 2:22 (NIV), which urges, "Flee the evil desires of youth and pursue righteousness, faith, love and peace, along with those who call on the Lord out of a pure heart."

Fleeing sin means turning our backs on it and literally running in the other direction. This is always our best option when it comes to the stuff that Satan throws in our path. Jesus reminds us that He came to give us life, but the enemy comes to steal and kill and destroy. When you flee your sin, make sure you run straight to Jesus.

GET REAL

Can you really say you're fleeing the sinful situations in your life? Are you lingering around places of sin that you shouldn't? If so, confess those areas to God, and ask Him for strength to run away.

A Friend Forever

Rusty Wright

In high school, I found success through athletics, academics, and student government. But my achievements didn't bring the personal satisfaction I wanted. Guilt, anxiety, and a poor self-image often plagued me on the inside. I nearly got myself expelled from school.

My first year in university, I encountered some students whose joy and enthusiasm attracted me. They claimed to have a personal relationship with Jesus of Nazareth. I couldn't believe it all. I kept returning to their meetings because I was curious and, even more important, because it was a good place to find a date.

They explained that God loved me but that my own self-centeredness and sin had separated me from Him. They said His Son, Jesus, died to pay the penalty for my sins and rose from the dead so I could receive forgiveness as a free gift.

Eventually it made sense. Through a simple heart attitude, I invited Jesus to enter my life, forgive me, and become my friend. No rainbow appeared in the sky, I didn't hear any angels sing, and I definitely didn't become perfect overnight. But I found a new inner peace, freedom from guilt, assurance that I would be with God forever, and the best Friend I could ever have. He won't ever let me or you down: "For God has said, 'I will never fail you. I will never abandon you' " (Hebrews 13:5).

GET REAL

Have you come to know God personally? Why not ask Him to forgive you and become your best friend forever? If you have, then share this friendship with others.

My Bad
Melanie Stiles

My mom had a musical ceramic figurine. I didn't think much of it, but she loved it because my grandmother had given it to her. One day I was goofing around with my friends. We were chucking throw pillows at each other, and—you guessed it—off the table it flew. I picked it up and inspected the damage. A dab of super-glue and everything would be fine—as long as no one looked too close. I swore my friends to silence and fixed the figurine.

A few days later I realized I couldn't live with the guilt. Every time I looked at my mom's face, I felt bad. I also wasn't happy with the reputation I now had with my friends. I kept thinking if they wondered how many times I'd tricked *them* in the past. I was going to have to let them know I had to tell my mom. The only way to fix things was to fess up like it says in James 5:16: "Confess your sins to each other and pray for each other so that you may be healed."

My mom wasn't happy, but I felt better afterward and earned back integrity with my friends.

It's always best to make things right with others and God—even if it's uncomfortable. A clear conscience is worth the effort.

GET REAL

Is there a situation you need to make right with God and someone else? Confess your mistake or sin and apologize. There's no better time than today.

Parent Frustration

Steve Russo

Being a teenager can be frustrating. You're caught between two worlds—being a child and being an adult. Frequently, your parents are a big part of the frustration because they can be embarrassing and overprotective.

Parents are part of God's protective plan for you while growing up. They're responsible to guide you on the right path of life. Chances are, you won't appreciate this about your parents until you have kids of your own someday. The big picture: God has a purpose for parents in your life.

Look at things from God's perspective. He has plenty of advice for situations like this. In Colossians 3:20 God tells us, "Children, always obey your parents, for this pleases the Lord." If you have a relationship with Jesus, you should want to please Him. It's always the right thing to do, and God promises rewards for your efforts. Ecclesiastes 2:26 is a promise that God will give you wisdom, knowledge, and happiness if you please Him. Obeying your parents isn't always easy, but it pleases God.

This is going to sound strange, but have you ever thought about being thankful that you have parents who love you enough to care about where you go and what you do? Even if it feels like they are being overly protective, thank God for them.

GET REAL

If you're frustrated with the way your parents treat you, talk with them about how you feel. You might be surprised by their response. And remember, it's not easy being a parent today.

Operation Lifesaver
Chris Haidet

Why is it that more of us don't tell people about Jesus? Maybe it's because we have the wrong mental picture. We view them as lost, blind, confused, or just wrong. So we ignore the issue, pretending it doesn't exist. However, we must understand that apart from Jesus, people are actually *dying*! The Bible says, "For the wages of sin is death, but the free gift of God is eternal life through Christ Jesus our Lord" (Romans 6:23).

One day in fifth grade, I was playing catch in my friend's backyard. We were having fun throwing the ball when all of a sudden my friend stopped cold. He said, "Did you hear that?" I listened, and there it was again. In faint, muffled words, someone moaned, "Help me!" We both ran to the ivy-covered fence that separated his yard from the neighbor's. As I climbed up and peered over, I wasn't prepared for what I saw. An elderly woman was lying facedown in a pool of her own blood. I was frozen. Fortunately, my friend ran into the house and called 911.

What would you do? Would you help? Or would you not care, or maybe even pretend she wasn't there? Of course you wouldn't. But what about those people dying spiritually—apart from Jesus? We need to do everything in our power to tell people the good news of Jesus, no matter how hard it may be.

GET REAL

Write down the names of seven friends who don't know Jesus. Pray for them and that God would give you the courage and opportunity to become a lifesaver.

Crying Time
Lesha Campbell

Ever had a day when you smiled all the way through your classes, at ball practice, around your friends, and even at home with your family, but when your bedroom door closed and the lights faded, your true self shone through, and your heart was breaking? All day you were surrounded by people, yet nobody, not even your best friend, actually saw through your mask of laughs.

I've worn a mask like that many times and always, always wished someone had cared enough to see through it. More often than not, no one acknowledged it if they did. After all, if someone got behind the mask, they might not know what to do with the real me.

So often I've wanted someone to know me without having to explain myself every time. Sometimes I don't understand myself or even like myself. That's usually when I've had my guard up all day long and forced smiles and laughs when I really felt like crying. If only someone cared enough to cry with me. No judgments, no advice, just a caring heart.

But you and I do have Someone who will do just that for us. Psalm 56:8 says, "You keep track of all my sorrows. You have collected all my tears in your bottle. You have recorded each one in your book." Wow! God knows my heart is breaking even when I don't say a word. That's a comforting thought.

GET REAL

Next time you think nobody sees the "real you," remember God is keeping track of all the tears you cry, even those that no one sees.

Cling, Don't Bail

Steve Russo

Have you noticed that when something really bad happens—a friend dies, a relationship falls apart, or parents get divorced—God is usually the first one we blame? We want to scream at Him, shake our fists, and say, "God, where were You? How come You didn't do something to help?"

It's okay to be angry with God, but it's not good to bail on Him. There are no easy answers when something tragic goes down for you or a friend. But no matter what has happened, God still cares about us, and nothing takes Him by surprise. When we're experiencing tough times, we need to remember the promise found in Romans 8:28: "And we know that God causes everything to work together for the good of those who love God and are called according to his purpose for them."

This doesn't mean that everything that happens to us is good. But God is able to turn around everything—not just isolated things—that occurs for our future good. Keep in mind, God is not working to make us happy, but to accomplish His goal for our lives. Part of His plan is that we would be able to help others who experience the same things in their lives that we have experienced in our own.

God wants us to have a different way of thinking when bad things happen. He wants us to trust Him.

GET REAL

Learning to cling to God and not bail on Him when bad things happen takes time and effort. Start by building your faith through everyday life things. What is one concern you need to trust God with today?

Relationship Killer

Danny Ray

What's the biggest destroyer of relationships? Sin. All relationships are affected by it. Try being "normal" around your parents when you've totally lied to them and they just haven't found out yet. Or try hanging out with your best friend after you've gossiped about them in front of others at school.

Same goes with your relationship with God. The big difference is that He already knows what you did. You can't hide it. It's no use trying to spend time with Him, pretending like nothing ever happened last night online when everyone else was asleep. It's dumb to act like you didn't gossip about your best friend or like you didn't lie to your parents: God isn't fooled—He knows *everything*, and He *still* loves you.

That's why the words of Hebrews 10:22 are such an awesome truth to live by: "Let us go right into the presence of God with sincere hearts fully trusting him. For our guilty consciences have been sprinkled with Christ's blood to make us clean, and our bodies have been washed with pure water."

God *can* help us get closer to Him when we confess our sin. He can clean the slate, clear our conscience, and bring us back into the incredible closeness that He wants with us.

GET REAL

Is there sin in your life that's killing a relationship? Talk with God about it. Let Him help you.

Deep Pain
Ramona Richards

You never see it coming. When it hits, your entire world changes. Your stomach feels shredded, your mind numb, your heart shattered. It's ceaseless pain, as if you've been buried alive with no way out.

Loss. Grief. Agony. Whatever word you use doesn't come close to describing how you feel. Whether the pain is caused by a death, a chronic illness, a terrible breakup, or something else, it remains almost unbearable for a long time. From that time on, your life is different than how you thought it would be. Maybe your dreams were shattered—which is almost as painful as the loss itself.

It helps to have people around who share the loss, who love and care for you. You know in your mind that God loves you and cares about what has happened. He really does understand—maybe more than you realize. Remember what Jesus experienced on the cross. There's no doubt that He can relate to what's happening to you. Check out Isaiah 53:3: "He was despised and rejected—a man of sorrows, acquainted with deepest grief." Jesus has walked the harshest of journeys.

Believe in your heart that there is hope that comes from Jesus wrapping you in His arms to comfort you.

GET REAL

Give yourself time to grieve. Ask God to mend your broken heart. The loss will always be there, but each day brings more healing and a greater ability to move forward in your life.

Better Than Dirt

Dale Robert Hicks

I've stood on the shore of the Pacific Ocean and been amazed at its majesty. I've sat high in the Rocky Mountains and been in awe of the splendor before me. But I will never forget one day at the edge of the Grand Canyon. A five-year-old boy was called to come look at the canyon's scenic beauty. He walked over to the edge of the canyon, shrugged his shoulders, and said, "Big hole." The boy then walked back a few feet, sat down, and began playing in the dirt. He was blind to the awesome scene because what he was doing in the dirt was more important to him.

Consider these words from the Bible: "For ever since the world was created, people have seen the earth and sky. Through everything God made, they can clearly see his invisible qualities—his eternal power and divine nature. So they have no excuse for not knowing God" (Romans 1:20).

Why is it that people don't see God in His creation? Just like the boy at the edge of the Grand Canyon, people are too busy with things that they think are important. They fail to pause and consider nature and what it tells them about God. Some people find "dirt" much more interesting and focus there rather than on what God has revealed about Himself.

GET REAL

Take a moment to look at creation and ask yourself what it shows you about God. What is more important or fascinating than observing the splendor of God Himself?

Packaging
Melanie Stiles

Are you into the latest styles and trends when it comes to clothes? I'm not exactly a trendsetter, but I don't ignore them either. I have my own taste and style. That doesn't stop me from checking out what everyone else is wearing, though. And a lot of what I see other people wearing I don't like.

One day while I was people watching at the mall, I realized that I was judging other people's style (or lack of style) and was forming pretty negative opinions about them.

Not long after that, I had to participate in a group project. I got to know someone I normally wouldn't talk to—mostly because of her clothes. It was hard to admit that I had been labeling and judging her for a long time. Check out Isaiah 11:3: "He will delight in obeying the LORD. He will not judge by appearance nor make a decision based on hearsay."

Now I realize that seeing a high school girl wearing black polish only tells me she likes to do her nails. The same is true for an elderly woman wearing a hat with feathers—she likes feathers. Neither polish color nor hat style tells me any more than how they have chosen to decorate their bodies. More importantly, it says zero about what's in their hearts—which is what I need to take the time to find out.

GET REAL

Focus on the person, not the package, with each person you meet today.

BFF
Steve Russo

Friendships are important. Everyone needs to feel wanted, accepted, and loved. A "Best Friend Forever" can meet these needs. But human friendships are fragile and don't last. No one is perfect—except Jesus.

Jesus, the best friend we could ever have, sticks closer than a brother, totally gets us, and is loyal—*forever*.

He wants to be our top BFF, but the choice is ours. If we want this kind of friendship, we need to realize it involves a major life change.

Romans 3:23 (NCV) teaches that "everyone has sinned and fallen short of God's glorious standard." *Sin* is wrong thoughts, words, and actions (according to God's measure) with disastrous consequences. It's trying to live our life without Him.

To restore our friendship with Him, God did something unimaginable. He sacrificed His only Son, Jesus, on a cross. It's the only way for us to be forgiven and become a new person.

GET REAL

Nothing in this book will make sense unless Jesus is your BFF. Use this prayer to get started:

Jesus, I was born in sin and need Your forgiveness. I want to turn away from my sin and surrender my life to You. I believe You died for my sin and came back to life. Help me become the person You created me to be. Thanks for Your love. Amen.

If you made a decision to make Jesus your BFF, contact me using the information in the back of the book. I have something to help you grow in this new friendship. Then pass it on! Share this information with a friend.

Baggage
Brian Sumner

One thing I learned during the years I spent touring on my skateboard is that I don't like baggage. Some of us on the team would show up at an airport or take off in a van with the goal of taking the least amount of stuff possible. Other guys brought everything—all kinds of decks, trucks, wheels, clothes, CDs, DVDs—resulting in lots of big bags. The extra stuff made us late to airports, to hotels, and ultimately to getting out to skate. The baggage hindered not only the guys toting the extra load but the rest of us as well.

If I told you to wear ankle weights when you went swimming, or to take a bag of rocks with you to go mountain climbing, you would think I was crazy. Because it would hinder you—slow you down. Why then do we continue to carry around the weight of past baggage in our day-to-day lives? Jesus has set us free from our past, released us from our baggage. Paul, a follower of Jesus, wrote that "anyone who belongs to Christ has become a new person. The old life is gone; a new life has begun!" (2 Corinthians 5:17). Whatever pain or hardship you've experienced in the past, leave it at the feet of Jesus. He's a baggage handler from way back, with a disposal method all His own.

GET REAL

What are you holding on to from the past that's slowing you down? Remember, you can't change the past—only today and tomorrow. Ask Jesus to help you lighten the load today, my friend!

Satan Is Not God's Equal

Ron Merrell

My neighbor used to have a German shepherd named Rommel. He was the scariest attack dog I've ever seen. Every time I'd walk by he would run at the fence, spitting and growling. I'm pretty sure Rommel dreamed about eating bunnies, kitty cats, and small children every night. Needless to say, I kept my distance.

I think this is the idea in 1 Peter 5:8 (NIV), which says, "Your enemy the devil prowls around like a roaring lion looking for someone to devour." It's a sobering, scary picture of the reality of what the enemy has in mind for people. And that picture is so opposite to the picture our culture has painted of Satan.

Most of us would describe the devil visually as a little cartoon character. Red. Pointy tail. Horns. Handlebar mustache. Carrying a pitchfork.

Scripture reminds us that as a fallen angel, Lucifer is actually quite powerful and quite beautiful. However, he is *not* as powerful as God. Satan is *not* God's equal. He is *not* God's alter ego. Satan is a created being who has some power—limited by God—and who is destined for failure.

GET REAL

How have you pictured Satan in your mind? Remember that he is intent on your destruction and the death of those around you. Don't take that lightly. But also remember that God is infinitely more powerful than Satan and sin—and God has limited Satan's power now and eventually forever.

Take a Chance

Steve Russo

Think about the future. What dream do you have for your life? What can you do right now to start pursuing it? Take a chance. Become a risk taker and see what happens.

As you learn to become a risk taker, you start to feel more comfortable with letting go and trusting God. Trusting God is not a crutch; it's childlike confidence we put in Him. It's believing that God is able to do what He promises.

Is it tough for you to trust God? Why? What areas of your life do you need to trust God with? Slowly read the following verses and think about how they apply to you: "Trust in the LORD with all your heart; do not depend on your own understanding. Seek his will in all you do, and he will show you which path to take" (Proverbs 3:5–6).

We need to learn to trust God completely in every choice we make—believing that He knows what's best for us. And we have to be willing to listen to and obey what's in His Word.

GET REAL

What's something new that you've been afraid of trying? This week try some different things; for example, eat something different for breakfast, listen to a different style of music, introduce yourself to a new person at school, change the order of your daily routine, or comb your hair a different way. It's a lot easier to start small when trying something new than to try to accomplish something huge right off the bat. And don't forget the power you have available through Jesus.

How Far Would You Go?

Steve Russo

How far would you go to rescue a friend who was caught in a life-and-death situation? I hope you and I would do everything humanly possible to rescue a friend who was trapped in a burning building, confined in a wrecked car, or drowning in a lake.

What about someone dying spiritually? It's easier to have a sense of urgency about saving someone who is dying physically rather than spiritually.

It's not easy to look at someone who's young and healthy and make the connection that, without Jesus, he or she is doomed for all eternity. That's why we need to ask Jesus to help us see people as He sees them—confused and helpless. He was overwhelmed with compassion for people. We also should have a deep concern for those who don't know Jesus.

You don't have to look very far to find people who are dying spiritually, their future and eternal destiny hanging in the balance. Paul, a follower of Jesus, reminds us that we're official representatives of the living God: "So we are Christ's ambassadors; God is making his appeal through us. We speak for Christ when we plead, 'Come back to God!' " (2 Corinthians 5:20).

As God's ambassadors we have a responsibility to clearly communicate His message of hope, love, and forgiveness to the world—starting with our family and friends. That's why we should do everything possible to rescue them by influencing them to live their lives for and like Jesus.

GET REAL

How are you doing as an ambassador of Jesus? Make a list of friends and family who don't know Him. Ask God to give you an opportunity to play a part in rescuing them.

Mountain Climbing

Melanie Stiles

I've discovered mountains aren't always made of stone. We all have personal mountains to climb in our lives. My biggest mountain used to be my own self-image. When I looked in the mirror, the person I saw couldn't go out and grab any opportunity she wanted. I didn't have enough confidence to take risks, so my choices centered more on feeling safe than living my life. I lost out on many opportunities to see, join, and do—all things I really wanted but didn't feel I was good enough to try.

Finally, I snapped while reading about creation in Genesis 1:26: "Then God said, 'Let us make human beings in our image, to be like us. They will reign over the fish in the sea, the birds in the sky, the livestock, all the wild animals on the earth, and the small animals that scurry along the ground.' "

If I am made in the image of God and have access to His power in my life, that means I can do anything He says I can do—whether I feel that way or not. If God intended humans to reign over the earth, then any event in my life was included. I started saying yes more often after applying the truth of this verse to my life. Not because it was comfortable, but because I could depend on God's power to give me the courage I needed in my life.

GET REAL

Are you saying no because you don't have the courage to say yes? Does God believe in you more than you believe in yourself? Remember who you are in Christ.

An Old Dog

Carson Pue

We have a family dog named Connor. He has outlived every dog in his litter. He has indicators of his old age, the most noticeable being his increasing blindness due to cataracts on both eyes.

The other day I took Connor for a walk in the forest, a place he has been thousands of times before—but this time was different. It was early in the morning and still dark, making it impossible for Connor to see his way. Unable to rely on his eyes for sight, he raised his nose in the air and began to rely on scent for direction in the darkness. It was amazing to me how he was able to stay on the path—almost as if he could see. Dogs are able to smell one thousand times better than humans, which is why they make such good "sniffers" for airport security.

When Connor needed to see in the darkness, he relied on his nose. As I ran along trying to keep up with him, I remembered the Bible verse, "Your word is a lamp to guide my feet and a light for my path" (Psalm 119:107). God is able to guide us with His Word whether or not we can see what lies ahead.

GET REAL

Are there times when life seems dark or confusing to you? It can get scary if we try to go it alone. The Bible helps us to "live" life. If you rely on God's Word, God will show you which way to go and how to stay on the path.

Be Still
Susie Shellenberger

We're a culture of fast-paced people trying to go even faster. We drive fast, eat fast, talk fast, walk fast. But as we study the life of Jesus, we notice He was never in a hurry. He took His time with people. He looked them in the eyes. He listened to them. He prayed with them. He spent time with them.

The Bible tells us to be still. "Stand silent! Know that I am God!" (Psalm 46:10 TLB).

That's the exact opposite of how most of us live, isn't it? Though Jesus had an extremely full ministry and was followed by endless crowds of people, He still took time to pace Himself, to be still, to get alone with His heavenly Father.

What's so important about being still? you may be thinking. When we take a little time to be still on a daily basis, we're more apt to increase our intimacy with God.

And when we make time to read the Bible, we're being still before God. It's usually while we're being still that God's voice becomes more recognizable.

But God never speaks to me! Yes, He does. He speaks to you every day. But it could be you simply haven't yet learned the sound of His voice. Doing so requires being still.

GET REAL

Ask God to teach you the discipline of being still. Tell Him you want to recognize His voice, and respond in obedience when He speaks.

Work Hard at Being Godly

Ron Merrell

I got into weight lifting in college but had a hard time sticking with it. I am skinny and have trouble bench-pressing a pack of Starburst. I sit down on those weight-lifting machines that look like medieval torture devices and can barely push the bar up!

But I know that if I don't exercise I won't stay healthy. I recognize that the best athletes are the ones who discipline themselves, train well, eat right, and work hard at what they do. My relationship with God needs to look more like that. More discipline. More training. More healthy eating by taking God's Word into my system. More hard work.

This is what Paul was talking about in his letter to Timothy: "Exercise daily in God—no spiritual flabbiness, please! Workouts in the gymnasium are useful, but a disciplined life in God is far more so, making you fit both today and forever. You can count on this. Take it to heart" (1 Timothy 4:7–9 MSG).

GET REAL

How would you rate yourself right now on how well you're doing with spiritual discipline? How hard are you working at connecting with God, taking unhealthy thoughts captive, and surrounding yourself with good coaching? It's a battle worth fighting, because your physical health is temporary, but your spiritual health lasts for eternity. Start a new exercise routine, working out daily by reading God's Word then obeying it and applying it to your life.

Fascination with Evil

Steve Russo

Evil and the occult have become huge! It's like people are trying to see how close they can get to the fire without getting burned.

Some are enticed to play with evil because they're looking for power to deal with the issues of life. Others find evil fascinating and appealing because their lives lack meaning and direction. Wickedness and things of the occult look pretty exciting when you're bored to death with life.

The fascination can turn into a growing obsession with darkness. Things evolve so gradually that people don't even realize what they're getting into.

One of the most deceptive ways that evil can be appealing is when it's portrayed as fun and entertaining. Movies, websites, books, music, and video games can have an element of wickedness that baits and hooks our curiosity. Such entertainment can appear to be funny, crazy, or even scary.

When evil comes packaged as entertainment or recreation, it disarms us to the dangerous truth that we're playing with spiritual fire.

In 1 Thessalonians 5:22 we are reminded to "stay away from every kind of evil." As followers of Jesus we need to avoid tempting situations and focus on obeying God so that we don't give evil a foothold. Through His Son, His Spirit, prayer, and the Bible, He has given us all the resources we need to enable us to shun every form of evil in our lives.

GET REAL

Evaluate your entertainment. Are you playing with spiritual fire? Is there something that needs to go? Ask God to give you the strength to avoid that form of evil.

Okay to Brag

Steve Russo

Most of us like to brag. We boast about places we've been, our athletic or musical abilities, our academic accomplishments, and the people we know—especially if they're celebs. When it comes to celebs, even if we've met them or had the opportunity to hang with them, do we really know them or just know about them? Bragging can be a subtle reminder to others of what we want them to admire about us.

Usually we admire three things about others—their looks, their power, and their wealth. What do you brag about? What is it that most people admire about you? Are they things that will last?

The most important thing to brag about and be known for—in a good way—is having an intimate relationship with the living God. Why? Because our relationship with God affects every area of our lives.

The Lord said, "Don't let the wise boast in their wisdom, or the powerful boast in their power, or the rich boast in their riches. But those who wish to boast should boast in this alone: that they truly know me and understand that I am the LORD who demonstrates unfailing love and who brings justice and righteousness to the earth, and that I delight in these things. I, the LORD, have spoken!" (Jeremiah 9:23–24).

God puts the highest priority on knowing Him intimately and living a life that reflects more than head knowledge. He wants us to know and understand things like his kindness, justice, love, and forgiveness.

GET REAL

If we truly know God, we will trust, obey, and share Him. How well do you really know God? What are you doing on a regular basis to grow in your relationship with Him?

Timing Is Everything
Ramona Richards

Mike had been saving for a car since he turned twelve, working at just about any job he could find. Mowing lawns, doing odd jobs for the neighbors. By sixteen he had just about enough for a good used car, but his dad asked him to wait one more year. Mike complained, but he waited, still working. A year later his dad matched him dollar for dollar, allowing Mike to buy the car of his dreams.

Waiting on something important annoys most people. It's not easy to be patient living in our culture. We prefer instant gratification. Whether it's waiting on something we've ordered, the next big movie, even a new album to download—we hate it. Most of all, we don't like waiting on God.

But trying to take action without Him is always a disaster. We can't see the big picture that God has planned for our lives; we just know what we want—and we want it now! But just as we have to learn to walk before we can run, God wants us to understand some things first.

God may have something bigger and better waiting for us, something beyond our wildest imagination. As Isaiah 64:4 reminds us, "Since the world began, no ear has heard, and no eye has seen a God like you, who works for those who wait for him!"

GET REAL

A little patience can make awesome dreams come true. In what area do you need to exercise patience? Ask God to help you wait on Him.

Random Kindness

Danny Ray

I was walking down the streets of Washington DC when I saw a homeless man setting up his spot for the day. It was pretty early, and I had just come out of Subway with a large, piping-hot breakfast sub. As I walked away, I realized that this man probably hadn't eaten in a while. I didn't need to pray; I knew what God wanted me to do. So I crossed the street, cut my sandwich in half, and offered it to the old man. He was incredibly thankful.

Some would call it a "random act of kindness," but not me. It was an "intentional random act of kindness"—in other words, I was intentionally asking God to use me to encourage and care for people that day. When I left Subway, He had already prepared a divine appointment for me—I just needed to be ready and be intentional about my desire to be used by God for His "random" meeting.

Consider what God's Word says about showing kindness: "Suppose a brother or a sister is without clothes and daily food. If one of you says to them, 'Go in peace; keep warm and well fed,' but does nothing about their physical needs, what good is it?" (James 2:15–16 NIV).

Practice "intentional random acts of kindness" every day— you won't be disappointed.

GET REAL

Ask God to use you to be an encouragement to someone today. Be intentional in your desire to be used; then let God show you His "random" appointment for you. When you're willing and available, it's amazing what He puts in your path.

Reducing the Drama in Life
Chris Haidet

Have you ever dealt with someone who says one thing but acts totally different? They become an actor, a poser, a fake, a hypocrite! Let's be honest—we all put on an act every once in a while. But what do we do if our leaders, teachers, coaches, and, yes, even our parents take center stage in the role of "hypocrite"?

We watch as they ignore the very same rules they enforce. But for some reason they hold us to a different standard. We're told, "Don't drink, don't smoke, don't cuss, and don't you dare hang out with anyone who does." We are to act responsible, dress respectable, work hard, and be courteous to all. But then we watch our coach drop the F-bomb, Dad lose his temper, Mom dress like a teenager, and our leaders cheat and steal with ease.

We ask, "But what can I do? Will they even listen to me?" The Bible says, "Don't let anyone think less of you because you are young. Be an example to all believers in what you say, in the way you live, in your love, your faith, and your purity" (1 Timothy 4:12).

Sometimes it's hard to do right while the people we love do wrong. We must realize that everyone will make mistakes, even those who love us. But if we focus on doing what is right, God will use our example to impact others, even those in authority over us.

GET REAL

When the hypocrisy starts, focus on yourself first. Ask God to help you become a positive example; then have patience for Him to do the same for others.

Guilt Free
Steve Russo

How do you feel when you do something you know you shouldn't? You probably feel a little sting inside.

This emotional response is guilt—taking responsibility for doing wrong, whether it's a sinful thought, word, or action. God promises that if we agree with Him about our sin, we can be guilt free: "But if we confess our sins to him, he is faithful and just to forgive us our sins and to cleanse us from all wickedness" (1 John 1:9).

This inner alarm is good, but we have to be careful we don't let guilt consume us. Sometimes we're weighed down with guilt that has its source in something other than sin. False guilt can afflict us when people impose legalistic standards of what it means to be a "true Christian"—things like attending a certain number of Bible studies each week or supporting a starving child in a foreign country. While these are good things to do, they're not a measurement of how spiritual you are.

False guilt also can stem from painful childhood memories of abuse and feelings of responsibility for what happened—even though the sin was committed against you. If the guilt is not biblically based, it's a lie from the devil. Remember, God forgives our sins and chooses to forget them.

GET REAL

Are you struggling with guilt? Ask God to search your heart to see if you have any sin that needs to be confessed. If you've done this and still feel burdened by guilt, it could be from legalism or lies. Ask God to help you get rid of these feelings.

Dealing with Drama
Dale Robert Hicks

A girl I know got busted by a teacher for smoking pot in the school bathroom. As she stormed out of the teacher's classroom on the way to the principal's office, she yelled, "I don't need all this drama in my life." Later she told me she was smoking because she was stressed out.

I realized that a lot of different things can cause pressure in our lives, and this verse came to mind: "Don't worry about anything; instead, pray about everything. Tell God what you need, and thank him for all he has done. Then you will experience God's peace, which exceeds anything we can understand. His peace will guard your hearts and minds as you live in Christ Jesus" (Philippians 4:6–7).

Let's be honest—we live in a stressful world, and sometimes it's easy to get overwhelmed. Issues with friends and family weigh us down daily. The Bible provides a way to deal with the stress and drama, giving us the promise of peace. We all need help managing the daily pressures. Letting God know we are feeling overwhelmed is a valuable escape valve that will ease the pressure and help us address those problems.

GET REAL

The key to dealing with the stress in your life is trusting God to take care of it. You just need to believe that He will. Next time you have problems in your life that cause stress, rather than worry about them, tell God what you need and trust Him to do something about it. When He does, be sure to tell Him "thanks."

Willing
Brenda Pue

I was reading a story in the Bible that made me pause. Imagine this scene. Jesus has been speaking to large crowds of people all day. He finishes and is walking away from the mountainside when a man with an infectious skin disease (leprosy) approaches Him. I imagine that this man had been listening to Jesus from a distance and had figured out that Jesus was his last and only hope.

The man falls to his knees before Jesus. He is broken. He is at his wits' end. He's done. The man looks into Jesus' eyes and says, "Lord, if you are willing, you can make me clean" (Matthew 8:2 NIV).

Next Jesus says three astounding words: "I am willing," which He follows with, "Be clean!" (Matthew 8:3 NIV). Immediately the man was cured of his leprosy.

Think about Jesus' words: "I am willing." He wants you to take those words to heart. He wants you to take those words into your very soul. Whoever you are—Jesus is willing. Wherever you are—Jesus is willing. Whatever you're facing—Jesus is willing. Whenever you need help—Jesus is willing. However badly you've blown it—Jesus is willing. Jesus is willing to love you, help you, heal you, and clean you. He hung on a cross for you and me because He *is* willing.

GET REAL

Are you at your wits' end? Do you feel like giving up? All you need to do is fall on your knees before Jesus (humble yourself) and tell Him the longing of your soul. . .knowing that He is willing!

Who Do You Think You Are?

Tracy Klehn

I watched a TV show called *Who Do You Think You Are?* Celebrity Brooke Shields was traveling the world in search of her family roots. As Brooke looked into her father's side of the family, she found out that one of her relatives was an extremely successful businessman in Italy, having started the first bank there. That was exciting to her, but her search didn't stop there. The further Brooke went back in her family history, the more impressive her ancestors became. She ended up finding out that one of her relatives was actually born at the Louvre (yes, the famous museum in France) when it was a palatial residence. Even more amazing than that, Brooke discovered that some French kings are directly related to her!

As I watched this show, it occurred to me that if we were to go back in history and look into our family roots, we could get excited, too, because of the royalty we might discover. Romans 8:15 says, "So you have not received a spirit that makes you fearful slaves. Instead, you received God's Spirit when he adopted you as his own children. Now we call him, 'Abba, Father.' "

Isn't it awesome to realize that you could be loosely related to some form of aristocracy from your family tree but also that you are an actual child of the King of kings?

GET REAL

The next time you are feeling lost or confused about where you fit in, take the time to remember who you are and who your Father is!

No Excuses

Melanie Stiles

When my friend asked me why I hadn't shown up to help her study, I hesitated. I didn't want to lie, but the truth wasn't going to sound so great either. I had decided to go out with other friends instead of meeting her at the library the day before.

I'd had the best of intentions when I said I would help her. Sure, I wanted her to pass. I simply did not follow through with my promise. When I saw the hurt in her eyes, I started to feel bad for what I had done to her. I had put my own desires in front of the commitment I had made. I could have made up some excuse, but God already knew what I'd done, and I'd only be digging a deeper hole. The best option for both of us was for me to come clean and try to make it right. The friendship was important, but being able to look at myself in the mirror with a clear conscience was even more important. Look at Luke 16:10 (NIV): "Whoever can be trusted with very little can also be trusted with much, and whoever is dishonest with very little will also be dishonest with much."

Fortunately for me, my girlfriend forgave me quickly, and we set a new study date. In the end, she was more understanding than I might have been if she had ditched me.

GET REAL

Have you not kept a promise recently? Lame excuses only make the situation worse. Maybe it's time to come clean—with God and the person you've hurt.

Success Redefined
Steve Russo

How do you define success? For some it's measured by the position and power they've achieved. Others define it by the size of their bank account and the bling they've collected. How do you define success, and how important is it for you to achieve success?

Some of the most successful people I've met are unhappy. And they have it all: position, power, bank, and bling.

Success in this life is never certain. It can be like trying to chase a leaf blowing in the wind. You never know where it's heading and where it will land.

The Old Testament includes an amazing story about a man named Joshua who took on a challenge that seemed insurmountable. It was the biggest challenge of his life, and God kept telling him to be "strong and courageous" (Joshua 1:6–7, 9, 18). God gave some other specific instructions for Joshua to follow to be successful: "Study this Book of Instruction continually. Meditate on it day and night so you will be sure to obey everything written in it. Only then will you prosper and succeed in all you do" (Joshua 1:8).

God gave Joshua a set of criteria to achieve success that is just as appropriate today in a totally different culture. To succeed we must be strong and courageous, because it won't be easy; we must obey God's instructions and consistently read and study the Bible. We may never be successful by the world's definition, but we will in God's eyes—which is what matters the most.

GET REAL

Based on the strategy God gave Joshua, what changes do you need to make in your life as you pursue success redefined?

Poked

Nicole O'Dell

Have you poked someone lately on Facebook? A poke is a popular app included with every account that looks like a hand with a finger pointing. Poking someone is basically a simple way of saying "hello."

But there's another kind of poke we should be experiencing frequently. Jesus talked about it in John 16:8: "And when he comes, he will convict the world of its sin, and of God's righteousness, and of the coming judgment." Jesus sent the Holy Spirit to help us live the Christian life. God's Spirit is the One who "pokes" us about sin in our lives.

Ever feel that little twinge of regret deep down inside after you did or said something unkind? What do you do? Start by taking care of things with God. Confess or "agree with Him" that you've sinned. Then "turn away" from that sin back to God's way. The Bible uses the word *repent* for this action. The plan is that with God's help you'll try not to sin like this again. And then accept God's forgiveness.

It's also important to apologize to those you may have hurt and to try to make it right if possible.

Ultimately, the Spirit's poke should cause us to want to change our behavior in the future. Feeling the poke means the Holy Spirit is at work in your life, convicting you of sin.

GET REAL

Have you been poked by the Holy Spirit lately? Pray that you never become so hardened that you don't feel His poking.

Intimidated?

Brian Sumner

How did you begin your day? With confidence and sureness, or doubt and fear? The majority of your life can be lost by not living in the moment and seizing the opportunities that come your way. We often hear "You can do it" from athletes, musicians, and even parents, but how does that apply specifically to our lives?

Whatever gifts, whatever talents we have are given to us *by* God to use for serving Him. If we don't really understand this, we'll find it difficult to fulfill our destiny. God has a plan and a purpose for each of our lives that only we can fulfill. When the apostle Paul wrote to Timothy to encourage him, he said, "For God has not given us a spirit of fear and timidity, but of power, love, and self-discipline" (2 Timothy 1:7).

When I was younger, had I known where I would be now, I would have stepped up to everything without any intimidation or fear. God has given us everything we need to be who He designed us to be. But we have to put our faith and trust in Him. You can step into the future with confidence and courage. God will use His power to support you as you use your gifts to serve Him. You can fulfill your destiny if you depend on Him!

GET REAL

What or who intimidates you? How are you being held back from being who you were made to be? Apply what Paul wrote to Timothy to your situation. Then watch how your life can be fulfilled beyond anything you could imagine.

Out of Air

Nathan Finfrock

I love the ocean—its smell, its waves, and the beautiful, captivating world that lies only a few feet beneath the water's surface. When I was very young, I started scuba diving so I could explore the sea. On a diving excursion in my late teens, I dove off a Pacific island with a good friend of mine. In the middle of a great dive in beautiful conditions, I suddenly couldn't breathe. I was forty feet under the surface, which seemed miles away. I panicked. I couldn't find my partner. Despite my years of training, my thinking was paralyzed. Out of air and disoriented, I swam up on a slow but steady ascend. When I broke the surface, I blacked out while inflating my BC (buoyancy compensator) vest. The next thing I remember was my friend grabbing me and demanding to know what had happened. He found that one of my air hoses had blown out. I was lucky to be alive.

You never know when it's your time to die. However, it's refreshing to know that "those who have been called. . .are loved in God the Father and kept for Jesus Christ" (Jude 1:1 NIV). But what does it mean to be *kept*? God has you here on this planet for a specific amount of time. He loves you as His own. God is in control of your existence. So don't be freaked out. God holds you in the palm of His hand, and He'll never let you go.

GET REAL

Stop worrying! Your life is in God's hands no matter what. Learn to live in God's peace.

Only You
Ramona Richards

Sometimes it's a little intimidating to think how much God knows about you. He made every bone and blood cell as you grew inside your mom. He knows your darkest secrets, your wildest fantasies. He knows where you've been, where you're going, and what His plans are for you. If you've surrendered your life to Jesus, you are God's child. There's only one of you, and He loves you, no matter what.

Wise people have learned this powerful truth. The prophet Jeremiah realized it. "I knew you before I formed you in your mother's womb. Before you were born I set you apart and appointed you as my prophet to the nations" (Jeremiah 1:5).

You may look like your dad or have your mother's eyes. You may sound like your brother or run like your uncle. But you are unique on this planet. No one else looks, sounds, thinks, or acts exactly like you, and you fit into God's plan for the world as only you can. Only you can achieve what you're meant to.

No matter what anyone else tells you, you are important to God and others around you. Some people may not value you, but God does, and He always will. You have a lot to achieve, and God wants to help you do it.

GET REAL

Only you can do the job of being you. Hang in there, and rely on God. Ask Him what He wants you to achieve—today, tomorrow, and the day after that.

Matchless

Steve Russo

I had a mind-boggling thought while driving down the freeway in LA. Jesus created Muhammad, Buddha, and even Satan. Turn this over in your mind. Now check out Colossians 1:15–16: "Christ is the visible image of the invisible God. He existed before anything was created and is supreme over all creation, for through him God created everything in the heavenly realms and on earth. He made the things we can see and the things we can't see—such as thrones, kingdoms, rulers, and authorities in the unseen world. Everything was created through him and for him."

Jesus is unmatched. Everything got started and has its purpose in Him. Jesus holds everything together. Awareness of these truths is crucial to our growth in our relationship with God.

The natural world we live in was His idea. It's amazing, beautiful, and mystifying because He made it that way. Yet the world also can be evil and ugly. It was never intended to be this way, and the living God has acted to heal the world of the wickedness that has so deeply infected it. That's why Jesus died on the cross.

The more we get to know Jesus—who He is and what He's done—the more we'll understand who we are and why we're on this planet. And what it means to live our lives for and like Jesus.

GET REAL

When the world's beauty takes your breath away, thank Jesus for making it. When the wickedness gets you down, ask God how you can make the world better.

Moja
Chris Haidet

Have you ever had one of those life-changing moments, the kind that left you speechless? I have. I had the wonderful experience of working in an orphanage in Africa for two weeks. Our team was there to paint, build, fix, and serve in any way possible. We were to teach lessons, play games, hang out, and befriend 154 poor, hopeless orphans in Nairobi, Kenya. But what happened was not what I bargained for.

When we got there we were met with songs, smiles, laughter, and hugs. I'd never experienced this before and surely didn't expect it in this situation. Why were they so happy? They had no parents, little food, and dirty clothes. They slept twelve to a room, and 25 percent of them were HIV infected. But over the next two weeks it was the orphans who taught us this timeless principle: "How wonderful and pleasant it is when brothers live together in harmony!" (Psalm 133:1).

We live in a world that is totally caught up in things that don't matter. But for them, there was so much more. Now, did the orphans want parents, homes, clothes, and food? Of course they did. But until that day would come, they placed their hope in God and trusted Him with everything. They taught us a word in Swahili, *Moja*, which means "one." They lived together as *one* and lived for *One*. You see, all they had was God and each other, and that was all they needed.

GET REAL

When life seems to take things away, look to God for comfort. When life gives you more than you need, look for others to share it with.

What Lasts?

Tracy Klehn

Our family went on what we call our "trip of a lifetime." It was a cruise of biblical places. One of the stops was Ephesus, Turkey—one of the locations the apostle Paul visited. He spoke to the citizens of this city and wrote a letter to the early church there. It's the book of Ephesians in God's Word.

It was fascinating to walk around this two-thousand-year-old city and to see things like the remains of a library, shops, and temples to pagan gods. At one time this port city was one of the most powerful ones in the world, second only to Rome. It had a population of more than 250,000 people. But now it was broken and abandoned. It was a great reminder of what Psalm 33:10–11 says: "The LORD frustrates the plans of the nations and thwarts all their schemes. But the LORD's plans stand firm forever; his intentions can never be shaken."

After our day of touring the city ruins, I wrote in my journal: "Thank You, Lord, for our time in Ephesus and for the reminder that great cities and civilizations rise and fall, but You stand firm, and Your Word remains forever. This makes me want to spend more and more time with You in Your Word."

GET REAL

Take some time today to think about where you are investing your time and energy. Are you making wise investments in things that will last? If not, ask God to help you make the necessary changes in your life.

Get Dressed
Danny Ray

Chances are you put some energy into choosing the clothes you wear. Everything has to be just right—including accessories if you're a female. Sometimes there's a "look" for school and an entirely different style for when you're hanging out with your friends on the weekend.

Did you realize that God cares about what you wear? It's more than just the modesty thing. The Bible has a "put off, put on" principle: whenever God tells us to take something out of our lives—to "put off"—He also tells us what to put back in—"put on."

In Colossians 3:9–10 Paul writes, "Don't lie to each other, for you have stripped off [put off] your old sinful nature and all its wicked deeds. Put on your new nature, and be renewed as you learn to know your Creator and become like him."

What should we put off? Paul tells us: sexual immorality, impurity, evil desires, greed, anger, rage, malice, slander, filthy language, and lying (Colossians 3:5, 8–9). Wow, that's quite a list! Yet each of us is probably struggling with at least one item from that list right now.

God also wants us to get dressed with new clothes like "tenderhearted mercy, kindness, humility, gentleness, and patience" (Colossians 3:12).

What kind of "spiritual clothes" are you wearing right now?

GET REAL

Take some time today to "take off" your old dirty clothes. Ask God to help you put on a new wardrobe, one that He wants all of His children to wear.

Work of Art

Ron Merrell

I have a huge face. And it's getting bigger every day. From space, satellites can pick up huge masses on their radar like oceans, the Sahara, glaciers. . .and my face. It's really big. Now that I'm going bald, I kind of look like the offspring resulting from a coupling of Howie Mandel and an alien.

I'm not the only one worried about how they look. Most people wish they could look different than they do. Girls. Guys. Older. Younger. Everyone struggles with image at some point. But we need to anchor our self-perception on how God sees us. A king named David said in Psalm 139:14 (NIV), "I praise you because I am fearfully and wonderfully made; your works are wonderful, I know that full well." Paul describes us in Ephesians 2:10 as "God's masterpiece." You are a wonderful work of art by God.

God didn't make any mistakes when He created you. Your worth is not found in how you look physically. Our culture may operate on a different system, but that's part of the journey in living as a Christian in this society. You learn to operate more on how God sees things than on how you or others see them.

GET REAL

Take a moment to thank God for how He made you, even if you don't feel that great about yourself. Ask Him to show you how He sees you. Ask Him to help you find your worth in Him and not in the passing opinions of others today.

Idol and You
Steve Russo

American Idol seems light-years away from primitive people in a far-off land bowing down to stone idols. But there's a connection. Idols are people and things we give excessive devotion to. They don't have to be primitive manmade objects you'd find on a remote island. Athletes, actors, and singers can be idols.

Idols can be everyday objects like smartphones, iPads, and cars. Popularity, power, and money can also be idols. We can make idols out of ourselves or our friends. All these people and things are not necessarily bad—unless they capture our hearts in an unhealthy way. The danger comes when we allow anyone or anything to come between us and God.

Idolatry is really about worshipping the creation instead of the Creator. We end up rejecting God for someone or something. Look at how this trade-off is described in Romans 1:23: "And instead of worshiping the glorious, ever-living God, they worshipped idols made to look like mere people and birds and animals and reptiles."

This doesn't sound like something an intelligent person would do. But there have been times in my life when I've rejected God for an idol; and chances are you have, too. It can happen subtly—without warning. When I think about it, I realize how lame it is to worship things God has made rather than being totally devoted to Him.

GET REAL

What have you allowed to come between you and God? Is it something you think you can't live without? Whatever it is that's consuming your passion and energy—even "good things"—take time to step back and carefully evaluate your priorities.

Think First

Lesha Campbell

I hate it when I open my mouth without first checking to see what's coming out. It never fails to offer a stinging word to whoever is in its path. Don't get me wrong; I love to offer quick-witted replies to people who appreciate my humor, but sometimes I act too fast and don't get the hoped-for response. Then comes the scramble to repair the damage that could have been prevented if only I'd thought before I spoke.

I guess that's where the saying "Put your mind in gear before you put your mouth in motion" originated. You will invariably find yourself at some point profusely apologizing for something you said that the hearer either understood or misunderstood. "No, really, I didn't mean it that way, seriously." "You took it the wrong way." "You took what I said out of context." How many ways can you try to explain what you said? Too many to count—take it from me, someone who's been there. It's not a part of me I'm proud of, but I do know it *is* a part of me.

When will I take words of wisdom from the Master Wordsmith—God—seriously? He puts it pretty plainly in Proverbs 13:3: "Those who control their tongue will have a long life; opening your mouth can ruin everything." Ouch! I think God's talking right to me.

GET REAL

Next time you find yourself with an especially good comeback to someone who really deserves it, remember to "put your mind in gear before you put your mouth in motion"; it could save a lot of confusion and make your life a whole lot easier.

No Neutral

Nicole O'Dell

If a car is in neutral, it isn't moving forward or backward. But if you've ever left a car in neutral on an incline, you know that neutral doesn't guarantee it will remain in the same place. Leave a car in neutral, and you're in trouble, because it will move whichever way the ground slopes.

We often think that being neutral in a certain situation means we can stay out of the drama by not getting involved. However, if you don't move at all, you'll become a victim of the landscape around you. If you aren't solid in your position—parked, moving ahead, turning left or right—the opinions and pressures of those around you direct your path.

God uses the example of being hot or cold when He refers to the church at Laodicea that was in neutral. "I know all the things you do, that you are neither hot nor cold. I wish that you were one or the other! But since you are like lukewarm water, neither hot nor cold, I will spit you out of my mouth!" (Revelation 3:15–16).

God wanted the believers in Laodicea to take a stand one way or another instead of being halfhearted and weak. The same is true for me and you when it comes to living out our faith.

GET REAL

Are you living in spiritual neutral? Ask God to help you take a firm stand in what you believe.

Negative Influence
Melanie Stiles

One morning I had a new lab partner in science class. No matter what the topic of conversation, he found the negative side of it. When I mentioned getting out early, he said we shouldn't have to show up at school at all. I talked about enjoying my free afternoon in the great weather we were having, but he complained for ten minutes that it was too hot, too bright, too something else. . . . By the end of lab, I noticed I had started to agree with some of his opinions. Why did we come to school for half days? We could have slept in. It wasn't until later in the day that I realized how easy it had been to change my attitudes and opinions.

Colossians 2:8 (CEV) is a good reminder to be careful whom we let influence our thinking: "Don't let anyone fool you by using senseless arguments. These arguments may sound wise, but they are only human teachings. They come from the powers of this world and not from Christ."

That morning reminded me that attitudes are like waves that wash over us. If we hang around negative people, it won't be long before we start seeing everything in our world the same way. We can't always avoid these kinds of people, but the sooner we leave their company, the better off we'll be.

GET REAL

Are negative people influencing your life? How much time are you spending with them? Find some more positive people to hang out with.

Payback
Tracy Klehn

Has anyone ever done something for you that was so amazing that it would be next to impossible for you to ever pay them back?

My in-laws took our whole family on a three-week international "trip of a lifetime." We ate delicious food, stayed in beautiful hotels, and cruised to many different ports. When I got home and started journaling about our extraordinary experiences, I realized there would be no way that we could ever "pay back" Grandma and Grandpa for this trip. How then do we say "thank you" for such a generous gift?

It reminds me of what Jesus did for each of us. He gave up His very life for us. Ephesians 2:8 (NIV) says, "It is by grace you have been saved, through faith—and this is not from yourselves, it is the gift of God."

If it's impossible to ever pay Jesus back, how then should we live? Maybe we could live with a deeper sense of gratitude that overflows into a life of service to others. One way of saying "thank you" to Jesus is by looking for ways—little and big—in which we can help other people.

GET REAL

Say a prayer thanking Jesus for the free gift of His grace, forgiveness, and eternal life. Ask Him if there is someone He'd like you to encourage today. Maybe you could tell your parents, "I love you and appreciate all you do for me"; or maybe you could help a friend with chores or homework. Why not do something nice for a stranger? Be open and ready to act.

Pick Your Audience

Steve Russo

Who's your audience? Everybody plays to one whether they realize it or not. We all try to please others in our lives. Whose approval do you long to have? It could be friends, parents, or even a teacher. But how far will you go to get their approval? Some people become masters at "selling out" to the audience of the moment. But that can become a vicious cycle with no end. We can't always please others, and when we are playing to the wrong audience, we lose sight of who we are.

Few decisions are as important in life as picking the right audience. The apostle Paul gave some good advice to people living in Asia Minor. His instruction is just as appropriate for us as it was for them. In Colossians 3:23 he writes, "Work willingly at whatever you do, as though you were working for the Lord rather than for people."

The ultimate audience we are to be playing for is small. It's an audience of one—Jesus. Gaining His approval is what counts. No one else really matters. It's weird, but when we decide to live in a way that pleases Him, Jesus gives us the courage and strength to resist playing to the wrong audience.

GET REAL

Step back and take an honest look at who your audience is. If it's not an audience of one, you're playing to the wrong audience. Starting today, set aside some time on a consistent basis to be alone with Jesus. This will help you stay focused on the right source for approval.

Overcoming Failure

Rich Thune

Everybody fears failure, yet we all fail. Our fear of failure keeps us from seizing opportunities—like not trying out for a team at school because we're afraid we won't make the cut. Yet when it comes to failing, even the best hitters in baseball fail two out of three times.

In the Bible, Peter is a sad example of being a failure, initially. In talking to Jesus, Peter said he would never deny Him. But when the Roman soldiers showed up to take Jesus, Peter claimed—three times!—that he never knew the Lord. Talk about fear and failing.

But when Jesus rose from the grave, He reached out to Peter and gave him a future through his failure. In John 21 Jesus asked Peter the same question three times: "Do you love me?" Each time Peter's response was, "Lord. . .you know I love you." Then Jesus told Peter to feed and take care of His sheep (vv. 15–17). The Lord gave Peter a purpose to fulfill and an assignment to carry out—to lead His followers. Peter went on to become one of the most powerful forces in spreading Christianity throughout the world. When he talked, thousands of people became followers of Jesus. Yet he experienced the bitter taste of failure before he could appreciate the savor of success.

GET REAL

Has your fear of failing kept you hostage on the sidelines of life? Do past failures keep you from saying yes to opportunities? You may feel inadequate, but God promises to provide strength for the challenges you face. What purpose does He want you to fulfill? Take courage and do it—with God's help.

Greetings

Brenda Pue

People in every country have a unique way of greeting one another. In Australia it's "How ya going, mate?" In Taiwan it's "Have you eaten?" In Botswana it's "How did you wake?" In Bhutan it's "Is your body well?" In Jamaica it's "What's happenin'?" In Canada it's "How's it going, eh?" In America it's "Hello" or "Hi." In Ireland the English translation is "A hundred thousand welcomes." In Germany it's the equivalent of "Best regards." In England it's "Aye up" or "Now then." In Japan it's the equivalent of "Good to meet you."

But my all-time favorite spoken greeting is from South Africa. It is *"Sawubona,"* or "I see you." What a remarkable thing to say to another person.

In our stressed-out, fast-paced, and self-absorbed culture, it is so easy to miss people. We look at them, but we don't actually "see" them. Others look at us but seldom "see" us.

How amazing it is that there is a God who "sees" you and me. First Samuel 16:7 (NKJV) says, "Man looks at the outward appearance, but the LORD looks at the heart." Not only does He see our outer world; He sees our inner world. God sees what no one else can see. He sees our potential. He sees beyond the here and now into what we are capable of in the future. He sees what a healed, restored, and fulfilled version of each one of us looks like. He sees us—past, present, and future. He *sees* us. He *gets* us.

GET REAL

Do you know what it feels like to be overlooked? Forgotten? Ignored? God is saying, "Sawubona," to you. He wants you to feel loved, accepted, and favored by Him. He sees you in all the ways that matter.

It's What You Do with It

Ramona Richards

Bobby threw for five touchdowns in a football game. He was being watched by one of the top sports scouts in the country. Later that night, his girlfriend broke up with him.

Mara's promotion at work meant she could pay for college without asking her parents for money. But when her top three schools turned her down, she began losing hope of even getting into a great university.

Bobby and Mara both succeeded. . .and failed. Or did they?

It's the same question you hear lots of times: How do you define success?

A lot of people think it has to do with how much money they have. It can bring stability and bling. But it can also be unpredictable and easily lost. Stock markets crash and jobs get cut. You can be wealthy today and broke tomorrow.

Yet there's also nothing wrong with having money and being successful. As 1 Timothy 6:10 reminds us, we have to be careful where our heart is when it comes to money. "For the love of money is the root of all kinds of evil. And some people, craving money, have wandered from the true faith and pierced themselves with many sorrows." It's all about our attitude toward it.

Money is a tool, nothing else. It's what you do with it that's important. As with any other kind of success—a good education, a promotion at work, possessions, fame—true success is based on acknowledging that God is the one who gives success and honoring Him when we do succeed.

GET REAL

What's your attitude about money? Do you handle it wisely, or does it handle you? Ask God to help you have a healthy way of thinking about money. Start today.

What Happens When We're Still

Susie Shellenberger

How well do you know the voice of God? Are you making a genuine effort each day to get alone with Him—to be still—to actually learn the sound of His voice?

As we set aside time each day to be still, here's what happens:

We become more aware of God. When we choose to focus on Him during the still moments, it's easier to see Him at work during the rushed times.

We learn what His voice sounds like. When we make time to shut out all the other noises of our lives for a few minutes each day and talk to God, we can hear Him respond. Turn off the TV, the music, the Internet, the noises of life. Get alone. Listen for God's voice.

We get in the habit of waiting for God. Sometimes God acts quickly, and other times He asks us to wait for Him. When we establish a daily quiet time with Jesus, we learn the process of slowing down, of waiting. And it's during these times that God brings important things to our minds, such as someone who needs our prayers, ways that we could serve Him today, and His love for us.

God blesses us. "For Jehovah God is our Light and our Protector. He gives us grace and glory. No good thing will he withhold from those who walk along his paths" (Psalm 84:11 TLB).

When we first learn His voice in the silence, it becomes much easier to hear His voice through the noise.

GET REAL

Sometime today, find a quiet space to be alone. Turn off everything for fifteen minutes. It may seem like an eternity, but just be still. Listen to God. Try to do this each day for a week and see what happens.

Pressure Test
Steve Russo

Ever find yourself in a situation that you know is wrong but you play the "why not" game? Life can be dangerously seductive if we're not prepared.

The first book of the Bible relates an interesting story of a young guy who survived a major pressure test in his life. Joseph went through a tough trial but never caved in to a very enticing situation.

Sometime after his brothers tossed him into a pit and then sold him as a slave to a passing caravan, Joseph was bought by the household of Potiphar, an official of the pharaoh of Egypt. While Potiphar was out on business, his wife would hit on Joseph, trying to get him into bed. At first, Joseph might have thought, *Hey, why not? I've been abandoned by my family, sold into slavery. Life stinks right now. . .might as well have some fun.* But because of something deep inside Joseph—his values and morals—he refused to give in. Genesis 39:10 records it this way: "She kept putting pressure on Joseph day after day, but he refused to sleep with her, and he kept out of her way as much as possible."

At some point before this pressure test, Joseph had decided to follow the Lord no matter what the situation. The best time to choose is when we still have options—before we are tempted. When we're in the middle of the pressure test, chances are we won't have the perspective we need to say no.

GET REAL

Where are the lines that you refuse to cross in your own life? Decide now before the pressure test.

Following God's Example
Dale Robert Hicks

Our world is filled with pain. A great deal of it is the result of the wounds we inflict on each other. Sometimes those wounds are physical. Sometimes they are emotional. On occasion the pain we cause others is intentional, while other times it's accidental, but only the one being wounded knows how much it hurts.

It's hard for someone who has been abused to let go of what has been done to them. It is difficult to be kind to someone who has spread rumors and gossip about you. It's tough to stop blaming a parent for the pain a divorce has caused you. However, as Christians, we have been asked to do just that.

Consider Ephesians 4:32: "Instead, be kind to each other, tenderhearted, forgiving one another, just as God through Christ has forgiven you."

The truth is that those who have hurt us are not always going to come and ask for forgiveness. They are not always going to admit that they were wrong, so, just as God did for us, we need to take the steps to forgive them even before they realize they have hurt us. However, that doesn't mean their actions have no consequences. God forgives us, but Jesus still had to pay the penalty for our sins.

GET REAL

Take a moment to ask God to help you forgive those who have hurt or wronged you. Now develop a plan for how you can show them kindness and tenderheartedness. Don't let your forgiveness be in words only; let it show in your actions as well.

Earworms

Carson Pue

You wake up listening to your favorite radio station and hear a great song. On the way to school you have it running through your head. You hum it at your locker, you tap it out on your desk during class, and by five o'clock even *you* are tired of it.

So how does a song get stuck in your head? Search *earworm* in Wikipedia for an answer. Earworms are usually songs, although the term can also refer to TV and movie themes, advertisement jingles, and even video game tunes.

I have an earworm. It is a Bob Dylan song called "Gotta Serve Somebody." Check it out on YouTube or iTunes. The thing is, while it's a catchy tune, it actually borrows wisdom from the Bible and reminds us that everyone is a servant of some master.

The Bible says we either serve God or serve sin (things not of God). "No one can serve two masters," Matthew 6:24 tells us. Paul explains it this way: "Thank God! Once you were slaves of sin, but now you wholeheartedly obey this teaching we have given you. Now you are free from your slavery to sin, and you have become slaves to righteous living" (Romans 6:17–18).

Everyone is a slave to somebody or something. You have to serve somebody or something. The question is, who or what are you going to serve?

GET REAL

There isn't any middle ground here. You go toward serving sin or serving God. You have to make up your mind which way you are going to go. Personally, I'm a slave for Christ. Whose slave are you?

The Knockdown

Nathan Finfrock

When I was on the freshman football team, I had to learn to keep an eye on the punt returner rather than the football. I didn't just listen to Coach tell me; I learned the painful way. During a game with fans, friends, and cute girls in the stands, I was running down the field, watching the football sail through the air for what seemed like days. Out of the corner of my eye, I saw a kid at least a foot and a half shorter than me flying toward me like a torpedo. When he hit me, his helmet smashed my chest so hard I felt it for two weeks. The game had to be stopped while the medical team carted me off the field.

Life happens fast. We focus on one thing, and out of no-where temptation hits and knocks us down. Through the apostle Paul, God warns us about just this kind of situation in 1 Corinthians 16:13: "Be on guard. Stand firm in the faith. Be courageous. Be strong." It's hard to be true to your beliefs if you don't even see temptation coming.

GET REAL

What is something that consumes you to the point that you forget about the rest of life? It may be a perfectly harmless thing, but focusing so intently on it causes problems. Remember to listen to people you are close to, because they can help point out problems waiting to knock you down.

No Comparison
Melanie Stiles

It's human nature to compare ourselves to others. Maybe you want to be a writer. Maybe a pro tennis or basketball player. Whether we dream of becoming another J. R. R. Tolkien, Stephenie Meyer, Venus Williams, or Kobe Bryant, we have to be prepared for the journey. Somewhere along the way we will face the temptation to compare ourselves to our heroes.

When that happens, it would be easy for us to feel mediocre. But rather than spending time putting ourselves down, we can look at the example of John the Baptist. John lived in a time when miracles were performed frequently all around him. But he was never used by God to do a single one. In John 10:41 we read: " 'John didn't perform miraculous signs,' they remarked to one another, 'but everything he said about this man [Jesus] has come true.' "

John wasn't famous for doing miraculous signs, but he was the guy Jesus chose to baptize Him. Jesus sees us in a totally different way than we see ourselves and others. Our accomplishments can contribute to something bigger than we may realize, no matter what we or others may think or say about them. That's why it's important that we are faithful and obedient in serving God instead of comparing ourselves to others.

GET REAL

You never know when you will be chosen to do something special for God. It may seem small or inconsequential to you, but not to Him. Stop comparing and be ready.

Quiet
Steve Russo

I have trouble with quiet. It's more than the fact that I like to talk. I guess it's partly because I like my music so much. Before I even start the engine in my Honda Pilot, I have tunes playing on a CD or my iPod. We live in a very noisy culture. Some kind of noise is always happening—our mobile phone is beeping with a new text message, the guy driving next to us has his music blasting (usually hip-hop or rap), or someone is trying to get our attention when we're online. Sometimes we do it to ourselves. It's almost like we can't function in quietness. But we desperately need quiet—even though it's hard for a lot of us to handle—especially when it comes to getting to know God better. We have to make time to clear the clutter from our minds and think about spiritual things.

The sons of Korah (temple assistants) spoke about the importance of quiet in our lives in Psalm 46:10: "Be still, and know that I am God! I will be honored by every nation. I will be honored throughout the world." It's hard to think about how amazing God really is when we have so much "noise" coming at us from so many different sources every waking hour.

GET REAL

Take thirty minutes each day to turn off all the sources of noise in your life. Find a quiet place to be alone and be still. As you become comfortable with being quiet, thank God for who He is and what He's doing in your life.

Turn It Around

Ramona Richards

Joy tormented Carla for most of their junior year. She made fun of Carla's clothes, flirted with her boyfriend, and called her names, even in front of teachers. She posted embarrassing pictures of Carla on her Facebook page and sent insulting text messages. She even stole Carla's iPod at a basketball game, deleting all of her music.

Carla started to fight back, and the battle escalated. So when Carla's mother suggested she respond by loving Joy instead, Carla didn't think she could do it. Still, she decided to give it a try. The situation couldn't get any worse, and nothing else had worked.

At first it was a disaster. Joy's attacks actually did get worse. But Carla discovered that she could be just as stubborn as Joy, except in a positive way. She engaged her friends in a "Love Joy" campaign. They prayed openly for Joy. Carla responded to Joy's attacks with kind words—trying to encourage her.

Unfortunately, they never became friends. There's no positive ending to the story. But slowly and steadily Joy backed off. By the time their senior year started, Joy had moved on to other victims. Carla's stress level dropped, her other friendships grew stronger, and she became a leader among her peers. Carla also experienced what happens when you take Jesus' advice seriously: "You have heard the law that says, 'Love your neighbor' and hate your enemy. But I say, love your enemies! Pray for those who persecute you!" (Matthew 5:43–44).

Jesus knew that the principle of loving our enemies isn't primarily about improving the lives of those who despise us. It's about helping us become better people and grow in our relationship with God.

GET REAL

Is it time for a "love campaign" for someone in your life? Ask God to help you get started.

Being Patient
Ron Merrell

Recently I ordered five hundred burritos from Taco Bell to take them to a big party. I called ahead of time, placed the order, and then went to pick them up. I walked up to the cash register and told the girl, "I'm here to pick up the five hundred burritos." She asked, "Oh, is that for here or to go?" What?! I wanted to say, "Yeah, it's for here. . . . Just bring *all* five hundred to table 12 and I'll chow down!"

I have a lot of pet peeves. Sometimes people say or do things that really irritate me. That's when verses like Ephesians 4:2 hit me the hardest. It says, "Be completely humble and gentle; be patient, bearing with one another in love" (NIV). I realize I'm not very patient with other people. And when I'm not patient, it's actually a sign that I'm not very humble. My pride gets the best of me, and I start to think I'm better than others.

God has a totally great plan for the world to see how amazing He is. In order for people to see how patient God is, they need to see us being patient first!

GET REAL

Think about how many times this week you've lost your patience with someone. Think about some people to whom you may owe an apology. Pray for God to give you an extra amount of patience this week; then practice being patient—especially around people or in situations that normally bother you. See what God does in others and in you when you're patient.

Mirrors Don't Lie

Chris Haidet

Have you ever been caught checking yourself out in a mirror? You turn side to side, pucker your lips, and maybe even flex your muscles. Be honest—sometimes you even talk to the reflection staring back at you.

Mirrors are a common part of our lives. We use mirrors daily to wash our face, brush our teeth, and comb our hair. Mirrors give us the ability to see the minor imperfections of life, from eye boogers to bed head. Mirrors reflect the truth about us, no matter how disturbing. Mirrors don't lie and can save our day—but only if we use them.

Did you know the Bible works in the same way? But instead of mirroring the outside, the Bible reflects our inside. Through God's Word we see the truth and are given insight into the areas of our lives that need adjustment. But like mirrors, the Bible only helps if we respond to what the reflection tells us. Look at this: "For if you listen to the word and don't obey, it is like glancing at your face in a mirror. You see yourself, walk away, and forget what you look like. But if you look carefully into the perfect law that sets you free, and if you do what it says and don't forget what you heard, then God will bless you for doing it" (James 1:23–25).

GET REAL

God wants you to open His Word, reflect on the truth, and let it guide your thoughts and actions. Set aside time each day to study God's Word. This book you're holding in your hands is a great start. Look carefully into the truth, and let God reflect it in your life.

Bungee Cord Friends
Tracy Klehn

One night I decided to get coffee with a group of friends. As we waited in line, I felt something brush up against the back of my knee. I looked down and was surprised to see a bright yellow bungee cord hanging off the strap of my purse! Apparently when I set my purse down on the floor of my friends' car, it was on top of a pile of bungee cords. One of them decided to go for a little ride! When I showed my friends my new dangling pal, they all burst into laughter—well, most of us did. (One of our friends, completely embarrassed by our rowdy laughter, hid!)

This experience reminded me of how we "carry" our friends around with us even when we don't realize it and aren't physically together. Friends have a huge impact on us. This influence can be positive or negative. Our friends can build us up or tear us down. Either way, we end up carrying this effect around with us. Perhaps that is why the Bible warns us, "Become wise by walking with the wise; hang out with fools and watch your life fall to pieces" (Proverbs 13:20 MSG).

What kind of "bungee cord" friends are you carrying around?

GET REAL

Take a minute to think about the friends you spend the most time with. What kind of influence are they having on you? Are they drawing you closer to the Lord or pushing you away from Him? Ask the Lord to help you choose to hang out with the right kind of friends.

The Forgiven Drifter
Steve Russo

A seventy-year-old woman said that she has forgiven and feels no anger toward a drifter who tried to rape her and cut her throat. Madge Rodda said she only wants to help the twenty-three-year-old man change his life.

Her attacker pleaded guilty to charges of attempted rape, sexual assault, and robbery. Authorities said the man had slit Madge's throat nearly ear to ear. Just before he was sentenced to seventeen years in prison for attacking her in the bathroom of a restaurant, Madge gave him a Bible.

Why would a woman who was almost killed want to help the man who had brutally attacked her? Jesus said, "If you forgive those who sin against you, your heavenly Father will forgive you. But if you refuse to forgive others, your Father will not forgive your sins" (Matthew 6:14–15). That's why!

An unwillingness to forgive others causes bitterness, which stresses people out and destroys their lives.

Forgiving someone means we are "letting go" of how they hurt us. Forgiveness is the responsibility of the one who has been hurt. Jesus said that there should be no limit to the number of times we forgive someone who has hurt us.

GET REAL

If you're struggling with bitterness and having a hard time learning to forgive, take a few minutes to list those who have harmed you. Then pray for them by name, asking God to heal the specific hurt they've caused you. Ask for God's help to forgive.

Awesome Power

Steve Russo

People want power. They want power to change their lives, feel special, and sometimes even to get vengeance on others who have hurt them. You should hear about some of the crazy places people look and the things they do to try to get power. But God is the only source of real power—the kind we need to change our lives.

You can't totally understand what God is like until you begin to grasp how awesome his power is. Not only is God all-powerful and able to do anything; His power is also infinite—limitless. Look at what he did in Genesis. Chapter 1 tells how God spoke things into existence: "Then God said, 'Let the earth produce every sort of animal, each producing offspring of the same kind—livestock, small animals that scurry along the ground, and wild animals.' And that is what happened. God made all sorts of wild animals, livestock, and small animals, each able to produce offspring of the same kind. And God saw that it was good" (Genesis 1:24–25).

That's just one example of what God spoke into existence. It's amazing! Have you ever tried to speak something into reality? Only God has the power to create something out of nothing. His power never runs out, and it's available to us whenever we need it.

GET REAL

What do you need God's power for in your life today? Ask Him to give you courage and strength. Remember that no problem is too small—or too big—for God.

Listen and Learn
Ramona Richards

What's your passion? What are you good at? Rebuilding engines, cooking, doing graphic design, sports, playing an instrument, writing, acting? Getting good at something takes time, practice, and usually instruction from someone else.

We learn things all the time, every day, by watching and listening to other people as well as by doing. Practicing. We watch the coach throw a ball, or a teacher shows us how to play a song. Then we practice it so we can do it ourselves.

But one of the hard things about life is that to survive and succeed, we often have to learn stuff we don't really want to, whether that means paying attention in the most boring class on the face of the planet or not letting our egos close our ears. Jesus talks about the importance of listening and learning in Mark 4:24: "Pay close attention to what you hear. The closer you listen, the more understanding you will be given—and you will receive even more."

We have no idea what's going to happen tomorrow, next week, or next month. And we probably don't realize what skills we'll need when we get there to make life even better. Pay more attention to who you're with and what's going on around you. Listen—you may learn something you need to know. It could change your life.

GET REAL

Think about the people God has placed in your life and the things you are experiencing right now. Are you listening? What are you learning? Be specific.

The Right Thing to Do
Nicole O'Dell

A lot of young adults are dealing with their parents' divorce. Often that means a stepparent is in the mix. What about your family situation? Do you struggle with respecting a stepparent?

My brother is in the Air Force. He has strong political views that don't always match up with those of the president of the United States. Even if his views are the exact opposite of those of our top government officials, my brother will still stand at attention and salute them when they walk into the room. My brother would even take a bullet for the president—whether he voted for that particular individual or not. Why? Because he first respects the position of the president. Then the person.

Stepfamily relationships can be viewed in much the same way. Check out what God's Word has to say in Ephesians 6:1–3: "Children, obey your parents because you belong to the Lord, for this is the right thing to do. 'Honor your father and mother.' This is the first commandment with a promise: If you honor your father and mother, 'things will go well for you, and you will have a long life on the earth.' "

This means if someone new is filling the role of Dad or Mom in your life, you need to respect their position in your life.

GET REAL

If your relationship with your stepparent lacks the respect you need to show, ask God to change your attitude. Remember, He has a reason for the relationships in your life. He wants to create unity in your home and in your heart.

Mean People Perspective
Chris Haidet

Have you ever had one of those days when everybody is mean to you? Even though you've done nothing wrong, you're yelled at, laughed at, picked on, and treated like dirt. You ask yourself, "When did I become ground zero for everyone else's miserable day?"

My school years were fairly normal, but there were definitely days that didn't go so well. I had a few schoolmates who called me names, pushed me around, and made me feel like I didn't belong. They made fun of my size, my clothes, my hair, and, oh yeah, apparently I had four eyes. *I hated them!* In fact, there were days I just wanted to stay home. But you want to know what the really sad thing is? There were also days when I did those exact same mean things to others.

So how do you respond? Do you strike back, or do you forgive? The Bible says, "If you forgive those who sin against you, your heavenly Father will forgive you" (Matthew 6:14).

Even when we don't deserve it, God forgives us, and we should do the same. Nobody likes to be the target of a mean person, but we never know what someone is dealing with, or why he or she chose to take it out on us. Sometimes it helps to take a breath, dig a little deeper, and find a different perspective.

GET REAL

If mean people suck the joy out of your day, try something brave. Ask God to give you the strength to forgive, and then do it. You never know—the next day it may be you who needs forgiveness.

Expensive Cribs

Steve Russo

The MTV show *Cribs* gives us an inside look at celebrity houses without the risk of getting arrested for trespassing. With bowling alleys, massive pools, movie theaters, gigantic closets, and garages built for a dozen cars, some houses look like they've been made for a king. I can't imagine living in a place like that—or trying to keep it clean.

Have you ever toured a royal palace? Everything is perfectly kept. Each room is decorated with exquisite art and costly furniture. The floors sparkle. Maintaining the palace takes a team of people working full-time to keep everything just right for the royal family.

That's because members of royalty—a king and queen or a prince and princess—don't live in run-down shacks. They live in palaces as a result of who they are.

God, the King of the universe, has chosen you and me as His dwelling place because we are His children (see John 1:12). First Corinthians 3:16 teaches, "All of you together are the temple of God and. . .the Spirit of God lives in you." Think about this awesome truth. God's Spirit makes His home in us. This is huge!

Because the Holy Spirit lives within us, we are never alone no matter where we go. All the power we need to take on the challenges of life is readily available because God's Spirit dwells inside us.

GET REAL

Your body is holy. Do you treat it that way? Is everything in order for the King? Have you abused the palace of God by entertaining impure thoughts, dulling your senses with drugs and alcohol, or engaging in other behaviors that don't honor God?

Move On
Melanie Stiles

My brother was going out of town and asked me for a favor. "Watch my mutt, sis," he said, throwing a bag of dog food my way. The first week went great. I'd wake up, open the front door, and Pickles (don't ask me why he named her that) would run out, do her thing, and run back in. No problem. . .until the day a car drove up while the dog was outside. Much to my surprise, the driver opened his door and Pickles jumped inside. The car sped away while I stood on the porch with my mouth hanging open.

Telling my brother was horrible. For months—even though he continually reassured me he knew it was a freak incident and he didn't hold it against me—I was miserable. Even though I apologized and asked my brother to forgive me, I just couldn't seem to let myself off the hook.

Guilt can consume us. The Bible never talks about forgiving ourselves, but it does offer a principle that can be helpful. Think about how these words from Jeremiah 31:34 could set you free from guilt: "And I will forgive their wickedness, and I will never again remember their sins."

God chooses to forgive and forget our sins. He wants us to move on after we ask for His forgiveness.

I finally forgave myself for Pickles's abduction and moved on. Four months later I heard a scratch at the front door. I couldn't believe my eyes. Pickles had somehow found her way back home!

GET REAL

Are you weighed down by guilt for something that happened in the past? Confess it and ask God to help you move on.

Following the Evidence
Dale Robert Hicks

Hope is an awkward word for most of us. We tend to use it in the same category as the word *wish*. But the difference between wishing and hoping is the difference between dreaming that it might happen and having confidence that it will happen.

If I go to a restaurant and hope to have ice cream for dessert, I do so because I believe it is possible for me to get ice cream. My confidence is not in someone granting my wish but in the evidence that it's possible. I have seen ice cream on the menu and even witnessed others eating ice cream. It's not a dream but something built on the possibility presented by the evidence.

Consider the following Bible verse: "Such things were written in the Scriptures long ago to teach us. And the Scriptures give us hope and encouragement as we wait patiently for God's promises to be fulfilled" (Romans 15:4).

The Bible shows us that others have experienced the fulfillment of God's promises. We can read about God's promises, and we can see others experience the promises of God. All this should give us hope that we will see God's promises fulfilled.

GET REAL

When you are struggling with doubt in your life, where do you turn? Consider turning to those who have experienced the hope of God, both in the scriptures and in modern life. Let them be a source of encouragement.

You Can Do It!
Chuck Poe

One of my favorite movies is *Water Boy*. During one of its scenes, a hillbilly, played by Rob Schneider, yells, "You can do it!" Living in today's society, you may believe all the negative news on the airwaves. We've all been told by friends or family members that we can't accomplish something—like make the team or get into college. But understand that nothing is impossible with God.

Philippians 4:13 (NKJV) says, "I can do all things through Christ who strengthens me." When we think we are hopeless, we begin to believe it. According to scripture, we don't have to fall prey to this negative mind-set. We have a promise from God that we *can* do it: "He who is in you is greater than he who is in the world" (1 John 4:4 NKJV). God has our best interests in mind; He says, "I know the plans I have for you" (Jeremiah 29:11). Trust that God can help you through. Are you inviting Jesus along on your life's journey?

God is yelling to us, "You can do it!" We must be willing to obey and trust that God can and will accomplish His purpose in and through us. Are you willing to be used? Don't take the easy way out. As Michelangelo said, "The greater danger for most of us lies not in setting our aim too high and falling short; but in setting our aim too low, and achieving our mark."

GET REAL

Why aren't you letting God use you? Quit listening to people, and start listening for God to yell, "You can do it through Me!"

Out of the Car

Nathan Finfrock

My younger brother was insanely active. I think the word *hyperactive* was coined especially for him. Obedience was not high on his priority list, and he always needed to learn things the hard way. One day my father, sister, Tasmanian-devil brother, and I were heading to town in our SUV. Despite being told a hundred times to stay seated and buckled in, my brother decided he didn't want to sit or even stay in the vehicle.

We were driving fast on a dirt road when I watched him open the door and jump out of the car. It was like the kid was a stunt man in a movie. He hit the ground, rolled a few times, and stood up as if it were no big deal. My father slammed on the brakes and backed up. After dusting off his clothes, my brother jumped back in the car, and my father said in a calm, stern voice, "I told you to stay seated." My brother never again jumped out of a moving vehicle!

Obedience is a tough thing to learn sometimes. Yet even Jesus learned it: "Even though Jesus was God's Son, he learned obedience from the things he suffered" (Hebrews 5:8).

GET REAL

We all learn through trial and error. That's reality. It's easier to learn to be obedient in the little things while you are young. Today, start listening to those people of authority in your life, or you will eventually learn the hard way.

Lollipop Palace
Steve Russo

When I was in junior high, my parents opened a store called Lollipop Palace. Unbelievable! This was huge for my stomach and my popularity at school. We sold every size and shape lollipop imaginable, along with Moo's Ice Cream, McFarland Candies, and our own caramel and candy apples.

The first week the store opened, my parents told my brother, sister, and me that we could help ourselves to whatever we wanted. *We must be dreaming,* I thought. So we took them up on their offer. Any self-control I had was gone. You should have seen my friends at school when I told them the amazing news. But by the end of the second week, reality hit my stomach. I was sick of sweet stuff. Just the smell of chocolate nauseated me—especially weird for a chocoholic like me. If only I'd used a little self-control, maybe my stomach wouldn't have ached so badly.

How's your self-discipline? Not just with food, but in other areas of life? Solomon, the wisest man who ever lived, reminds us how important willpower can be: "A person without self-control is like a city with broken-down walls" (Proverbs 25:28). Just like city walls restricted the movement of residents, self-control can limit us. But it's necessary. An out-of-control life is not only a mess but also opens us to a variety of attacks from Satan. Look at self-control as protection for your life.

GET REAL

A person with self-discipline controls his moods and reactions, watches his words, sticks to his schedule, and stays healthy. How are you doing in each of these areas?

An Honest Response

Ramona Richards

Do you struggle with doubt when it comes to who God is and what He's capable of doing? Who hasn't had doubts? We read about all the great stuff that Jesus did when He was here on earth. He healed the sick, raised the dead. God split open rocks, seas, and city walls. Mark 9 relates the story of a father who brought his son to Jesus to be healed. " 'How long has this been happening?' Jesus asked the boy's father. He replied, 'Since he was a little boy. The spirit often throws him into the fire or into water, trying to kill him. Have mercy on us and help us, if you can.' 'What do you mean, "If I can"?' Jesus asked. 'Anything is possible if a person believes.' The father instantly cried out, 'I do believe, but help me overcome my unbelief!' " (vv. 21–24).

The cry of this father was an odd response to Jesus. But an honest one. He believed, but he didn't.

The Bible is full of stories of miracles and wonders like this one—some we may never get to experience during our lifetime. There's nothing wrong with doubts. If we don't ask questions and wrestle with things, we never grow in our faith. That's why God sends us wise people in our lives, most of whom asked the same questions when they were younger.

GET REAL

If you ask a question and don't get an answer, keep asking. And keep praying that God will give you courage to face your doubts and help you to believe.

Rescuing Your Friends

Ron Merrell

One night my cat, Paul, got stuck about thirty feet up in a tree. Saving him was going to take some serious work. I grabbed a ladder and a backpack and started climbing.

Once I got up to Paul, I grabbed him by the head and began jamming him into the backpack. But every time I thought I had all of his hugeness in the bag, one leg would poke out before I could zip it up. I finally got him in and climbed down, excited to free my feline friend. I realized then that in all the confusion, I'd accidentally crammed Paul into that tiny pocket on the front of the backpack! It didn't turn out as I'd planned, but I did manage to get my friend out of the tree. And it had taken some work.

You may have friends who desperately need your help. They need you to take an active part in rescuing them from their poor choices and leading them to God. No matter what the cost to you, your friends need you. The Bible says, "Be merciful to those who doubt; save others by snatching them from the fire; to others show mercy, mixed with fear—hating even the clothing stained by corrupted flesh" (Jude 1:22–23 NIV).

GET REAL

Think about one friend you know who needs rescuing, whether from their own choices or from other people. A good starting place might be to ask your friend if they need anything or to let them know they don't have to feel stuck in a situation all alone.

Radar Deflectors

Carson Pue

My wife and I have an old sailboat that I sail in a sometimes very busy coastal area. Larger cruise ships and freighters around us have radar they use to identify boats, islands, and logs so they can avoid us even when it is foggy.

While sailing one day, a friend asked me, "What is that?" He was pointing up one of the mast stays (a cable holding the mast upright).

"That's a radar deflector," I replied.

"Why do you need that?" the landlubber puzzled.

"Well," I replied, "sailboats don't show up very well on radar because they are low to the water. With that radar deflector hoisted up there, it makes us look like an aircraft carrier."

I thought about this conversation afterward. The radar deflector makes us appear to be something we aren't; many people carry around deflectors like this in life. We find ways to deflect people from finding out who we really are.

You have probably known friends at school like this. You're trying to get to know them, but all they tell you about is what they do. Others deflect through their choice of clothing or jewelry, and still others by becoming very, very knowledgeable about music or sports, others by using foul language.

Maybe it's time to take down the deflector. "You can't keep your true self hidden forever" (Luke 12:2 MSG).

GET REAL

In what ways are you deflecting others from knowing the real you? Why do you do that? Stop deflecting and start reflecting Jesus in your life.

Slow and Savory

Susie Shellenberger

By making time to be still each day, you're choosing to allow God to mold you to His image. That's not an instant process. It works kind of like a Crock-Pot—a slow cooker for food. Allow me to challenge you: you can choose to be either a microwave Christian or a Crock-Pot Christian.

If we spend only a few minutes with God each day, we're microwave Christians. We don't take enough time to get to know God, to let Him permeate our hearts, minds, and spirits. His aroma doesn't stick. We "cook" so quickly, no scent permeates our being or extends to others.

If we allow God to make us Crock-Pot Christians, we'll be much more effective in spreading His aroma. Think about it this way: The fragrance of a roast inside a Crock-Pot permeates the entire house. As soon as you walk through the door, a smile spreads across your face, and you're immediately aware that something very good is cooking. Your hair and clothes pick up that pleasing aroma.

"Thanks be to God, who. . .uses us to spread the aroma of the knowledge of him everywhere" (2 Corinthians 2:14 NIV). Start "cooking" today. Ask God to make you a Crock-Pot Christian. That's the kind of relationship God wants to develop with *you*.

GET REAL

When people are around you, God wants them to "smell the aroma" of your faith. Wouldn't it be exciting if people smiled when you walked into the room and became acutely aware that something good was happening inside of you? They'd crowd you. They'd want what you have. You'd be so tender, people would be attracted to your "scent"—to God's presence within you.

Thought Shaper
Steve Russo

Every day various sources influence our thoughts, which in turn shape our attitudes. Our attitudes determine how we live and what we do. Who or what is your thought shaper? Daily we have to choose to let either the world's way of thinking or God influence our thoughts.

Websites, blogs, music, and other forms of media offer a huge amount of information and advice about life that can be either helpful or harmful. Friends and family are also available to give advice—even when we don't ask for it. But how solid are their opinions, and what are they based on? Because our thoughts shape our beliefs and lifestyle, it's important to make sure we're listening to the right thought shaper. Our best resource for answers and advice is always God's Word.

The book of Hebrews reinforces this truth: "For the word of God is alive and powerful. It is sharper than the sharpest two-edged sword, cutting between soul and spirit. between joint and marrow. It exposes our innermost thoughts and desires" (4:12). The Bible isn't just a collection of words and ideas from God. Because it's alive, it changes lives. Just like the precision of a surgeon's knife, God's Word cuts to the very core of our lives to reveal who we are and what struggles we have.

GET REAL

We need to listen to God's Word and let it shape our lives. What do you need advice for in your life today? Have you looked in God's Word for direction yet?

Daredevil

Lesha Campbell

Risk takers seem to be admired by everyone. In the 1970s one of the greatest daredevils of all time—Evel Knievel—would perform his death-defying motorcycle leaps over rows of cars and trucks, and once he even attempted to jump the Snake River Canyon on a rocket cycle.

Evel Knievel was one crazy dude. My friends and I loved to watch his wild stunts and try to repeat them on our bikes in the front yard. Of course, I wasn't crazy enough to seriously try to do something that could really hurt me or scratch my beloved bike.

After a lot of Evel's jumps, he'd have wrecks and broken bones and blood transfusions. Whew, I didn't want to go that route. So I simply took the risks in my mind as I flew down the street with my hair blowing in the wind as I braved the downhill pace of a racer. I couldn't even "pop a wheelie" like most of the other kids could.

We all loved the daredevil, but we loved having our bodies in one piece even more. I'm reminded of Proverbs 14:16: "The wise are cautious and avoid danger; fools plunge ahead with reckless confidence." I think I'll stick with wisdom and watch the daredevil.

GET REAL

When you find yourself in a situation in which you need to be wise rather than foolish, remember that caution goes before the wise one: if you stop to think, maybe wisdom is leading the way.

Flavorful Living
Nicole O'Dell

If all of the salt was somehow evaporated from the ocean and spread evenly over the earth, it would create a layer about five hundred feet thick. That's a lot of salt! If you compared the taste of ocean water to the taste of tap water, you'd definitely taste the difference. Lots of people don't like to swim in it because of the taste.

Salt can be used in many different ways, including as a weed killer and to preserve food. Salt even has some medicinal purposes. But it's most commonly used to flavor food. Jesus said that we should be like salt in the way we live. "You are the salt of the earth. But what good is salt if it has lost its flavor? Can you make it salty again? It will be thrown out and trampled underfoot as worthless" (Matthew 5:13).

How's your saltiness? You're meant to add flavor to the lives of those you connect with and have the opportunity to influence. If you lose your saltiness, your purpose is diminished. Think about it. What good would it be to sprinkle an empty saltshaker over your food? You could shake it all day long, but it would have no "tasteful" effect on what you're eating.

You want to be so salty that you make a noticeable difference through the things you do and in the lives of those you come into contact with. Salt the world around you with truth and the love of God.

GET REAL

Do a salt check in your life today. Are you adding some flavor in your family and on your campus? Ask God to show you what you need to do.

Deep Waters
Melanie Stiles

I once had the opportunity to go on an Alaskan cruise. I was very excited; I had never been on a ship before. On the first day, I stood on the deck, watching as the crew members struggled with a gigantic rope that kept us tied to the dock. As they pulled it loose, I realized in that moment all connection with land was now gone. We were headed out to deep ocean waters.

The idea of deep water was scary to me. Not only would there be no swimming for shore if something went wrong, but the water itself looked dark and cold. As the trip continued, I learned the same ocean I was fearful of before held unique and unusual perks. Much to my surprise, seals floated around on icebergs, sunning themselves. Orcas gathered in groups to play. Massive black-and-white beasts defied gravity as they leapt through the air. These pictures are still vibrant and clear in my memory. I could never see them anywhere else but in those murky waters.

The experience reminded me that God wants to bless us in special ways if we are willing to go out into deep places and trust Him. Just like in Luke 5:4 (MSG): "When he finished teaching, he said to Simon, 'Push out into deep water and let your nets out for a catch.' " The disciples received God's blessings as they pushed out and watched their nets overflow.

GET REAL

Are the deep waters of your spiritual life calling to you? Are you ready to distance yourself from the shores of comfort? The first step is always the hardest.

Making Plans
Dale Robert Hicks

Have you ever sat around with a group of friends, trying to figure out what you're going to do? Does the conversation go something like this: "What do you want to do?" "I don't know. What do you want to do?" The problem with making plans is that no one wants to commit to something that no one else wants to do. No one wants to be responsible for an idea that their friends think is bad. Sometimes determining what you are going to do, whether with friends or with your life, is difficult.

We spend a lot of time worrying about the direction of our lives and whether what we're doing is the best for us. Read the following promise from God: " 'For I know the plans I have for you,' says the LORD. 'They are plans for good and not for disaster, to give you a future and a hope' " (Jeremiah 29:11).

This promise assures us that even when things seem to be going really wrong in our lives, God's plan is at work now and forever. It encourages us that God will work things out for us—if we allow our plans to be His plans.

GET REAL

What plans are you making in your life? Are you including God in your strategy? Whether your plans are big or small, ask God to help you bring them in line with His will for your life.

Looking for Love

Steve Russo

Everyone I know wants to be loved. Some people find love in the strangest places. . .like a Los Angeles freeway. It was rush hour and the 110 Freeway was like a jammed parking lot. No one was moving. Bob looked out his driver-side window and into the car next to him. The driver was a beautiful girl. Bob jumped out of his seat, ran around the car, and started a conversation that would change his life. Eight months after Bob and Jenna met on the freeway, they were married.

Are you looking for love? You don't have to go to a freeway. Love has already found you. It's not like ordinary human love, which has conditions, limitations. The love that has found me and you is unconditional—no strings attached. It never fails and isn't self-centered. Paul, a follower of Jesus, tells us about this love in Romans 5:8: "God showed his great love for us by sending Christ to die for us while we were still sinners."

Before we even knew Him, God showed us how much He loves us in an amazing way. He sent Jesus to die for us, not because we were good enough, but just because He loves us.

We don't have to go looking for the amazing gift of God's love. All we have to do is accept it. When we begin to grasp how much God loves us, our lives will start changing dramatically.

GET REAL

Read the verse above several times. Think deeply about it. Ask God to help you start grasping how great His love is for you. How would your life be different without God's love?

In the Beginning, Lars
Chris Haidet

I remember sitting in my high school science class, learning about how the universe began in what was called the Big Bang Theory. I began to think, *What caused the bang? My textbook seems to say we came from nothing.* So I thought to myself, *If that's possible, could it happen again, but this time slightly differently? What if the next thing to pop into existence is not planets and stars, but a Viking named Lars?* Wow, I couldn't escape the realization that none of this seemed possible or, to be honest, even made sense. I was confused. . . . Where *did* the universe come from? What's real?

Look at Genesis 1:1: "In the beginning God created the heavens and the earth." In these first ten words of the Bible, we find the foundation of all that exists. There was a beginning, and that beginning was God. God created everything we know, from the largest of stars to the smallest of atoms. He designed the universe with you and me in mind. Instead of being the product of time and chance, an accident of astronomical odds, we are, in fact, a priceless work of art, created in God's image, and are loved beyond measure.

You see, with God, life simply makes sense. When we put God at the beginning, what seems impossible becomes reality. Vikings named Lars, however, should only pop out of one's imagination.

GET REAL

When life gets confusing, ask God to help you gain understanding. When others try to claim everything is an accident, thank God for His creation and for giving you life.

What's Our Purpose?

Mike Thune

I had this random thought: What if friendly space aliens showed up at my door and asked me questions about the things they saw in our world? If they said something like, "What is this metal boxlike thing stationed outside your dwelling place?" I'd say, "It's called a 'car,' and it was manufactured by a company called 'Toyota' for the purpose of transporting human beings from place to place." I'd explain that the refrigerator in my kitchen was built to cool and preserve perishable foods, and so on.

But what if they asked me this question: "What are you?" What would I say? One popular answer, even among Christians, is, "I am a human being created by God so that I can be happy and enjoy good things in life—things like love, family, romantic relationships, and material possessions." While it is certainly true that we are human beings created by God, the hard reality we must face is that our own earthly happiness is not God's primary purpose in creating us. Instead, our Manufacturer tells us in our instruction book, the Bible, "I have made them *for my glory*" (Isaiah 43:7, emphasis added).

We glorify God when we reflect His character and goodness to others. The awesome news is that when we fulfill this central purpose of ours—to glorify God and enjoy Him forever—we will experience real happiness.

GET REAL

In what specific ways are you pursuing real happiness? Does your pursuit of happiness match the very reason for your existence in the first place?

When Life Gets You Down

Ramona Richards

Clay curled the blankets around his body and shoved his face into the pillow. His alarm had gone off an hour ago, but he still couldn't get out of bed. Clay just wanted to sleep.

Get up? For what? School was awful and was getting worse every day. His grades had bottomed out. His friends had turned their backs on him. Clay didn't want to go anywhere or do anything. He wondered why he should go on living.

Ever felt this way? Lots of people get depressed. Maybe you've faced dark times when your soul ached and the pain seemed endless. When life gets you down, the first place to go is God. "O my people, trust in him at all times. Pour out your heart to him, for God is our refuge" (Psalm 62:8). Our heavenly Father cares about us more than we realize.

Paul, an early Jesus follower, reminds us that talking with friends can also be helpful. "Encourage each other and build each other up, just as you are already doing" (1 Thessalonians 5:11). The words of a good friend can help during a tough time.

Sometimes our depression can be a deeper issue. It could be a matter of just needing more sleep. Or the result of a chemical imbalance in our bodies. If you want to beat your depression, you may need to see your doctor.

Figuring out what's causing your depression isn't easy. Just remember it's nothing to be ashamed of and there is hope.

GET REAL

God wants us to be healthy mentally, spiritually, emotionally, and physically. Get help for yourself or help a friend.

Walk the Talk

Danny Ray

A major university's women's fast-pitch softball team was playing in a crucial game at the end of its season. The game was tight when a senior from the other team hit a home run. It was her last year, her last game, and her first career home run. She was excited. In fact, too excited.

In her enthusiasm over hitting the homer, she missed first base; when she backed up to touch it, she broke her knee and collapsed on the ground. According to the rules, she had to touch each base or the run wouldn't count. And her teammates couldn't help her or she'd be called out.

That's when the opposing team's pitcher did something amazing, bringing the stadium crowd to tears. She called over a fellow teammate, and the two of them carried their opponent around the bases, helping her touch each one. You see, while the rules didn't allow for the girl's own teammates to help her, they said nothing about the other team assisting her. When asked after the game why she did it, the young pitcher said, "It was the right thing to do. We talk about sportsmanship all the time; this was an opportunity to practice it."

That's what James says about living the Christian life: "Don't just listen to God's word. You must do what it says. Otherwise, you are only fooling yourselves" (James 1:22). In other words, don't just say you know God; show it by what you do! Walk the talk!

GET REAL

What is one area of your life in which you've been "talking" more than "walking"? Ask God to help you— and be specific.

Memory

Steve Russo

Have you ever been to a concert and heard people all around you singing the words to just about every tune perfectly? Think for a second about the lyrics of your favorite song. The crazy thing is you never made a decision to consciously memorize those words. You know them because of repetition—you've heard the song so many times you ended up learning the lyrics.

Advertisers are banking on the fact that you and I will hear their commercials so many times that their product will stick in our minds. Then when it's time to buy, we'll purchase it. Think about all the other information you know by heart—names, phone numbers, facts and figures about your favorite sports team or band. Our memories are amazing. Anything is easy to memorize when you're interested in it.

How about God's Word? Have you ever thought about memorizing specific verses? The author of Psalm 119:11 reminds us of the importance of scripture memory: "I have hidden your word in my heart, that I might not sin against you." One benefit of memorizing God's Word is that it helps keep us from sin.

Hiding God's Word in our hearts can also give us confidence when we tell others about Jesus.

GET REAL

Choose four verses to memorize. Print them on three-by-five-inch cards or pieces of paper. Pick one to work on each week for the next month. Keep the verse with you. At least twice a day read the verse out loud. Before long you'll have each of the four verses memorized.

A Frequent Trap

Melanie Stiles

It was the night before a huge project was due. I didn't realize until it was too late that I didn't give myself enough time to finish it. I was depending on tossing a bunch of information together at the last minute to get me through. By midnight, it was obvious I wasn't going to finish the project.

Once again I was caught in the frequent trap of procrastinating. I caused my dilemma by not planning ahead and by assuming I could do the project quickly without checking out what would be required. I hadn't even completely read the instructions until the night before the assignment was due. Once again there would definitely be consequences. At best, a partial grade or a chance to turn my work in late with a lesser grade. At worst, a complete zero for the project. None of those options looked good. Ever been there?

Someone once said, "Don't do today what you can put off until tomorrow." Talk about bad advice, but it's easy to find yourself in this trap. We get lazy and put off what we know needs to be done. The Bible has some strong words about procrastinators: "Lazy people want much but get little, but those who work hard will prosper" (Proverbs 13:4).

I had gotten lazy and didn't care about the project as much as I should have. After getting a lower grade, I knew I'd have to make some changes if I wanted to fulfill my goals.

GET REAL

Are there areas of your life in which you've been procrastinating? Ask God to help you plan better and work harder.

Little Things
Nicole O'Dell

Do you have a set of tasks you do daily—a routine? Doing the same things every day, like exercise, chores, and homework, can seem boring and not a whole lot of fun.

Life isn't always cool; it takes hard work and discipline in little tasks to succeed. There's always something to maintain—to strive for and improve.

That's why being disciplined in the little tasks matters to God. He says that if we're faithful in the little things, those every-day disciplines, we'll prove that we're trustworthy for the bigger, more exciting things. "The master was full of praise. 'Well done, my good and faithful servant. You have been faithful in handling this small amount, so now I will give you many more responsibilities. Let's celebrate together!' " (Matthew 25:21).

From some people's perspective, a missionary living in a foreign country appears to have an exciting life. But do you think God calls someone to this kind of work who doesn't know the Bible? Of course not. He chooses those who have prepared through a regular discipline of Bible study.

The same is true with what God has called us to do right now in our lives. Even our daily tasks are part of the work God wants to do in and through us.

GET REAL

It's okay not to like the seemingly dull tasks and responsibilities of life. Remember that God uses them as building blocks to get you ready for an awesome future. Pray for God to help you discipline yourself to prepare for bigger, more exciting things!

Standing against the Current
Dale Robert Hicks

Watching people try to cross a fast-moving mountain stream can be a humorous experience. The rocks underneath the water are often covered with moss that makes them slippery. This unstable footing combined with the push of the current often causes people to slip and fall into the water. To avoid humiliation and hurt, you need to make sure you are standing firm in the stream before taking your next step.

Certain forces in life are working against us to knock us down, hurt us, or cause others to laugh at us. Even (maybe especially) as followers of Jesus, we face times when the currents of life push against us, causing us to lose our balance and fall. Just as we need to make sure we have a safe place to put our feet when we cross a stream, we need solid footing when taking spiritual steps so we don't slip and fall: "Therefore, put on every piece of God's armor so you will be able to resist the enemy in the time of evil. Then after the battle you will still be standing firm. Stand your ground, putting on the belt of truth and the body armor of God's righteousness" (Ephesians 6:13–14).

GET REAL

Do you know the truth about God, or do you have doubts? What's pushing against you and creating an unstable footing in your spiritual life? Who do you know who can help you find answers to your questions and help you plant your feet and stand firm?

Purity
Doug Jones

Some of you reading this might be wearing a purity ring on your hand right now, signifying that you have made a commitment to God and to your future spouse that you are saving sexual activity for your marriage. Not only does this commitment show sweet respect to God and your future spouse, but saving yourself also makes practical sense.

When we have premarital sex with our future spouse or someone else entirely, we are, without meaning to, telling our future spouse that we are willing and able to have sex outside of a marriage commitment. Jealousies and suspicion of affairs are much more common in marriages in which the partners have subtly told each other they are capable of having sex outside of their current marriage.

Statistics show that divorce rates are 50 percent higher for couples who had sex with each other before they got married than for those who waited for their wedding night.

Older generations look at kids today and think things are much worse than when they were kids. But you have a chance to reverse that opinion, as expressed in 1 Timothy 4:12 (NIV): "Don't let anyone look down on you because you are young, but set an example for the believers in speech, in conduct, in love, in faith and in purity."

GET REAL

Let's show the world that young adults have smarts, respect, self-control, and, yes. . .purity. And if you feel impure, God's forgiveness means you can reclaim that purity today.

Psychic Octopus
Steve Russo

Paul the Psychic Octopus became a media sensation during the 2010 World Cup by correctly predicting Germany's seven victories and Spain's win in the championship match. He picked game winners by choosing a mussel from a container marked with a country's flag.

But now Paul has gone digital. A smartphone app—"Ask the Octopus"—is available that allows a cartoon version of Paul to help users make decisions. Two possible options are entered, and the animated octopus swims to the sea floor, making his prediction by selecting one of two boxes. Hopefully it's a choice that guides a person's life in the right direction.

Are you ready to have this media sensation tell you if it's going to rain or shine or who will win the next NBA title? Or maybe there's critical life information you need to know. Do you trust this dynamic sea creature? Since the main idea was to create a fun way to randomly choose between two options, Paul isn't the best option for finding answers.

Many sources offer help in making decisions for the future. But only one is totally reliable. Isaiah, one of God's special representatives, was clear about whom we should trust with future decisions: "Only I [God] can tell you the future before it even happens. Everything I plan will come to pass, for I do whatever I wish" (Isaiah 46:10).

GET REAL

What is the one question that concerns you the most about your future? Spend some time today talking with God about it. Trust Him to guide you to make the right decision.

Love in Action

Chris Haidet

I am sometimes puzzled at how celebrity relationships last. I stand in line at the store and glace down at the various gossip magazines. In big bold letters I see the torrid details of romance, sex, betrayal, scandal, and, of course, true love. But is that really what love is? I remember when I was in school—people were dating, going to dances, taking moonlit drives with that special someone. . . I always wondered if I would ever fall in love or if anyone would love me back.

Have you ever fallen in love? Have you met someone who completes you? Do you even know what love is?

Here's how the Bible describes what love is and what love is not: "Love is patient and kind. Love is not jealous or boastful or proud or rude. It does not demand its own way. It is not irritable, and it keeps no record of being wronged. It does not rejoice about injustice but rejoices whenever the truth wins out. Love never gives up, never loses faith, is always hopeful, and endures through every circumstance" (1 Corinthians 13:4–7).

Love is more than just telling someone, "I love you." Love is not a passive feeling—love is a verb! It takes work, humility, patience, and loyalty. It's the act of putting others ahead of self. Love waits, love respects, and love puts God in the middle.

GET REAL

Ask God to give you wisdom in your relationships. Pray that He will guide you in how to authentically love another and that He will give you patience to wait for His direction.

It's Not about Me and You

Brian Sumner

We live in a culture that wants us to think that everything revolves around us. We're supposed to believe that it's all about me and you. We expect everything done yesterday, questions answered two seconds before we've asked them. Everybody and everything had better be on time, because we don't want to be kept waiting. The clothing store must have the right size, and the waiter had better serve us as if we were royalty.

We live as if the moments were made for us to direct them, but nothing could be further from the truth.

As I think about approaching God, more times than not I've looked to Him as my own special waiter or some magical genie, waiting to see what I will want next. When did God step down from His throne and decide to take orders from you and me? He never has and never will. I like the reminder Solomon gives us in Ecclesiastes: "As you enter the house of God, keep your ears open and your mouth shut. It is evil to make mindless offerings to God. Don't make rash promises, and don't be hasty in bringing matters before God. After all, God is in heaven, and you are here on earth. So let your words be few" (5:1–2).

It's not about me and you. It's about Him. Slow down, be quiet, and remember all God has done for you. Show Him the respect that He deserves.

GET REAL

Do you approach God as King or as some type of personal servant to cater to your every whim? Ask Him to change your attitude about Him and yourself.

Dark Times
Ramona Richards

Jenn's parents had moved three times in five years. She'd begged them not to move the last time, since she'd finally started to make a few friends.

But it happened again just after Christmas. A new school, a new set of strangers who had no time for her.

I don't know why I fight it, she wrote in her journal. *Life is purple and black, dark and spiraling.* After several attempts at making friends and failing, Jenn withdrew, stayed to herself, and stopped eating. She was so frustrated with her life she wanted to scream.

Sound familiar? Even when you haven't had the life shifts that Jenn experienced, the feeling of being alone, frustrated that nothing ever goes your way, can be overwhelming. There seems to be no light at the end of the tunnel.

There are no easy answers when you feel this way. Having a relationship with God doesn't mean you'll be able to avoid times like this. But it does mean that these dark times don't have to break your spirit. Look at Jesus' words in John 16:33 (MSG): "I've told you all this so that trusting me, you will be unshakable and assured, deeply at peace. In this godless world you will continue to experience difficulties. But take heart! I've conquered the world." Dark times don't last forever. Knowing God means that you recognize that the dark times will pass and the pain will eventually fade away.

GET REAL

No matter how tough the dark times are, don't give up. Cling to God and trust that He'll be there for you, bringing hope and light.

Stressing
Melanie Stiles

Stress can get to you. I got stressed about career choices. Business? Teaching? Other options? It wasn't like I had to have the answer that second. I wasn't even a senior yet. I just got caught up in thinking about my future. It seemed like I should have known all these answers.

Another related factor added more stress: How was my education going to be paid for? Scholarships? Probably not. Could my parents swing the cost of university up front or would I have to go to community college for a while? Was college away from home possible or would I be living with my parents for four years after high school? Too many questions with too few answers.

It took me half a day to figure out two things. First, I wasn't getting any closer to the answers, just worrying about them. Second, worry and stress can be magnified endlessly.

Do you feel like there's way too much stress in your life?

Jesus had a way of dealing with the stress the disciples were feeling. Carefully look at Luke 12:22–23: "That is why I tell you not to worry about everyday life—whether you have enough food to eat or enough clothes to wear. For life is more than food, and your body more than clothing."

Since Jesus said not to worry about what to eat or what to wear, I knew that school would work out also. You may not have it all sorted out today, but trust God to have a plan.

GET REAL

What are you stressed about today? Trust God to have a plan and your back.

Justice
Steve Russo

Down deep everyone has a thirst for justice. But justice is different than charity or compassion. It can be defined as a view of moral rightness based on fairness and moral values. But who decides what's right and fair? It's a hotly debated subject that has often been associated with fate, reincarnation, or even a cosmic plan for life. There are countless examples of injustice—acts that inflict undeserved hurt—in our world today. Many people are crying out for justice as they observe or personally experience human suffering, whatever form it may take. But we have to keep in mind that the God of the Bible is a God of justice and will one day right all wrongs.

Sometimes we are so enraged by what we see happening that we want to take justice into our own hands. We want vengeance, and we want it now. But Romans 12:19 teaches that retribution has to be left up to God: "Dear friends, never take revenge. Leave that to the righteous anger of God. For the Scriptures say, 'I will take revenge; I will pay them back,' says the LORD."

But knowing this should not be an excuse for us to ignore the acts of injustice in our world. As followers of Jesus, we are called to do everything we can—with God's help—to seek justice for those who cannot do it for themselves.

GET REAL

Are you convinced that God will avenge all injustice? What are you doing until that time to help those who cannot help themselves on your campus or in your neighborhood?

Fearing God
Ron Merrell

I had the opportunity to perform a wedding between two ninety-four-year-olds. It was incredible, except for the fact that the little old lady couldn't hear me well enough to repeat most of her vows. When we got to the end, I asked her to repeat after me: "With this ring, I thee wed." She scrunched up her face at me and with a puzzled look said, "With this ring, I beware?"

I couldn't stop laughing! There was *nothing* this woman needed to beware of in her ninety-four-year-old husband-to-be. Nothing! He didn't have any teeth! He had his pants hiked up to his neck. He was the safest, gentlest man ever.

I used to think of God as a little old man. In my mind He had gray hair and a beard and was kind of hunched over. He had funny old stories and crazy little sayings that He'd throw out when His children were listening. My view of God was totally off.

Psalm 111:10 (NASB) says, "The fear of the LORD is the beginning of wisdom." To have a healthy fear of God is to respect Him. Your wisdom starts in seeing God as He really is—and as He really isn't! Far from being a frail old man, He is the God who created the entire universe and allows you to take each breath.

GET REAL

God is calling you into a close, marriage-like relationship with Him, but He isn't a weak, timid partner. He's God. What are some ways you can show God that you respect and fear Him in light of who He really is?

Hopes and Dreams
Brenda Pue

Do you ever look at the people around you—you know, the amazing athletes, the good-looking guys and gals, the supersmart ones, the gifted and talented ones—and wonder where you fit in?

I used to wonder what I could possibly "bring to the table" in this world. Then one day a very wise person asked me a question that would be life-changing for me. He asked, "If there were no barriers at all—if money, time, education weren't a consideration—what would you love to do with your life?"

When I pondered that question deep in my soul, without being blocked by all the "buts," the answer came to me with clarity. My heart was opened to consider these further questions:

What would I love to do for God?
What would I love for God to do through me?

In Habakkuk 1:5 (NIV) God says, "Look at the nations and watch—and be utterly amazed. For I am going to do something in your days that you would not believe, even if you were told." How awesome is that!

GET REAL

Could it be that God also is going to do something in your days—something that you would not believe? What would you like to see God do through you in your lifetime? Take time to journal your answers to the above questions. With God, all things are possible! Stop comparing yourself to those around you and begin to focus on loving God and doing great things for Him.

Temple Thinking
Melanie Stiles

"Want a burger?" my friend asked as she pulled up to the drive-thru.

"Nah," I said, hoping she wouldn't push it. I really didn't want to explain I was trying to eat healthier to shed a few pounds. Losing the weight was turning out to be a lot harder than I thought it would be. Lately I couldn't help but notice every social event I attended revolved around food. I also counted over twenty fast-food restaurants in my neighborhood. On every menu were all kinds of mouth-watering selections designed to tempt my taste buds. We won't even discuss the aromas as I entered each eatery.

I was constantly arguing with myself about choices—until I started reading 1 Corinthians 6:19 every morning: "Don't you realize that your body is the temple of the Holy Spirit, who lives in you and was given to you by God? You do not belong to yourself."

Reminding myself that my body belongs to God gave me an awareness I didn't always have before. It caused me to think about the purpose God has for my life and the importance of being in shape for it. I decided God doesn't mind the occasional banana split, but He probably doesn't intend for me to have one every day. Knowing He values me enough to call me His temple helps me to recognize my body as a place of honor and respect. It gives me the strength to say no to the burgers and fries and opt for a salad instead.

GET REAL

What kind of physical shape are you in? Take a step toward temple thinking today.

Dealing with Letdowns
Nicole O'Dell

Disappointment is a part of life, a part of being human. Anytime our hopes, expectations, or desires are unfulfilled, we get disappointed. It's natural and it's a very real emotion to experience. Disappointment can be temporary and pass quickly, or it can hit us hard. When we get blindsided by a major disappointment, it can stay with us a long time and can affect our attitude about life.

The Bible is filled with stories of people who experienced disappointment. Sometimes it's caused by people; other times it's a result of our circumstances. It can also be part of Satan's strategy to bring us down to the level where we feel completely abandoned and defeated.

We can deal positively with disappointment in two ways. A great antidote is learning to be thankful. "Be thankful in all circumstances, for this is God's will for you who belong to Christ Jesus" (1 Thessalonians 5:18). It's not an easy thing to do, but it's a great reminder that God is still in control.

Another good antidote is found in 1 Peter 5:7: "Give all your worries and cares to God, for he cares about you." God not only understands our disappointments; He cares.

GET REAL

If you're struggling with disappointment today, let God know. Get alone and pour out your heart to Him. Let the tears fall if it helps. Ask Him for strength and encouragement to get through this difficult time.

Trash Talk

Steve Russo

Walking ahead of me in a parking lot were two girls and a guy who looked to be in their early twenties. The guy started trash-talking. The more he talked, the more the girls laughed. The more they laughed, the more trash came out of his mouth. It went from bad to worse.

I couldn't believe the girls thought this guy's language was funny. I kept thinking they were going to shut him down. I wanted to say, "Hey, dude—do you eat with the same mouth you talk with?"

Foul talk is like vomit. It spews out from deep inside our hearts and makes a disgusting mess wherever it lands. It can make you feel better temporarily, but it's an awful experience for anyone who gets in the way!

Distasteful language in all its forms—obscenities, gossip, criticism, lying, and crude humor—is tainted and ugly. Someone always gets hurt by it. Remember, the words we speak have the power for harm or for good in someone else's life.

The apostle Paul writes about trash talk in Ephesians 4:29: "Don't use foul or abusive language. Let everything you say be good and helpful, so that your words will be an encouragement to those who hear them."

No one is perfect. We should all pay attention to the kind of talk coming out of our mouths.

GET REAL

What has been coming out of your mouth lately? Are your words helpful and encouraging? If you don't like what you hear, ask God to forgive you and put fresh words on your tongue.

Still Cooking?

Susie Shellenberger

It's hard to become a Crock-Pot Christian if you're living in a microwave. We need to cook slowly and be filled with the heavenly Father's savory Spirit. Think about the disciples. They slowly "cooked" in the presence of God for three years. So after Christ returned to heaven, it's understandable they were ready to begin organizing the first churches. They spread the Good News, fulfilling God's mission. They were filled with His savory Spirit. They had been tenderized. They were ready!

When you decide to become a Crock-Pot Christian, God's Spirit through you will sweetly fill the atmosphere. Be willing to go for the long haul. Don't be in such a rush in your relationship with Jesus that you're not fully cooked. Take Jesus up on His invitation: "Come with me by yourselves to a quiet place and get some rest" (Mark 6:31 NIV).

God has a mission for *you*. How can you discern what it is? By spending time in His presence daily, becoming savory and tender before He reveals His full plan.

GET REAL

How can you know how to fulfill His mission for your life? By quieting yourself on a daily basis and truly learning the sound of His voice. You can't *respond* to His voice until you know what it *sounds* like. You can't know the *sound* of His voice until you *hear* it. You can't *hear* His voice until you've learned the discipline of *being still*. And you need to practice being still *every single day*. Amazing how it all fits together, isn't it?

Outside the Box

Danny Ray

Are you a risk taker? Do you think outside the box and sometimes find yourself doing crazy things? Or would you rather be comfortable and safe? When we decide to follow God, we take a risk because we start living by faith. But sometimes we try to make God safe. You know, we put Him in a nice little box. As long as He stays in there, we're okay with following His directions.

But you can't keep God in a box. And if you read the Bible for any length of time, you'll see how much He loves to do crazy things with those who are willing to live with Him outside the box. Things like telling an old man to build a big boat while waiting for something to happen that had never happened before in history —rain. Or prompting a young man to fight a giant with pebbles for weapons. Or telling a man to get out of a comfortable boat and walk on stormy waters. Or what about asking His followers to give up everything for Him?

Are you ready to step outside the box? Memorize Philippians 4:13 for all the courage you will need: "For I can do everything through Christ, who gives me strength." Get ready for the adventure of your life!

GET REAL

Close your eyes. Take God out of the box you've placed Him in. Ask Him to fill you with His presence in a new way. Pray that God will give you the power to be a risk taker, however crazy and uncomfortable it might seem.

Jesus and Text Messaging

Carson Pue

How many text messages, Facebook comments, and e-mails do you receive in a week?

You're probably one of those multitasking, cool people I see using their laptops, sending text messages, and listening to their iPods simultaneously with their thumbs typing away at a speed I envy. Millions of SMS messages are sent every day. Who answers all of these?

Have you ever wondered how God handles receiving prayers from people all around the world at the same time? Doesn't God get tired? Does He even hear my prayer?

When John the Baptist was in prison, he was feeling very perplexed, so he sent messengers from the prison to ask Jesus if He really was the Messiah. Guess what? Jesus told them, "Go back to John and tell him what you have heard and seen—the blind see, the lame walk, the lepers are cured, the deaf hear, the dead are raised to life, and the Good News is being preached to the poor. And tell him, 'God blesses those who do not turn away because of me' " (Matthew 11:4–6).

Jesus listens to all our prayers and even hears our whining and doubts. His heart must be pained at times by our lack of faith, but He is patient and kind as He answers us nevertheless. Jesus knows us inside and out and sends reassuring answers out of His love for us.

GET REAL

Pause right now and pray to God. He will answer. So listen and watch carefully. Next time you get an e-mail or text message, thank God for always answering your questions and prayers.

The Father's Call

Nathan Finfrock

Have you ever had one of those dreams where you seem lost for days? I experienced that in real life. When I was six, my cousin and I set out on an adventure in a large wash near our grandparents' house. At that age, we didn't have much concept of time. We told our fathers where we were going, and they told us to be back before dark. Well, time escaped us, and we forgot about our curfew. When night began to fall, our bearings in the once-familiar landscape deserted us. We searched and searched for the path home but could not find it. Out of the daunting darkness, we heard our fathers calling for us. It didn't take long to find them; we just followed their voices.

Throughout my life, I have found that most people are wandering in darkness. They take for granted the time on this earth that God has given to them. And they often forget to listen to His voice. Matthew, who knew Jesus personally, quoted His words: "Then the righteous will shine like the sun in their Father's Kingdom. Anyone with ears to hear should listen and understand!" (Matthew 13:43). Do you hear your heavenly Father calling?

GET REAL

Are you wandering in the darkness? If you are looking for direction and purpose, maybe you need to listen for the Father's call in your life. He has great plans for you! This week make it a priority to spend time with God and just listen.

Expensive Books

Steve Russo

Books can get pretty pricey. A copy of *Treasure Island* sold online for $4,870. A first-edition copy of *Grimm's Fairy Tales* sold for $11,388.

A rare first-edition copy of *Harry Potter and the Prisoner of Azkaban*, signed by the author, sold for $12,874. It included a misaligned block of text that was corrected later.

There's another book that contains priceless content. It's by far the most unique book ever written and is the bestseller of all time. The wisdom it holds—when practically applied—can transform individuals, families, and nations.

Countless people own a copy. Yet in many homes it's rarely ever read. What's the name of this book? The Bible. An early follower of Jesus spoke about its power in 2 Timothy 3:16: "All Scripture is inspired by God and is useful to teach us what is true and to make us realize what is wrong in our lives. It corrects us when we are wrong and teaches us to do what is right."

Throughout history people have attempted to destroy the Bible in a variety of ways. Today it's banned from being read in some school classrooms. And yet others wait years just to receive a small portion of the Bible.

With so much effort being made to keep people out of God's Word, you'd think we would smarten up and acknowledge that there must be something supernatural about this book.

GET REAL

Do you own a Bible? What's it worth to you? Has it changed your life? If not, begin reading a portion each day.

Stuck Outside

Tracy Klehn

A shuffling sound caught my attention as I made my tea. My eyes met my dog's gaze as she sat staring at me through the screen door. Our yellow lab sat in the darkness of the predawn morning, looking lonely and somewhat pathetic. I shook my head and laughed at my silly pooch, who didn't realize that the screen door stood ajar. It was not until I called to her by name, "Eve, the door is open," that she realized she had access to the warmth, light, and love of her home.

Have you ever felt "stuck outside"? Maybe some bad choices you've made have left you feeling unforgivable. Perhaps you have experienced rejection from family or friends. Or maybe nobody has ever told you that God wants you. God wants you to come and enter into the warmth of His unconditional love. Will you accept His personal invitation?

"Here I am! I stand at the door and knock. If anyone hears my voice and opens the door, I will come in and eat with that person, and they with me" (Revelation 3:20 NIV). Are you listening?

GET REAL

At different times I've experienced God's invitation through a song on the radio, a conversation with a friend, or a verse that resonated with me during a sermon. Ask God to show you the times and ways He has been personally inviting you to enter into His love.

No Fear?

Ramona Richards

Ever heard the phrase that bravery means being the only one who knows you're terrified? Or how about the saying that courage isn't the absence of fear—it's going ahead even though you're scared to death?

We read a lot of stories about people facing their fears in the Bible. Moses was so fearful that God sent his brother with him to face Pharaoh. Queen Esther reminded her cousin that she could die if she approached the king without an invitation.

"No fear" is, for the most part, a joke. In 1 Samuel 25, Nabal shows no fear of David, but everyone knows he's a fool. On the other hand, Abigail, Nabal's wife, was terrified but still faced down four hundred angry, heavily armed men in order to save her household. Described as intelligent as well as beautiful, Abigail knew the risk but made her stand anyway.

Have you ever thought about the connection between fear and love? Check out 1 John 4:18: "Such love has no fear, because perfect love expels all fear. If we are afraid, it is for fear of punishment, and this shows that we have not fully experienced his perfect love."

Courage isn't about taking foolish chances. It's about having experienced the love of God and trusting Him to guide you. There is no weakness in fear itself. Only in surrendering in the face of it because you haven't experienced God's perfect love in your life.

GET REAL

Is fear holding you back from accomplishing something or helping someone? It's normal. Everyone struggles with fear. Ask God to give you the courage to be bold and move forward.

Lies
Melanie Stiles

Have you ever been lied to? Most of us have. It took one lie, told by my closest friend, to mess up my ability to trust for quite a while. She hurt me very deeply. I found I was no longer so quick to believe anyone for fear of being lied to again. It felt like all my friends changed overnight. But really the problem was my lack of trust.

After a while, I noticed even more fallout. My relationship with God was different. I couldn't connect the way I did before. I put off praying. My worship didn't go as deep. I finally decided to tell a camp counselor about what I was going through. I found that I'd been applying the same lack of trust I had for people to God without realizing it. But check out Numbers 23:19: "God is not a man, so he does not lie. He is not human, so he does not change his mind. Has he ever spoken and failed to act? Has he ever promised and not carried it through?"

My friend may have let me down, but God would not.

Because of my relationship with God—and the assurance that He is totally dependable—it wasn't long before I was able to have confidence in Him and others again.

GET REAL

Are you able to not let what people do to you affect your relationship with God—especially in the area of trust? Remember, no matter what people say or do, you can always rely on Him.

Can't Take It Back

Nicole O'Dell

Have you ever said something that you wish you could take back? Unfortunately, no matter how much you might apologize for something you said, you can't take it back.

The same is true once you text, tweet, or post something on Facebook. Once you share something, there's no telling how many people will see it. As great as technology is, we also need to think about the harm it can cause to us and others as well. We have to be more careful about what we share and with whom. Being wise and knowing whom we can trust are crucial in today's world. It all comes down to the way we live and whether it honors God.

Paul has some interesting advice in Ephesians 5:15–17: "So be careful how you live. Don't live like fools, but like those who are wise. Make the most of every opportunity in these evil days. Don't act thoughtlessly, but understand what the Lord wants you to do."

These words are powerful and seem to scream one word—*think*! It's way too easy to go with the moment—to let our emotions get the best of us—without thinking about the consequences of our choices. God doesn't want us to be paranoid and stop using technology. He expects us to be wise instead of living foolishly.

GET REAL

Think about some of the things you have posted on Facebook, tweeted, or texted lately. Are there any you wish you could take back? If they were harmful to someone else, apologize. Ask God to forgive you and help you to think before you do the same thing again.

Coming to America
Steve Russo

Today, over 40 percent of Americans can trace their ancestry through Ellis Island, the premier immigration station until it closed in 1924. My grandparents came to America this way.

My Italian family members—along with all the other "steamship immigrants"—were tested to see how well they could read and understand English by reading a Bible verse.

Strange how much has changed since then. Now it seems like there's a concentrated effort to rid our society of God and His Word. In many places it's not legal to display the Ten Commandments publicly or for a high school senior to mention the name of Jesus in a valedictorian speech.

How did we drift so far away from God? Why are people so antagonistic? Maybe it has to do with the desire for personal freedom. But Jesus said in John 8:32, "You will know the truth, and the truth will set you free."

Then there's the spiritual battle. Even though we can't see it with human eyes, it's real and destructive. Maybe someday God will invade the hearts and lives of those living in America in such a dramatic way that we will become a nation that honors Him.

This will happen only if individuals like me and you decide to live our lives for and like Jesus. Then we can influence others to consider making this same choice, and they, too, can experience a transformed life. It sounds simple enough, but it won't be easy.

GET REAL

Do you know someone who has drifted away from God? Pray and find ways to connect with that person so you can influence them to come back.

Image Is Everything
Chris Haidet

In today's world, image is everything—or at least that's what we are told. We see it on the Internet, in magazines, and on TV. We must look, speak, dress, and be a certain way. But when we see these images, we sometimes feel as though we'll never measure up. Do you ever feel like what the world sees as beautiful, smart, sexy, and popular seems a long way away from your reality? The good news is that image *is* everything, as long as it's the right one. Look at this: "So God created human beings in his own image. In the image of God he created them; male and female he created them" (Genesis 1:27).

We don't have to live up to the fabulous and, quite honestly, fake images we see in the media. We already are the very image of God! You are exactly who God created you to be. You are unique, beautiful, smart, and loved more than you can ever imagine. Plus, what the world thinks is beautiful today might not be the same tomorrow. Just look at some of those old paintings in the museum. Their creators are long since dead. But God is forever, He is the creator of everything beautiful, and He will never change. What image are you living up to?

GET REAL

There is only one you, because that's how God planned it. You are fearfully and wonderfully made (Psalm 139:14). So if the world's image brings you down, go look in the mirror and remember. . .what you see is God's perfect image staring back at you.

When Growth Is Slow

Ron Merrell

Have you ever told God you'd never commit a specific sin again, only to find yourself falling back into the same temptation a week later? Have you ever wondered if you're going to conquer some specific issue in your life that's been with you for a year or more? If so, you're not alone. What are you supposed to do when your spiritual growth is slower than you'd hoped?

People in the book of Haggai had been instructed to start rebuilding God's temple, but after a month they were ready to give up. The work was hard and costly, and it wasn't going as fast as it should have been.

God gave the people some encouraging words: " 'But now the LORD says: Be strong, Zerubbabel. Be strong, Jeshua son of Jehozadak, the high priest. Be strong, all you people still left in the land. And now get to work, for I am with you, says the LORD of Heaven's Armies. My Spirit remains among you, just as I promised when you came out of Egypt. So do not be afraid.' For this is what the LORD of Heaven's Armies says: In just a little while I will again shake the heavens and the earth, the oceans and the dry land" (Haggai 2:4–6).

God tells them to take courage, to keep doing what they should do, that He's with them and He's building more than they can see—even when it's slow going.

GET REAL

Do three things if your spiritual growth is lagging: keep working at it, remember God is with you, and don't forget that He's working even when you can't see the change.

Midflight Refueling

Steve Russo

During the Cold War, the Strategic Air Command operated twenty-four hours a day as a shield of protection for America. This meant that at any point in a given day several fully combat-configured bombers were flying to assure the safety of the nation. Since these planes flew constantly, how did they keep them full of fuel? They used a procedure called midflight refueling. A refueling plane actually flew above and in front of the Strategic Air Command plane, docked in, and filled the plane with fuel.

The Christian life is a lot like combat flying. Staying alert for attacks from the enemy can be stressful, and then there's the issue of the fuel we need to keep flying. Going to church and youth group weekly doesn't provide enough fuel to keep us in the air the rest of the week. Just as we need food for our physical bodies daily, we need to have spiritual food, too.

What are you doing to refuel each day? Without spiritual fuel you won't get very far or last very long. The source for the fuel we need is the Bible. "But they delight in the law of the LORD, meditating on it day and night. They are like trees planted along the riverbank, bearing fruit each season. Their leaves never wither, and they prosper in all they do" (Psalm 1:2–3).

So don't forget to dock in and fill up every day!

GET REAL

If you haven't been doing a spiritual midflight refueling, it might be tough to start doing it every day. Set achievable goals to begin with, and gradually work toward a daily time alone with God.

Can You Afford It?

Susie Shellenberger

It's fun to dream of owning a luxury car. But it will take more than dreaming big to own a Maybach—the luxury sedan from Mercedes-Benz priced at $400,000-plus. Fortunately, it's not essential that any of us own a car of such quality. Let's draw a few spiritual parallels from this car scenario.

Salvation is expensive. Salvation is deliverance from the power and penalty of sin. And it's much more expensive than a luxury car. In fact, it's the most expensive thing in the entire universe. It's so expensive, none of us can afford it. But thankfully, because God loves us so much, He chose to pay the staggering price for us through the death of His Son, Jesus Christ.

Salvation is a gift. It's offered to all who will receive Jesus as their Savior. And you don't have to put down a $50,000 deposit or wait four months. Salvation can be yours right now!

Salvation is a necessity. Just as you need a dependable vehicle to get from one place to another, you need salvation to get from earth to heaven. The only dependable transportation is salvation through Jesus Christ. Without His salvation, you're lost for eternity.

Think about the value you place on things as you take a peek at this scripture: "If your profits are in heaven your heart will be there too" (Matthew 6:21 TLB).

GET REAL

If you've never asked Jesus to forgive your sins, you can place your faith in Him right now simply by admitting that you're a sinner and accepting His free gift of eternal life. By placing your faith in Him and walking in obedience to Him, you're a brand-new person!

Confident Waiting

Steve Russo

Waiting isn't part of most of our vocabularies. We live in a culture obsessed with instant gratification. We want what we want and we want it now!

Have you noticed how the new smartphone or iPad you just got isn't fast enough? It's like we can never be on top of things because there's always something newer and faster. An insatiable need for speed wells up inside of us and clouds our thinking. We're in such a rush that we end up making hasty decisions with no thought of the possible consequences.

This way of thinking creeps into many areas of our lives, enticing us to move ahead of God. But doing that is never healthy for us. The results can be disastrous and turn our lives inside out. The problem is that it's hard to surrender our dreams, goals, and relationships to God so things can happen in His way and His time. It takes willingness on our part to acknowledge that God knows what's best.

Waiting for God to help us, direct us, and provide for us is not easy—but it's the best thing we can do. King David knew this from personal experience: "I waited patiently for the LORD to help me, and he turned to me and heard my cry" (Psalm 40:1).

God encouraged and guided David as he lived day by day and obeyed Him. Sometimes we need to go through the trial of waiting to experience God's blessings.

GET REAL

Find a good friend you can call when you are tempted to move ahead of God. Ask that friend to pray for you and keep you accountable.

Stop the Smack
Dale Robert Hicks

Have you ever overheard someone talking about you behind your back? Ever read something that someone posted online about you? I read an online post by a high school student who was expressing his frustration with people who had made negative comments about him. That's when these words of wisdom came to mind: "Don't eavesdrop on others—you may hear your servant curse you. For you know how often you yourself have cursed others" (Ecclesiastes 7:21–22).

Social networking sites abound, and text messages flow so easily that sometimes things we aren't supposed to see end up being forwarded to us. That's why we need to practice the principle found in these words of wisdom: don't say anything about others that you wouldn't want them to say about you. Even more than that, we need to stop listening to what people are saying when they aren't saying it to us, although that can be difficult. To do it we need to decide whose opinion really matters.

Consider Jesus for a minute. In spite of all the things you've said or done, Jesus loved you enough to demonstrate that love. Jesus knows the unfavorable words that others speak against you, and He wants you to know that He loves you regardless. He gave His life for you.

GET REAL

Ask yourself what means more to you—the words spoken by others about you or the actions of Jesus for you. People will always talk, but very few of them will put their love for you into action.

Staying Sharp
Brian Sumner

Have you noticed how we give names to certain types of people and objects? The term we use often has something to do with its purpose. A knife is meant to cut, and a ball to be bounced. But what about a Christian—is this name an accurate reflection of how we live?

I grew up in Liverpool, spending evenings with my father cutting firewood. When the ax was sharp, I was more motivated to chop wood because I didn't have to work hard. If it was dull, I'd spend most of my time pulling the ax head out of the wood. The wood wasn't getting cut, and I was getting drained.

Maybe you've been feeling like your life is a dull ax. Situations you face are defeating you, and you don't have wisdom to make good decisions. In the process you're getting worn out. Check out the words of Solomon in Ecclesiastes 10:10: "Using a dull ax requires great strength, so sharpen the blade. That's the value of wisdom; it helps you succeed." Trying to do anything without the right tools is tough, including living the Christian life. If your life—"tool"—is dull, you need to sharpen it. But you need to know that there's a problem before you can address it.

The wisdom for living a sharp life is found in God's Word. As your "tool" gets sharp, you'll notice a difference in the quality of your life and your ability to face challenges.

GET REAL

Ask God to help you examine your life to see where your "tool" is dull. Look in His Word for help to sharpen your life skills.

Routines
Melanie Stiles

Routines are normal. I wake up, walk into the kitchen for a drink, make a U-turn, and sit on my bed for another fifteen minutes. I'm not a morning person. It takes me some time to get my mental motor running. Other people I know pop out of bed and instantly start zooming around, going full speed. God made everyone different on purpose. But there is one thing that He would like for each one of us to do when we start our day—take the time to connect with Him.

King David recognized this and talked about his morning routine in Psalm 5:3: "Listen to my voice in the morning, LORD. Each morning I bring my requests to you and wait expectantly."

David knew that God was in charge of his day, and it was his responsibility to seek Him for guidance and direction. He spoke to God first after waking up and waited for His direction. I've noticed that the more distractions, hassles, and busyness I have in my life, the more important that first connection with God becomes. It reminds me that no matter what occurs in the coming day, God knows what will happen, and He will be there helping me to get through it.

GET REAL

What does your morning routine look like? Do you begin each day with a time to connect with God? Try talking with God and maybe even reading a verse or two before your feet hit the floor. It will change your outlook on the entire day.

Ready for a Quiz?

Nicole O'Dell

How many times have you walked into a classroom to hear, "Have a seat and take out a piece of paper and a pen"? Those words can mean only one thing: a quiz! Either you forgot you were having one that day, or the teacher decided to surprise you. At that moment you wish you would have studied instead of hanging out with your friends the night before. And you hope—and pray—that you can recall the class discussions, because you know you're not prepared for the quiz.

Being prepared is also important in our spiritual lives. Look how Jesus describes the need to always be ready with this illustration: "A servant who knows what the master wants, but isn't prepared and doesn't carry out those instructions, will be severely punished. But someone who does not know, and then does something wrong, will be punished only lightly. When someone has been given much, much will be required in return; and when someone has been entrusted with much, even more will be required" (Luke 12:47–48).

God isn't in the habit of throwing a surprise quiz at us or trying to catch us off guard. But He wants us to be prepared for whatever He might call us to do. It's our responsibility to make sure we are ready physically, mentally, and spiritually for what each day holds—even if it's a surprise quiz.

GET REAL

Are you prepared? The best way to be ready is by spending consistent time alone with God in the Bible and prayer. Don't put it off—start today.

Family
Steve Russo

I come from a large Italian family. If you want a glimpse of how I grew up, take the classic movie *The Godfather* and put it together with *My Big Fat Greek Wedding*. Family gatherings were always a blast. There are a lot of us, we're loud, we like to have fun, and we love to eat! Underneath all of this is a strong sense of identity. When we're together, I know that's where I belong and where I'm loved.

Regrettably, families like mine are scarce these days. I wish more people could experience what I always thought was normal. But there is an even larger family we can all be a part of, if we choose to. And it can be loud, too. Although it's not perfect—after all, what family is?—there's an extremely strong sense of identity and love in this family.

I'm talking about the family of God. One of Jesus' followers, who was sometimes called a "Son of Thunder," wrote about how to become a member of this family: "But to all who believed him and accepted him, he gave the right to become children of God" (John 1:12).

The family of God is amazing. It will never break up, and no matter what we do, we won't be kicked out. Our new identity is even more amazing. It doesn't get any better when you *know* you're a child of the King!

GET REAL

Are you a member of God's family? If not, why? If you are a child of God, are you working to expand the family by inviting others to join?

Genuine Love
Danny Ray

A lot of problems at home and at school have to do with love. And it's worse for some friends than others—they just don't seem to get it. Driven by their emotions, they slam in and out of relationships, looking for love. But the problem is that they don't really understand what love is. A lot of adults have the same difficulty. You can't find something if you don't know what you're looking for.

Paul gives us an awesome description of what real love looks like—from God's point of view: "Love is patient and kind. Love is not jealous or boastful or proud or rude. It does not demand its own way. It is not irritable, and it keeps no record of being wronged. It does not rejoice about injustice but rejoices whenever the truth wins out. Love never gives up, never loses faith, is always hopeful, and endures through every circumstance" (1 Corinthians 13:4–7).

There are some interesting "love words" in these verses. Great stuff to apply to our own lives:

- Love doesn't give up just because of hard circumstances. Love is in it for the long haul.
- Being kind means backing up our "I love you" with heartfelt action.
- Genuine love is excited for others when they get good grades, the trophy, or something cool. It doesn't brag, because love knows everything is from God.
- Love doesn't act with a quick temper. It forgives just as Christ forgave.
- Love assumes the best in others—always.
- Love does not fail.

GET REAL

Pick one "love word" today and find a way to offer it to someone at home or at school.

Self-Aware

Brenda Pue

It was a hot and humid summer day. I attended an old Baptist church, and this Sunday was particularly uncomfortable. The ushers decided to open all the windows and doors to try to get a breeze moving through the sanctuary. The singing was finished and someone was getting up to pray, when something unusual happened.

A mother cat and her five kittens paraded down the aisle and across the front of the church—oblivious to the fact that they weren't where they were supposed to be.

Some people are a bit like those cats—not very self-aware. They don't think about the context they are in and how they may be impacting others. Self-awareness equals authenticity.

One way to become more self-aware is to invite feedback. Ask people you trust for their opinions. Jesus was known for good, solid feedback. Here's an example from Matthew 19:16–19:

"Teacher, what good deed must I do to have eternal life?"
"Why ask me about what is good?" Jesus replied. "There is only One who is good. But to answer your question— if you want to receive eternal life, keep the command- ments." "Which ones?" the man asked. And Jesus replied:
" 'You must not murder. You must not commit adultery. You must not steal. You must not testify falsely. Honor your father and mother. Love your neighbor as yourself.' "

It's worth the effort to search and pray for at least one person who can give you honest feedback in your life.

GET REAL

God knows that our lives will be so much better and fulfilling when we make the choice to embrace self- awareness. Ask God whom you can approach.

Shattered Glass

Ramona Richards

Maggie had done nothing wrong. She was innocent. But that was the problem.

Maggie had decided to wait for marriage to have sex. Not a popular decision among her friends. While Maggie wanted to stay pure for her husband, her girlfriends took her commitment as disapproval of them because they hadn't waited. Her boyfriend, who thought he'd waited long enough, broke up with her. One of his friends started a rumor that she'd slept with at least six other guys.

So while Maggie was just trying to pursue a good character, her heart shattered like glass because she felt so alone.

It has been said that character is who you are when no one is looking. For Maggie it turned out to be who she was when everyone was looking. She chose a tough path but decided to keep her commitment.

Life got a little easier. The rumors vanished, but so did all her previous friendships. Maggie made only one new friend by the time she graduated. In college her situation improved, and Maggie found a whole new set of friends who supported and loved her.

The qualities of a great character are outlined in Galatians 5:22–23: "The Holy Spirit produces this kind of fruit in our lives: love, joy, peace, patience, kindness, goodness, faithfulness, gentleness, and self-control. There is no law against these things!"

These qualities aren't easy to develop, but the payoff is more rewarding than you might think.

GET REAL

A broken character can be repaired, but it takes time. Start developing a solid character by letting the Holy Spirit control your life—one trait at a time.

Run, Don't Walk

Tracy Klehn

When was the last time you were really scared? Was it when you almost got in a car accident? Or during sudden turbulence on a plane ride? How about when you heard some weird noises late at night when you were home by yourself? For me it was at my son's basketball tournament. In a heated moment during one of the games, there was an exchange of words between our team's parents and those of the opposing team. Within several seconds a giant of a man leaped out of his seat and stood towering over and threatening one of the moms on our team. My heart started pounding, my stomach did a few flip-flops, and I broke into a cold sweat. All I could think of was to start quietly saying, "Jesus, Jesus, Jesus." Amazingly, that was enough.

God's Word says, "The name of the LORD is a strong fortress; the godly run to him and are safe" (Proverbs 18:10). There is power in the name of the Lord! Your prayers don't need to be full of fancy words. Sometimes all you need to know is who to call out to for help. His name is Jesus.

Within a few minutes of my "running, not walking" to the name of Jesus, coaches and tournament organizers had brought the situation under control, and by the end of the game everyone shook hands and exchanged apologies.

GET REAL

The next time your blood starts pumping in an anxiety-provoking situation, run—don't walk—to the name of Jesus. Whether you say it out loud or in your heart, it's sure to help.

Vagueness
Steve Russo

I found some vague questions that made me think. These are the ones that are a bit doubtful and can sometimes have more than one meaning. For example:

> If man evolved from monkeys and apes, why do we still have monkeys and apes?
> What do you do when you see an endangered animal eating an endangered plant?
> If a turtle doesn't have a shell, is it homeless or naked?
> If the police arrest a mime, do they tell him he has the right to remain silent?
> Why do they put Braille on the drive-through bank ATM machines?
> If one synchronized swimmer drowns, do the rest drown, too?

You and I may have our doubts about the answers to a lot of these questions, but some things we can know for sure, like God's grace and mercy. Paul, a follower of Jesus, encourages a young man named Timothy: "May God the Father and Christ Jesus our Lord give you grace, mercy, and peace" (1 Timothy 1:2).

It's amazing how God has blessed us with things that we, because of our rebellion and disobedience, don't deserve and could never get any other way. God's grace and mercy are two things we should never take for granted.

GET REAL

Take some time to thank God for His grace—giving you things you don't deserve. Also be grateful for His mercy—not giving you the punishment you deserve for your sin. Be specific. Peace!

Heartbreak in a Bottle

Chris Haidet

I walked into health class my sophomore year and saw several people crying. I asked what had happened. They told me four classmates, including my friend Jeff, were involved in a fatal car accident the night before. They were returning from a party where alcohol had been consumed. Only one died—Jeff, who was thrown through the front windshield.

The media makes drinking out to be fun, cool, exciting, and the popular thing to do. The problem is, they rarely show the heartbroken friend crying beside the casket. Alcohol, as well as drugs, can take over your life, make you into something you're not, and lead you down a road you don't want to travel. Listen to these descriptive and wise words from the Bible: "Who has anguish? Who has sorrow? Who is always fighting? Who is always complaining? Who has unnecessary bruises? Who has bloodshot eyes? It is the one who spends long hours in the taverns, trying out new drinks. Don't gaze at the wine, seeing how red it is, how it sparkles in the cup, how smoothly it goes down. For in the end it bites like a poisonous snake; it stings like a viper" (Proverbs 23:29–32).

God has wonderful plans for our lives, but we can throw them away. Giving up control to a substance is against what God wants for our lives and inevitably leads to heartbreak.

GET REAL

If you are ever pressured to drink or use drugs, have the courage to let it pass. If you or a friend is struggling with substance abuse, ask God for strength and get help.

What Are You Selling?

Ron Merrell

I only buy what I want. Except for random trips to Best Buy, it's very rare that I buy something on the spur of the moment. For example, we had dirty carpets for several months because our son liked to pour cherry cola on them. We talked about renting a carpet cleaner but never got around to it. Then one day a door-to-door salesman showed up offering to clean our carpets for free! I immediately invited him in. Halfway through his cleaning, he told us that his cleaning gadget cost approximately as much as a house in Malibu (not quite), but we didn't care. We had dirty carpets and his carpet cleaner gadget was working.

We bought it. We saw the need and the guy was nice. Done deal.

When it comes to buying things, I don't like being presented with arguments, bullied, or taken on a guilt trip. I think people are the same way when it comes to someone telling them about Jesus.

Paul encouraged Titus to make sure he presented, as attractively as possible, the good news of who Jesus was. "Slaves must always obey their masters and do their best to please them. They must not talk back or steal, but must show themselves to be entirely trustworthy and good. Then they will make the teaching about God our Savior attractive in every way" (Titus 2:9–10).

GET REAL

Which of your friends do you need to tell about Jesus? What can you do now to make sure you have the best relationship possible with them before you share? When you talk, avoid being argumentative or judgmental. Take the opportunity to gently and clearly tell them about Jesus.

Presidential Visit

Nathan Finfrock

Growing up as missionary kids in the Philippines, my two American friends and I were seriously into camouflage, guns, and war games. When others told us Filipino president Cory Aquino was coming to visit our island, we devised a plan to get a close glimpse of her. We were well acquainted with the airfield, which was only a few blocks away from my house. When we discovered what time her plane would arrive, we set our plan into motion. Security was tight, helicopters thundered overhead, and soldiers with machine guns patrolled the airfield. Our hearts pounding, we snuck through the barbed-wire-fence perimeter and began our slow army crawl across the rice paddies surrounding the airfield. Then we heard the roar of jet engines powering down the runway. The president had landed. Our combined efforts got us one hundred yards from the aircraft, and we saw the president wave to the crowd as she exited the plane.

It amazes me how many people try to achieve things by themselves. Every successful person I have ever known regularly accepts help and advice from others. Even Jesus, when He fed five thousand people, requested help. " 'But we have only five loaves of bread and two fish!' they answered. 'Bring them here,' he said. Then he told the people to sit down on the grass. Jesus took the five loaves and two fish, looked up toward heaven, and blessed them. Then, breaking the loaves into pieces, he gave the bread to the disciples, who distributed it to the people" (Matthew 14:17–19).

GET REAL

Jesus achieved so much because He's God and worked through people like me and you. Develop healthy relationships; they will be essential for a successful life.

Uncertainty
Steve Russo

Our world is filled with uncertainty today: families breaking up, terrorist attacks, earthquakes, the environment, wars, people losing their jobs and homes. . . How do we make sense out of what's happening so that we can make wise decisions?

The Bible teaches that there will be trouble but cautions us not to give up hope. God is in charge. Solomon, the wisest man in all of history, encouraged, "Trust in the LORD with all your heart; do not depend on your own understanding. Seek his will in all you do, and he will show you which path to take" (Proverbs 3:5–6).

God wants us to have a steady, childlike confidence that makes us totally dependent on Him. And to believe that He will always do what is best for us.

When we are living in uncertain times, it's easy for us to get sidetracked. That's why it's so important to consistently spend time reading and studying the Word of God. Then the Holy Spirit will help us to apply it to the challenges we are facing. We also need the encouragement of other people—especially those who have experienced similar situations. God will often use them to help us make it through the tough times of life.

God will not abandon us. He just wants us to trust and obey. It's not always easy, but it's the best thing we can do. Remember God has it all figured out.

GET REAL

In what ways has God helped you in the past? What areas of your life do you need to trust God with today?

Clowns
Melanie Stiles

I've always liked the circus. I like watching all the high-wire and animal acts. One day I had a random thought—my family sometimes resembles the clown act. We have members running around doing crazy stuff that makes little or no sense.

I have a slightly odd auntie who is married to an equally weird uncle. For the most part, the relatives who come to visit amuse me far more than they irritate me, but it's a little different with the ones who live in my home.

My brother and I are absolutely nothing alike. And although I love him very much, he's kind of strange at times. He's a lot easier to communicate with if I practice Psalm 49:3: "For my words are wise, and my thoughts are filled with insight."

I have to use my mouth and ears in coordination with what my heart is telling me when we have a conflict. If I don't respond too emotionally, I'm able to see where he's coming from a little more clearly. I can also see some really cool stuff about him. Taking time to understand him helps me see a totally different side of him.

Does your family sometimes resemble the clown act of a circus?

GET REAL

Make it a point to spend some quality time with the "resident clown" in your family. You might be amazed at the great characteristics hiding under all that makeup!

Exam Time

Susie Shellenberger

So—how are you doing spiritually?

How are you *really* doing?

While on earth, Jesus referred to Himself as a doctor—the Great Physician. Maybe it's time to let the Great Physician give you a spiritual exam. King David sought the Great Physician's help when he asked God to search his life in Psalm 139:23–24: "Search me, O God, and know my heart; test me and know my anxious thoughts. Point out anything in me that offends you, and lead me along the path of everlasting life."

We've become accustomed to rushing through our daily routine in such a way that we're blinded by things in our lives that keep us from becoming all God wants us to be. That's why we need God's help in locating the stumbling blocks in our lives.

So—how are you doing spiritually?

How are you *really* doing?

Are you making time to read the Bible on a daily basis? Are you developing a solid prayer life? Are you actually *growing* in your relationship with God?

Or have you become stagnant? Are you comparing yourself to others? Have you started rationalizing things in your life that God never wanted you to get comfortable with?

GET REAL

I'm convinced that if we'll do our part to maintain an active, growing relationship with Christ, He'll do the rest. If we'll seek Him *daily*—through Bible reading and prayer—He'll be faithful to show us anything in our lives that can be a hindrance to intimacy with Him. And when He *does* bring specifics to our attention? It's our responsibility to obey. Ask God to examine your life today.

Dynamic Duo
Tracy Klehn

Two young boys approached a dark door on Halloween. As they knocked and called out, "Trick or treat!" they were startled by a grownup dressed in a scary costume. The pair ran screaming from the house until one of the boys stopped in his tracks. "Hey, what are we afraid of?" he said to his friend. "We're Batman and Robin!"

As my friend recounted this story about his little boy—"Batman"—I thought of the many times I have forgotten who I am in Christ, and instead have run in the opposite direction, screaming in fear. It's at these times that I need to stop to pray and remember this promise from God's Word:

> But now, O Jacob, listen to the LORD who created you. O Israel, the one who formed you says, "Do not be afraid, for I have ransomed you. I have called you by name; you are mine. When you go through deep waters, I will be with you. When you go through rivers of difficulty, you will not drown. When you walk through the fire of oppression, you will not be burned up; the flames will not consume you. . . . Do not be afraid, for I am with you." (Isaiah 43:1–2, 5)

There's absolutely nothing to fear. God is with us through flood, fire—anything and everything!

GET REAL

Next time you forget who you are, say this prayer: "Lord, please stop me in my tracks when I start to run away in fear. Remind me that I belong to You and that You protect me. Thank You that I can stand firm and face my fears, knowing that You are always by my side."

Honest Answers

Ramona Richards

Graduation was so close that Maxie could taste it. She'd plastered her walls with the logos of her dream college, along with her acceptance letter. Maxie talked so much about the school that her mother jokingly threatened to ban talking about it at the dinner table.

One thing stood between Maxie and success—passing trigonometry.

It was a test Maxie knew she'd never pass, so she bought the answers to it. They came in a sealed envelope. All she had to do was memorize just enough to pass.

She'd never cheated on a test before, and that envelope now haunted her. With the purchased answers she could succeed, but her conscience told her she'd be flying off to college on the wings of a lie.

Where do you land when it comes to cheating? It's actually a form of lying. To cheat can be defined as "to plunder" or "to take captive." To steal. To lie. To deceive. When you look at it this way, you realize a lot of cheating goes on.

Honesty is an important character trait for a Christian to have. Check out Proverbs 24:26: "An honest answer is like a kiss of friendship." Think about how this applies to cheating on a test.

Maxie decided not to use the answers she bought. She ended up failing the final but still passed the class. Maxie graduated honestly but lost one of her scholarships, which meant a part-time job instead of parties. That she could live with.

GET REAL

Do you cheat even in little ways? It's wrong, no matter how you try to rationalize it. Make honesty a priority in your life.

Savoring the Coffee

Steve Russo

A small group of alumni visited a former college professor. The grads' entire conversation was filled with complaints about their stressful lives.

The professor offered his guests coffee, encouraging them to help themselves from a large pot and an assortment of cups— expensive and cheap ones.

Once everyone had a cup of coffee, the professor said, "Notice how the expensive cups were taken first, leaving the cheap ones. While it's normal to want the best for yourselves, that's the source of your stress. The cup doesn't add to the quality of the coffee. What you really wanted was coffee, not the cup—but you consciously chose the best cups."

Life is a lot like coffee. Jobs, bank, and position are cups, tools to hold life. If we concentrate on the cup, we don't savor the coffee God has given us—a relationship with the living God, a relationship that requires our total surrender.

Jesus said, "Seek the Kingdom of God above all else, and live righteously, and he will give you everything you need" (Matthew 6:33). What's really important to you— people, bling, money, power? The struggle we have is figuring out the difference between what we want and what we need. It's easy to let the want overshadow the need.

We experience satisfaction when Jesus becomes our life. In order for us to recognize this truth, He must consume every dimension of our lives. He should fill our thoughts and be our motivation.

GET REAL

What's really important to you? What needs to change in your life for you to be able to savor the coffee God has for you? Don't put off making the necessary changes. . .do it as soon as you can.

Money, Money
Nicole O'Dell

Money is a very necessary part of life. Without it, we can't do things like go to a movie, buy a car, attend a concert, or buy clothes. It also plays a role in our relationship with God. He wants us to be aware that money comes from Him and to use it wisely, including learning how to be generous givers. Money can go a long way toward helping others to experience God's love and forgiveness. But it can also be a distraction and hinder our spiritual growth. Our culture seems to tell us to crave money. But God feels differently. That's why we need to understand His perspective on how to handle it.

First Timothy 6 is a great place to read about our relationship to money: "But people who long to be rich fall into temptation and are trapped by many foolish and harmful desires that plunge them into ruin and destruction. For the love of money is the root of all kinds of evil. And some people, craving money, have wandered from the true faith and pierced themselves with many sorrows" (vv. 9–10).

You see, it's not *money* itself that's bad; it's the *love* of money that causes all kinds of evil. When you love money and it becomes more important than anyone or anything else, you're on a self-destructive path. It will keep you from becoming the person God designed you to be.

GET REAL

How is your relationship with money? Do you crave it? Ask God to help you develop a healthy perspective on how to manage money.

Go Back
Lesha Campbell

I've traveled a lot in my line of work and have been on the road alone without a GPS. I had to learn how to read a map and follow the road signs along the way. Many times I found myself lost or at least on the wrong road simply because I had turned left instead of right, headed north instead of south, or taken the wrong path at the fork in the road.

Once I realized I was traveling the wrong way, I had to make a decision. Sometimes I'd think, *If I keep going, maybe I'll realize I'm not really on the wrong track,* and sometimes I'd stop in the middle of the road and make a U-turn.

I also did this in my personal life once. I was engaged and called it off six weeks before the wedding date. Lots of people thought that took loads of courage, but I just knew it wasn't right, so better safe than sorry.

We need to make decisions in our lives daily—choices for right or wrong, truth and consequences, with or without friends. Follow your heart and listen to God. "This is what the Lord says: When people fall down, don't they get up again? When they discover they're on the wrong road, don't they turn back?" (Jeremiah 8:4).

We all make mistakes, but they can't be corrected if we stay in them. Headed down the wrong road? Make a U-turn; you'll be glad you did.

GET REAL

Think about the road you're currently on. Using the Bible for guidance, make a U-turn if needed.

The Adventure

Dale Robert Hicks

When we think of learning, we usually think about school, a classroom, textbooks, and a teacher. When the last bell rings and school is out, we're done learning for the day. But the learning has really just begun.

After school we go to practice and learn to play a sport or an instrument or improve other talents and skills. We hang out with friends, learning what they like and dislike. We play a new video game, studying the directions so we can get to the next level. All these moments are learning moments, but we don't think of them that way. They're just the things we do in life.

A life of faith grows in much the same way. Our faith in Christ grows not just in church but also in the hallways of our schools, workplaces, homes, and bedrooms. Our faith grows in the every-day moments of our lives.

Think about Abram's journey of faith. It began with this encouragement from God: "The LORD had said to Abram, 'Leave your native country, your relatives, and your father's family, and go to the land that I will show you' " (Genesis 12:1).

God invited Abram on a journey, and along the way as he lived his life, God taught Abram what it meant to trust Him.

GET REAL

Does your faith life go outside the walls of your church? Do you see how God invites you to trust Him in the day-to-day moments of life? Your faith grows as you work what you learn and know about God into every area of your life.

Irish Golden Rule

Carson Pue

The Irish have a toast that goes like this:

Here's to you and yours and to mine and ours,
And if mine and ours ever come across you and yours,
I hope you and yours will do as much for mine and ours
As mine and ours have done for you and yours!

This Irish attempt at the Golden Rule stands as a reminder of how we should treat others. What has been called the Golden Rule is one of the most famous sayings of Jesus. It is found in Matthew 7:12 (MSG): "Here is a simple, rule-of-thumb guide for behavior: Ask yourself what you want people to do for you, then grab the initiative and do it for them. Add up God's Law and Prophets and this is what you get."

I was downtown and passed a person living on the street. He said, "Thank you," to me as I walked by. "Why did you say thank you?" I asked, for I had given him no money.

"Because you looked me in the eyes and treated me with respect," he said. "So many people treat me like I am a dog."

Whenever you see a Bible, remember that what lies at the heart of all of God's commandments is this—we are to love others and to love God. Jesus taught that this summed up all of the law.

GET REAL

Just imagine how different our world would be if everyone followed the Golden Rule and treated other people and countries the same way they'd want to be treated themselves. It could happen, you know. And it can start with you.

Living Hands-on
Steve Russo

There are two ways to live: hands-on or knee-jerk. Sounds pretty simple, huh? It is, but it's not easy.

Living hands-on means you have a high standard for the way you live and don't allow negative influences from others to drag you down. You take control in a positive way and use God's Word to guide you. You don't judge others or act like you're perfect. Rather, you follow principles for living that honor God instead of displaying a knee-jerk reaction to what others are doing.

Knee-jerk living is taking your cue from other people. For example, if people trash-talk you, then you do the same to them. It's all about payback. Paul, the author of several books in the New Testament, was pretty blunt talking about knee-jerk living. "If you are always biting and devouring one another, watch out! Beware of destroying one another" (Galatians 5:15). If you live this knee-jerk way, you give up control of your life and fail to honor God.

If our lives are motivated by love, we will stop "devouring" one another and look for the good. Keep in mind that Jesus wants us to love others as we love ourselves (see Matthew 22:39). This isn't easy—especially with the difficult people in our lives. But it's the right thing to do, and it pleases God.

GET REAL

Do you talk behind people's backs? Are you always focusing on other people's faults? Instead of criticizing someone, make a list of their good traits. Wouldn't you want them to do the same for you? Ask God to help you make a serious effort to start living hands-on instead of knee-jerk.

Eyes of the Wise

Chris Haidet

Has anyone ever stereotyped you because of your height, weight, clothes, or the music you listen to? What about your age, gender, nationality, or race? It's tragic when people show prejudice toward others. Wars have been fought, nations have been split, and hopes and dreams have been shattered because of something so meaningless. How does God view such things? Is He prejudiced, too?

The Bible says, "The Lord doesn't see things the way you see them. People judge by outward appearance, but the Lord looks at the heart" (1 Samuel 16:7).

A definition of *biblical wisdom* is seeing something the way God sees it. If we see others as precious creations made in the image of God, we will gain a wise starting point in our dealings with people.

God wants no part in singling someone out on the basis of outward qualities; His focus is on the heart. If we are to represent God's love to a fallen world, we *must* focus on the things that matter. Look past the divisive stereotypes of the world, and focus on the person's heart. Put yourself in their shoes; try to see their point of view. Realize others have hopes and dreams, fears and doubts, just like you. When we let God give us insight on the issues and the people behind them, our judgment becomes wise while our prejudgments disappear.

GET REAL

Ask God to give you wisdom to see things through His eyes. When people prejudge you, ask God for guidance. If you have prejudged someone, ask God for help in making it right.

Advice
Melanie Stiles

I have a friend who has an opinion on everything. While some of us seem to be asked for advice quite frequently, plenty of others give it without a request. I've also noticed that people who are very smart tend to request advice. Wherever you are in the circle of advice, it's useless to acquire it if you don't plan to at least consider what's being said.

We can receive valuable suggestions—even from those whom we might not consider very wise. In this way, we can all learn from one another. But there's a big difference between wise counsel from a person you respect and an opinion given without much thought. It's up to us to consider the source and compare the advice to God's Word.

Sometimes, even when I've asked for advice from the right people, I ignore it if I don't want to do what they're suggesting I do. It doesn't mean they haven't given me good advice. It means I'm not ready to do the work it takes to deal with my situation.

The Bible is clear on finding wise opinions and counsel: "Let the wise listen to these proverbs and become even wiser. Let those with understanding receive guidance by exploring the meaning in these proverbs and parables, the words of the wise and their riddles" (Proverbs 1:5–6).

It's important to listen to the right people. But it's only helpful if we follow through with the advice they give us.

GET REAL

Who do you go to for advice and guidance? Do you follow through with their suggestions? Remember to always compare their advice with scripture.

Best Friend
Kati Russo

One of my favorite classic sitcoms is *I Love Lucy*. Best friends Lucy and Ethel are always getting into crazy, wild, and sometimes serious situations.

Best friends are great. With them we create memories that last a lifetime. I remember once when my BFFs and I got lost on the way to a party. For an hour we drove around trying to find it. We missed most of the party but still had fun and will always remember that night.

It's great to have BFFs, but are you best friends with the One who really matters? Jesus talks about being our friend in John 15:13–15 (NIV): "Greater love has no one than this: to lay down one's life for one's friends. You are my friends if you do what I command. I no longer call you servants, because a servant does not know his master's business. Instead, I have called you friends, for everything that I learned from my Father I have made known to you."

Isn't that awesome to realize that we can have a close relationship with the Creator of the universe? Do you take advantage of His offer to be your friend, or do you blow Him off? Jesus wants to be your BFF and wants you to spend special, quality time with just Him.

GET REAL

The only way Jesus can be our best friend is if we've accepted Him into our hearts and allowed God to have control of our lives. Are you treating Him like your best friend or an acquaintance? Start spending time with Jesus daily so you can really get to know Him.

Care Enough to Share

Steve Russo

Pink's Hot Dogs has been a Hollywood legend since 1939. The restaurant has created an amazing lineup of dogs that you won't find anyplace else. On one visit I decided to try something different, so I opted for the *TODAY Show* Dog. It's two hot dogs in one bun with mustard, onions, chili, cheese, and guacamole. It tastes great, but I'm not sure how it rates on a healthy diet scale!

As I was walking back to my car, a twentysomething guy with a beard and a backpack approached me and said, "God loves you!" He never slowed down but kept on walking down the street smiling. I shook my head, laughed, and wondered how he was processing our "encounter." Had he completed his mission? Did he meet his quota for the day? What was the point? It seemed shallow and meaningless to me.

Why didn't he take the time to share the most significant news ever known to humankind—God loves us! In Romans 5:8 Paul describes how great this love is for me and you: "But God showed his great love for us by sending Christ to die for us while we were still sinners."

This news is too good to just "dump and run" with. But maybe we need to do an attitude check to see if we really care enough about family members and friends to share Jesus with them.

GET REAL

Think about the people in your life who need someone to share Jesus with them. Ask God to prepare their hearts and to give you the words to share and the courage to do it.

Heart Pollution

Steve Russo

I visited "Smoking Mountain" while on a trip to the Philippines. From miles away you can see the smoke. It's a mountain of garbage—one of the largest dumps in the world— that burns twenty-four hours a day, all year long. That's how it got its name. My friend Walter and I had to "buy" a taxi for the day (about five dollars) to get there. Once the cab went "up to the mountain," it would stink so bad no one would want to ride in it the next day. When we got halfway to this gigantic heap of trash, the smoke was so thick it looked like a wall. I don't even know how the taxi driver could see where he was going. As we approached the top of the mountain, the smoke cleared, and the first thing we saw was a huge wooden cross.

Smoking Mountain is a picture of our hearts. Many times they're filled with trash that's burning up our lives. A spiritual haze clouds our lives, and it's hard for people to know the real "us."

Our hearts are constantly storing things that we read, watch, and listen to. The stuff we store up affects our thoughts, feelings, attitudes, and actions. Solomon, the wisest man to ever live, talked about why it's important to protect our hearts: "Guard your heart above all else, for it determines the course of your life" (Proverbs 4:23).

The best way to guard your heart is to clean out the trash and fill it with Jesus and God's Word.

GET REAL

Are you guarding your heart? Is there some trash that needs to be cleaned out? Ask for supernatural help to get started today.

Revolution
Ron Merrell

At summer camp one year, some teenage friends and I experienced an entire week of walking closely with Jesus and hanging with others who were dialing in to Him. Then our time ended. School started. Jesus seemingly disappeared. Back to life as usual. Ever experienced this? Ever felt ready to tackle the world for Jesus and then been dead cold a week or two later?

This reality drove me to Acts 1. The disciples had three years of walking with Jesus, hearing Him teach, watching Him perform miracles, seeing Him die and then rise again. Then, after laying out the mission for His followers pretty specifically, Jesus disappeared into the clouds. The disciples stood there staring up into the sky, no doubt thinking, *What are we supposed to do now?*

We're supposed to start a revolution. In Jesus' words, we're meant to be His witnesses to the ends of the earth. How do you start a revolution for Jesus Christ? The disciples wondered this two thousand years ago. We wonder about it today.

Jesus' answer is straightforward: "But you will receive power when the Holy Spirit comes upon you. And you will be my witnesses, telling people about me everywhere—in Jerusalem, throughout Judea, in Samaria, and to the ends of the earth" (Acts 1:8).

Step one in starting a revolution for Jesus is to wait and pray for the Holy Spirit to guide you. Wait and pray.

GET REAL

If you're passionate about seeing your school, your team, your family, or your friendships turned around for Jesus, start praying for the Holy Spirit to come into those places and people. Pray and keep praying.

Family Time

Ramona Richards

Everyone is so busy with all the activities swirling around us, there's just not as much time for everyone to get together over pizza, lasagna, or a BBQ. Dinner used to be a time when everyone traded stories about their day and parents made an effort to know what was going on with their kids.

Sounds like a good idea.

But hanging out with the family isn't just about swapping tales over slices. It's about getting to know each other, understanding what's important in our individual lives. It's about parents listening and kids actually talking instead of texting.

In 2 Timothy 1:5 Paul praises Timothy's family life: "I remember your genuine faith, for you share the faith that first filled your grandmother Lois and your mother, Eunice. And I know that same faith continues strong in you." Timothy's family played a huge part in the type of man he became. They modeled strong family values for him, encouraging and helping him to grow in his faith. They also supported his hard work, which made him a great pupil for Paul.

Positive or negative, our families play a huge part in who we are. We may not like it, but we can't avoid it. God expects us to love them, even if they're toxic to us. He can use us to be a positive influence in their lives.

GET REAL

Family is forever. Make time to interact with your family and get to know them. Remember to pray for them, and ask God to help you be a good example of His love at home. It will change you and them for the better!

Thinking about You

Danny Ray

I love living by the ocean. I love seeing the power of God displayed in the mighty waves as they crash on the shore. I love playing with my kids in the waves and wrestling with them on a beautiful day at the beach. What I don't like is trying to clean up the sand afterward. Sometimes I feel like a human sandbox with sand in my pockets, in my shoes, in my hair, and even in my ears!

Here's a random thought: I know I've left the beach with thousands of grains of sand on my body, and yet if you went to the beach after me, you'd never notice any of them missing. I could walk away with millions of grains of sand, and you still wouldn't have a clue that they were missing from the infinite number of grains still on the beach.

Here's another random thought: According to Psalm 139, if you were to number the thoughts God has for us, it would be more than the grains of sand by the sea. "How precious are your thoughts about me, O God. They cannot be numbered! I can't even count them; they outnumber the grains of sand! And when I wake up, you are still with me!" (vv. 17–18).

God must love you and me a lot to think about us that much!

GET REAL

Since God thinks about you all the time, He knows a lot about you. Talk with Him today about any problems or challenges in your life you lack answers to and are having trouble making sense of.

The Backyard's on Fire!

Nathan Finfrock

I awoke to a knock on my bedroom door. My mother stood in the doorway with a strange smile on her face and said, "Come and see what your brother did this time, Nathan."

We had two acres out back, with a large brush area at the far end of the property. As we walked to the backyard, I noticed the brush was on fire! I heard the faint sound of fire trucks heading our way and saw my brother and his friend standing on the back porch with their heads hung low. They said that other kids were playing with fireworks near the back fence, but their expressions said otherwise. After the flames were extinguished, my brother finally admitted his lie to the fire chief. He had started the fire. He found himself spending two weeks of his summer vacation doing community service.

Why lie? We want to blame our situation on anyone or anything else. But words of dishonesty are a cheap escape. Lies come with consequences, and those penalties affect both us and others. Romans 9:1 talks about the importance of being honest: "With Christ as my witness, I speak with utter truthfulness. My conscience and the Holy Spirit confirm it."

Being honest is important to God and should be to us, too.

GET REAL

A simple spark can start a fire and leave you clinging to the ashes of your once-respected life. Even small words and actions can profoundly affect those around you, so speak the truth and don't play with fire!

The Battle

Steve Russo

Speaking at an event in Poundridge, New York, I met two federal law enforcement officers who were part of a Satanic Task Force. I learned there were more officers just like them in large metropolitan areas scattered across the country to investigate occult crimes. I was curious why the public wasn't more informed about the task force. Their response: "The public isn't ready to accept that this kind of activity is real."

Lots of people—even some who go to church—don't believe that Satan and demons are real. So if they don't believe these supernatural enemies are real, they aren't going to be prepared for the intense, unseen spiritual battle that is being fought in and around their lives. The Bible is very clear that they *do* exist, and this warfare inevitably takes a toll on our lives.

John, the brother of James, records Jesus' illustration of the contrast in goals between Satan and Jesus: "The thief's purpose is to steal and kill and destroy. My purpose is to give them a rich and satisfying life" (John 10:10).

The thief, Satan, wants to steal our purity, faith, and truth. He wants to kill our joy, our love, our relationship with Jesus, and our credibility in telling others about Him. Ultimately, Satan wants to destroy everything—our country, family, church, and each one of us trying to live for and like Jesus.

Put simply, the thief wants to take life while Jesus wants to give it—in amazing ways!

GET REAL

What's the devil stealing and destroying in your life? Ask for God's help to stop believing Satan's lies. Have you accepted Jesus' offer of life and the power to live it?

Find the Shoe That Fits

Melanie Stiles

The best and funniest rendition of *Cinderella* I've ever seen was an onstage presentation in which the "wicked stepsisters" were played by two guys. The men impersonating women in goofy ways were extremely funny. The comedic performance of a story that I already knew made the play original, and I enjoyed it hugely.

What isn't funny is when my friends, thinking it makes them cool, try to mimic others by dressing like someone else, hoping it will make them popular, or by imitating behavior just to get attention. They look just like what they are. . .posers. It's sad sometimes as I sense the desperation of people struggling to fit in and be popular. That's why it's important that we find the road to our own individuality, even if the ride isn't always comfortable. Just like in *Cinderella*, only one shoe will fit.

I'm glad I have a Helper, a Friend, to guide me the right way to discover and express who I am—one original thought and action at a time. Check out John 14:26 (MSG): "The Friend, the Holy Spirit whom the Father will send at my request, will make everything plain to you."

We don't have to imitate someone else in hopes of being a unique person. If we wait until we know the right way for us to express ourselves, we will eventually be the prince or princess at our own ball.

GET REAL

Do you ever feel the urge to copy someone to get the attention that they seem to be getting? Ask the Holy Spirit to help you discover the real you—and live it.

Picture This

Tracy Klehn

I am the official "team photographer" for my son's football team, so each year when a new group shows up at practice, I make sure to get the guys' e-mails so I can send game photos to them. One year my husband and I went on a sailing trip with friends, and I took pictures of all of our adventures. The only problem was that when I went to send the vacation pictures to the two other couples who went on the trip, I accidentally sent them to the new football group! Twenty-five families got to see pictures I had no intention of showing them! Fortunately, there was nothing all that embarrassing in those photos.

What if pictures were taken of everything you and I ever did in life—good, bad, and ugly—and forwarded to the world at large? We'd probably be *freaking* out, because there'd be some things we aren't proud of. The amazing thing is that God has seen every picture taken during our lives. If He were to send an e-mail reply, it would probably say something like this:

> *"I have loved you, my people, with an ever-lasting love. With unfailing love I have drawn you to myself."* (Jeremiah 31:3)

Nothing can change the eternal way the Lord cares about me and you. There's no need to hide or be embarrassed. He wants us to keep talking to Him, no matter what we've done.

GET REAL

Write one sentence that represents the "picture" you regret the most. Now rip up the paper into tiny pieces while saying, "Thank You, Jesus, for forgiving me for this, for forgetting this, and for still loving me."

Big Green Footprints

Chris Haidet

Are you going green? Do you care about the environment and those who live in it? These are important questions being asked by people today. My cousin is the definition of what it means to *go green*. He recycles daily, conserves energy, buys organic, wears natural fibers, uses less water, and rides a bicycle everywhere he goes. He sure does his part to reduce his environmental footprint. How about you? Is it even important?

To God it is. Shortly after He created humans, the Bible says, "God blessed them and said, 'Be fruitful and multiply. Fill the earth and govern it. Reign over the fish in the sea, the birds in the sky, and all the animals that scurry along the ground.' Then God said, 'Look! I have given you every seed-bearing plant throughout the earth and all the fruit trees for your food. And I have given every green plant as food for all the wild animals, the birds in the sky, and the small animals that scurry along the ground—everything that has life.' And that is what happened" (Genesis 1:28–30).

How amazing is that! The Creator and Designer of the universe gave us complete authority over the earth and everything in it. We are to govern, which means to take care of the earth and ensure that it will last for future generations. What a massive responsibility, something we shouldn't take lightly.

GET REAL

Make a list of ways you can go green—not littering, taking shorter showers, and recycling when possible, to name a few. Taking the little steps now might leave big green footprints in the future.

Make It Yours

Nicole O'Dell

Are you struggling with the whole church thing—going to youth group, listening to Christian music, studying the Bible? Maybe you were you raised in a Christian home, and the whole faith thing has become boring. Or maybe you made a commitment to Jesus a couple of years ago, and you're not sure about the relationship right now.

Whether you are feeling distant from God or are questioning your faith, you're not alone. It's not unusual at this time in your life to begin to question the things of God—even questioning His very existence. The important thing is to acknowledge where you're at and to start looking for answers. God's desire is to have a close, intimate relationship with us. It's so important to Him that He has given us all the resources we need, including His Word and the Holy Spirit. Start with 1 John 2:27: "But you have received the Holy Spirit, and he lives within you, so you don't need anyone to teach you what is true. For the Spirit teaches you everything you need to know, and what he teaches is true—it is not a lie. So just as he has taught you, remain in fellowship with Christ."

God wants our faith to be real for us. It's not to be based on what our parents or our friends believe. We can have a faith that's real with the help of His Spirit. There are answers to our questions if we ask God and apply the truth of His Word.

GET REAL

Ask God to give you answers for your questions and help you develop a deep, personal relationship with Him. Make your faith your own.

Important and Necessary
Steve Russo

We all want relationships that work. Whether it's friends we can rely on, a group to hang with and have fun with, or eventually the guy-girl thing—each of these relationships is important. So how do we develop healthy relationships? Let's check out the owner's manual and see what God has to say about healthy friendships.

The Bible instructs us to choose our friends wisely—because it's more important than we might think. Why? Because we become like those we spend the most time with. Check out 1 Corinthians 15:33: "Bad company corrupts good character." So who do you spend the most time with—people who encourage you to be the best you can be? Or people who are always trying to get you to do or say things that you know aren't right? Flip it around—what kind of friend are you? Do you think people will like you more if you're always at the center of all the "bad stuff" going on? Don't let your relationships lead you in the wrong direction. Also make sure that you're a positive influence on others.

Relationships are priceless gifts from God. Choose wisely. But remember, sometimes no matter how hard we try to work at a relationship, we will sometimes face disappointment when others don't meet our expectations.

GET REAL

Honestly think about the friends you currently have. Do you need to make some changes? Ask God to bring you some new friends—He's more than capable of doing it.

Step Out
Melanie Stiles

What if I told you that you'll be famous someday? Or how about successful in the career of your dreams? You may find that hard to believe right now. When God told Moses he would be the one to free the Israelites, his reaction might have been similar to yours. Not only did Moses refuse to believe, but he also complained and argued with God several times. He could not get his mind wrapped around the fact that God had chosen him instead of somebody else. His big stumbling block centered around one thought: *I am a nobody.* Check out Exodus 3:11: "But Moses protested to God, 'Who am I to appear before Pharaoh? Who am I to lead the people of Israel out of Egypt?'"

Everybody struggles with thoughts of being a nobody—until they step out. As Moses stepped out and took risks, being courageous inside a body shivering with fear, he was able to move his people out of Egypt. His journey was not always easy, but after he fell down, he did what he needed to do. He got back up and kept walking, looking to God for strength and guidance.

Think about your own future. Wouldn't you rather step out and walk through the wilderness than stay behind and struggle with feeling like a nobody?

GET REAL

Is God asking you to step out in some way? Are you willing to face fear, fall down, and get back up to succeed? Ask God to give you the courage to take the risk to do what He's calling you to do.

Answers
Brenda Pue

Have you ever been in a desperate situation? One where you needed help? A miracle? I have. I had saved up enough money for my school tuition with no wiggle room. Literally. And then it happened. . . . I got a speeding ticket. I didn't want to drop out of school. There were no borrowing options. I was desperate!

I decided to pray and ask God for help. I admitted to Him that I was in the wrong and knew I didn't deserve His help, yet didn't know where else to turn. I humbled myself before God, and although I didn't realize it at the time, I was now ready to see God at work.

Philippians 4:6 (NIV) says, "Do not be anxious about anything, but in every situation, by prayer and petition, with thanksgiving, present your requests to God."

God chose to answer the cry of my heart in such a way that I would know that He was behind it. Here's how. One day I received a letter in the mail—typewritten and anonymous. Enclosed was twenty-five dollars. The following day a friend stopped to say hello and blessed me with a hundred-dollar bill. The combined total was the exact amount of my speeding ticket! God delights in providing for us. God loves you and me. He cares about the smallest details of our lives, even when we don't deserve it.

GET REAL

Are you facing a difficult circumstance in your life? I encourage you to let God show you how much He loves you and cares for you. He wants to be there for you.

Dream On

Ramona Richards

Following your passion, your dreams, is never easy. Life can sometimes get in the way. Stuff happens—people move, change jobs, get married, have children, get sick. You may have to work a job that's not your passion in order to pay the rent and put food on the table. Reality checks hit. And it's all good if no matter what happens, you never totally give up on your dreams. Find a way to keep digging, keep growing, keep believing.

Paul, an early follower of Jesus, followed his passion in spreading the Good News to various parts of the world. No matter what trouble he got into—and he got into a lot—he stuck to his dreams, survived, and succeeded. Paul's life had a huge impact for God's kingdom because he didn't give up. "I have fought the good fight, I have finished the race, and I have remained faithful" (2 Timothy 4:7).

When you look back over your life, will you be able to say the same thing? Remember that true success is about obeying; it's about following God's call on your life and using the gifts He has given you. It's also about surrendering—which is the hardest part—to what God has planned for your life. You may be more than surprised what He does through you if you hang in there. Dream on.

GET REAL

Pursuing your dreams, following your passion can shape your entire life. Don't give up. Ask God to help you identify His dreams for you and give you the perseverance you need to realize them!

Friend Request
Chris Haidet

I opened my Facebook account to see something not too uncommon: a friend request. Not just 1, but 5, to go along with 2 friend suggestions, 9 group invitations, 34 cause invitations, and 157 other random requests. These fit nicely with my 736 accepted friends and 54 pieces of flair. I began to ask myself some questions: "What does it mean to be a friend? Is it more than a mutual agreement of acceptance?" And then came the nagging thought, *How many friends on my list am I really friends with?*

A wise man once said, "Two people are better off than one, for they can help each other succeed. If one person falls, the other can reach out and help. But someone who falls alone is in real trouble. Likewise, two people lying close together can keep each other warm. But how can one be warm alone? A person standing alone can be attacked and defeated, but two can stand back-to-back and conquer. Three are even better, for a triple-braided cord is not easily broken" (Ecclesiastes 4:9–12).

God did not design us to be alone; He loves us and created us to love others. Friendship goes beyond a simple mouse-click of acceptance—true friendship takes effort. It's a day-to-day relationship built on loyalty, humility, honesty, and respect.

GET REAL

It has been said, "In order to have a friend, you must be a friend." What kind of friend are you? Make an effort this week to reach out and become a friend. If you can't find anyone, take a look at your friend list on Facebook.

Unexpected Boast

Steve Russo

We all have things we want to show off about. It could be a sport we're good at or the ability to sing and act. Maybe it's a boyfriend or girlfriend who gives us bragging rights. It could be our cars or jobs. Sometimes it's a place we go or people we get to hang out with.

Paul, an early follower of Jesus, had lots of things he could boast about. For example, he was well educated and could speak several different languages. Yet despite his many credentials that gave him bragging rights, he chose to boast about something totally unexpected. Check out Galatians 6:14: "As for me, may I never boast about anything except the cross of our Lord Jesus Christ. Because of that cross, my interest in this world has been crucified, and the world's interest in me has also died."

Some people show off a cross necklace or ring they wear. But I can't remember hearing anyone brag about the cross of Jesus. Why would you want to boast about something that caused horrible pain and suffering?

But so much more was accomplished. The cross shows us how much God loves us. It's also the only way to be forgiven for our sins and experience a restored relationship with God. We could also boast about how it gives new power for living or guarantees us a place in heaven when we die. Sounds like quite a lot to brag about.

GET REAL

Does the cross of Jesus mean more to you than just a piece of jewelry to wear? Has it affected your daily life?

Who Is Jesus?

Steve Russo

Jesus is the most controversial person who ever lived. For centuries people have been confused about Him. Try asking people at school or in your neighborhood, "Who do you think Jesus is?" and you'll get lots of different answers. But it's the most important question in life. The way we answer this question will mean the difference between life and death; between a meaningful life and a meaningless one.

Jesus asked this same question of His followers. Look at the answers He got: "When Jesus came to the region of Caesarea Philippi, he asked his disciples, 'Who do people say that the Son of Man is?' 'Well,' they replied, 'some say John the Baptist, some say Elijah, and others say Jeremiah or one of the other prophets.' Then he asked them, 'But who do you say I am?' Simon Peter answered, "'You are the Messiah, the Son of the living God'" (Matthew 16:13–16).

At first the disciples answered Jesus' question like everyone else at that time did—He was one of the great prophets who was brought back to life. But Peter recognizes Jesus as the long-awaited Messiah—the Son of God. If Jesus were to ask you this question, how would you answer? Is He your Savior and Lord?

There are two things we all must be absolutely sure of if we are going to live the kind of life God designed for us: who Jesus is and what He has done.

GET REAL

It takes quality time praying and studying the Bible to get to know Jesus and what He has done. Do you need to change your daily schedule?

Video Games and Talking with God

Dale Robert Hicks

We can learn a lot from the world of the video gamer, and one of those things is persistence. There are times when I encounter a situation in a game and try to solve the problem, beat the boss, or learn the track, and it ends in failure. Game over. I could quit and move on to a different game, but I don't. I keep making attempts until I win the game. That's persistence—keep trying until you get it right.

Sometimes talking with God and letting Him know what you need requires persistence. Jesus had an idea that people would get discouraged and want to give up while they were praying: "One day Jesus told his disciples a story to show that they should always pray and never give up" (Luke 18:1). The story He told is about a woman who needs help from a judge. The judge doesn't listen to her at first, but because she keeps pestering him relentlessly, he finally agrees to help her.

Now think about how Jesus sums up the story: "Learn a lesson from this unjust judge. Even he rendered a just decision in the end. So don't you think God will surely give justice to his chosen people who cry out to him day and night? Will he keep putting them off?" (Luke 18:6–7).

It's worth being persistent when you talk with God.

GET REAL

Just as you would keep working at a video game until you beat it, keep praying even when you feel like giving up. Know that God will hear and answer your requests—in His time, not yours.

Changed Lives
Ron Merrell

No one can argue with a changed life. People might have questions about the Bible or whether God exists, and you may have a hard time coming up with proof. But then you find someone whose own life has been changed, or maybe your life has been changed. That's the best proof.

In the book of Acts, the early church is exploding, catapulting from 120 to 5,000 people in no time. Armed with the power of God, Peter and John come across a beggar who is crippled. Peter steps up boldly in the name of Jesus and heals the beggar. A crowd gathers and is amazed. More come to believe in Jesus as Peter and John explain what's going on. Lives are being changed.

Put in jail overnight for the act of healing, Peter speaks boldly again before the court. "The members of the council were amazed when they saw the boldness of Peter and John, for they could see that they were ordinary men with no special training in the Scriptures. They also recognized them as men who had been with Jesus. But since they could see the man who had been healed standing right there among them, there was nothing the council could say" (Acts 4:13–14).

The rulers of the court are silenced by his words. Silenced by the truth. Silenced by the evidence of a changed life.

GET REAL

The only way lives are changed for real is through a relationship with Jesus. How can you spend more time with Him so that He can continue to change you? Don't worry about words to convince people God is real. Focus on your own walk with Jesus.

Speed and Patience

Carson Pue

Don't you hate waiting for what seems like forever for your video game to load? What about being in a location where the Wi-Fi signal is so slow you can't use Skype to talk with your friends—isn't that just downright annoying?

Life goes pretty fast at almost every level you can think of—well, except for school days (they seem to drag on forever most of the time).

In our fast-paced world, one of the virtues that can be under-developed is patience. The *New Oxford American Dictionary* defines patience as "the capacity to accept or tolerate delay, trouble, or suffering without getting angry or upset."

The Bible puts patience in a list with other qualities we should be developing as Christians. "But the Holy Spirit produces this kind of fruit in our lives: love, joy, peace, patience, kindness, goodness, faithfulness, gentleness, and self-control" (Galatians 5:22–23). If the fast pace of our world today is eroding our ability to have patience, what can we do to learn to accept or tolerate delays, troubles, and suffering?

One of the ways God works to develop patience in us is through our parents, brothers, or sisters. It's easy to flare up with those closest to us, isn't it? So why not try being understanding and tolerant of the things that annoy us? Show some love and kindness and the other fruits of the Spirit. We can all start practicing at home.

GET REAL

Next time you notice yourself getting upset and impatient, pause for a moment, and ask the Lord to help you be patient. Ask Him if there is something He wants you to learn through waiting.

Gone Too Soon

Steve Russo

I was bummed when Michael Jackson died. What an amazing performer we lost! If you read the liner notes on his CDs, you'd realize just how talented he was. All that talent—gone too soon.

Michael was blessed with some awesome gifts from God. And even though I totally respect Michael's abilities, I also can't ignore the problems he had in what seemed to be a pretty pain-filled life. I wonder if Michael ever experienced God's forgiveness and peace. I can only hope that someone took the time to tell him about God's love.

When we're young, we think we'll stay that way forever. Then we get a wakeup call when we experience the first death of a friend. At first it seems like a bad dream, and we're sure that we'll wake up any minute. Then reality sinks in. Life is so fragile. David reminds us in Psalm 103:15–16 how brief our lives really are: "Our days on earth are like grass; like wildflowers, we bloom and die. The wind blows, and we are gone—as though we had never been here."

No matter how many years we live, life is short. It's too easy to fall into the trap of thinking that we have plenty of time to experience all the things we want to. Remember, God doesn't promise us tomorrow. We should live like today could be our last, because we could be gone too soon.

GET REAL

Check your life for two things. Are you living in a way that pleases God? Have you been telling those in your life about His love and forgiveness?

Revolving Door

Susie Shellenberger

Imagine entering a restaurant to place your order with an employee who's wearing pajamas. That's the norm at Cereality Cereal Bar and Café. You have your choice of several varieties of cereal and toppings. It's a cereal smorgasbord where the customer chooses everything!

Unfortunately, many people view Christianity this way. They casually saunter into church and filter out parts of the sermon they don't like. They flip through the Bible and ignore passages that demand our all. They assume Christianity, like cereal, can be mixed and matched to their personal tastes.

We're told in Matthew 7:13–14 something different. "You can enter God's Kingdom only through the narrow gate. The highway to hell is broad, and its gate is wide for the many who choose that way. But the gateway to life is very narrow and the road is difficult, and only a few ever find it." In other words, we *can't* pick and choose when it comes to being obedient and making Jesus the Lord of our lives. We do it either His way or our way. If we demand our own way, we'll never fit through the entrance to the kingdom of heaven.

Think of this narrow gate as a small revolving door. It's restrictive. You can't go through it holding on to people or things. You must go through alone, and you must be empty-handed.

GET REAL

Have you surrendered everything in your life to Christ? Has obedience become part of your lifestyle? If so, you're on the right road. If not, who or what is holding you back?

Using Your Weapon
Kati Russo

"Sticks and stones may break my bones, but words will kill me." A different take on timeless words of wisdom—but it's good truth. Do you know anyone who has been dumped and started a rumor about their ex to get back at them? Maybe you were jealous of someone who got the spot you wanted on the team, and you trashed their reputation. Have you ever told someone they're ugly or stupid?

Our words are a very powerful tool, and we need to be careful how we use them. Once we say something, we can never take it back. We can try to apologize and tell people we didn't really mean what we said, but that would be a lie. If you said it, you probably meant it. When people repeatedly hear something hurtful about themselves, they start to believe it—even if it's not true.

The Bible says, "Don't use foul or abusive language. Let everything you say be good and helpful, so that your words will be an encouragement to those who hear them" (Ephesians 4:29). Our words should be used to encourage our family and friends, not tear them down. We need to thank them for what they do for us and how much they mean to us. If we do, we'll see a difference in our relationships.

GET REAL

Words are the most powerful weapon we have; they can shoot someone down or lift them up faster than a bullet. Think before you speak, because what you say may be the breaking point for others. Lift up instead of putting down.

Climbing Out
Ramona Richards

Roger shoved every baseball trophy he'd ever won into his backpack and left the house before his dad got home. He moved slowly, even on his skateboard, because each twist of his body made his shoulder scream with pain. He gritted his teeth, anger gripping him.

At the river bridge, he stepped off the board and walked to the middle. One by one, he dropped the trophies over the rail, watching the silver batters disappear beneath the muddy water. As the last one sank down, Roger was tempted to follow it. At seventeen, he realized his ball career was over. The damage to his shoulder was so bad it couldn't be completely repaired. Surgery would only ease the pain, but he'd be able to live a normal life.

Roger didn't want to be normal—he wanted to play baseball. But he was finished.

Roger isn't alone. A lot of people face this kind of disappointment. Maybe you have, or maybe one of your friends has.

Climbing out of disappointment takes time, perspective, and encouragement. The Bible reminds us that Jesus faced deep disappointment, betrayal, and discouragement. "Think of all the hostility he endured from sinful people; then you won't become weary and give up" (Hebrews 12:3).

Jesus knows exactly what you or a friend is dealing with.

Nothing surprises God. He knows everything about our lives—even before it happens. Trust Him to use this disappointment as a part of His plan for you.

GET REAL

Accepting a loss doesn't mean giving in to discouragement. It means looking upward for hope. If you're struggling with disappointment, take it to God. He'll help you through. If someone you know is discouraged, pray for and encourage them.

Rocket Wars
Nathan Finfrock

Have you ever gazed into the sky on the Fourth of July and wondered what it would be like to have your own fireworks show? I grew up in the Philippines, where fireworks are cheap and there are no laws against them. My friends and I had an ongoing feud with some annoying neighbor kids who lived on the opposite side of a coconut tree grove. One day after school, we thought it would be fun to shoot rockets toward the neighbors' house. We all laughed as we launched rocket after rocket. The laughing stopped when a huge rocket exploded over our heads, and the battle began. Our rocket war ended swiftly with all of us on restriction for a month.

Some days we make good decisions; other days it's more difficult. I thought it was acceptable to launch rockets at the neighbors' house because I didn't like the people living there. God says, "Do not seek revenge or bear a grudge against anyone among your people, but love your neighbor as yourself. I am the Lord" (Leviticus 19:18 NIV).

GET REAL

It's hard enough to love the people we know well, let alone people who are difficult to like. So how are we to love our neighbors as ourselves? How do we let go of our grudges? We begin by changing our actions toward them. Today, think of someone you dislike and find a way to be kind to that person. Pray for them. Doing so may not change them, but it will definitely change you.

No Fuel, a Prayer, and a Sign

Steve Russo

Two New Zealand pilots ran out of fuel in a small microlight airplane. They did some serious praying rather quickly and were able to make an emergency landing in a field.

Grant Stubbs and Owen Wilson were flying up the valley of Pelorus Sound when their engine sputtered, coughed, and finally died. "My friend and I are both Christians so our immediate reaction in a life-threatening situation was to ask for God's help," Stubbs told the Associated Press. He said he prayed that the tiny craft would get over the top of a ridge and they would find a landing site that wasn't too steep—or in the nearby sea. "There was an instantaneous answer to prayer as we crossed the ridge and there was an airfield—I didn't even know it existed till then."

After Wilson glided the powerless craft to a landing on the grassy strip, the pair noticed they were beside a twenty-foot-tall sign that read, JESUS IS LORD—THE BIBLE.

Was it just by chance that they landed near the sign? I doubt it. Seems like a good reminder that God is in control and cares about everything in our lives. Check out this advice from Philippians 4:6: "Don't worry about anything; instead, pray about everything. Tell God what you need, and thank him for all he has done."

We may never need a landing strip. But God does know the needs we have and wants us to simply obey, worry less, and pray more.

GET REAL

What are you worried about? Stop and tell God the concerns you have. You'll be surprised what He'll do.

Need or Want

Nicole O'Dell

We live in a culture that blasts us with messages about all the things we are supposed to need. Think about the number of commercials we get hit with every day online, on the radio, and on TV. Most of them have a similar message—"You need this product." And it's everything from pizza to shampoo to the latest app for your smartphone.

Have you ever stopped to ask yourself, "Do I really need this stuff, or do I just want it?" There's a big difference, and our culture makes it hard to distinguish between the two.

The Bible talks about God taking care of our needs in Philippians 4:19: "And this same God who takes care of me will supply all your needs from his glorious riches, which have been given to us in Christ Jesus." This verse makes it clear that we can trust God to meet our needs, but it doesn't say anything about our wants.

As we grow closer to God, things change in a lot of areas of our lives, including our ability to discern between what we want and what we really need.

GET REAL

What do you need today—hope, courage, food, money for a car or college? Remember, the needs we have are not always physical. Talk with God about what seems to be a necessity in your life. Ask Him to help you discern if you really need it or just want it. Trust Him to provide all your needs.

Get the Truth

Melanie Stiles

When my friend told me she wished I would lose weight for my health, it really stung. How could she say something so cold? I had to stay away for a few days. But after thinking more about it, I realized she made a truthful statement because she cared about me—even though I really didn't want to hear it.

Jesus was always careful when He confronted people with the truth. He always spoke the truth in love and with a purpose. We should ask ourselves three questions before confronting others with the truth:

1. Do we have a relationship with this person? If we don't know anything about them or they don't really know us, we don't have the right to confront them.

2. Do we feel overly emotional, or do we have the right attitude about the problem? Sometimes we're more intent on getting our side out than on considering how our words might affect the other person.

3. Can we accept the truth with the right attitude? Proverbs 23:23 instructs, "Get the truth and never sell it; also get wisdom, discipline, and good judgment."

I had to have an honest conversation with my girlfriend, admitting that she was right. She cared enough to tell me the truth. Do you care enough to tell the truth and accept it?

GET REAL

Who are the truth tellers in your life? Ask God to give you the grace to willingly accept their honesty.

Working at Prayer

Danny Ray

We know that God wants us to pray, but prayer can be very challenging. Have you ever tried to pray only to find yourself thinking about your latest homework project? Ever wake up thirty minutes after you started praying and realize you'd fallen asleep? Prayer is hard work, yet Jude reminds us that through prayer we can be built up in our faith: "Dear friends, keep building on the foundation of your most holy faith, as the Holy Spirit helps you to pray" (Jude 1:20 CEV).

If you're struggling with prayer, here are a couple of ideas to try. They've helped me and might work for you.

Pray for at least three minutes at the top of each hour. If you were awake for fourteen hours a day, you'd be praying about forty-two minutes a day by practicing this idea. Spending an hour straight might seem overwhelming, but by using the top of the hour as a regular reminder, you could spend significant time in prayer each day.

If three minutes an hour isn't your style, try setting aside ten minutes twice a day—once in the morning and once at night. Try doing this for a week; then increase that time by two minutes. If you did this every week, at the end of four weeks you would be praying about a half hour each day.

Find out what works best for you and pray!

GET REAL

Sometimes it helps to write out your prayers. Write out the prayers of your heart in a journal, word for word. It's a good way to stay focused.

Who's Got Your Wheel?

Chris Haidet

When I was young, I couldn't wait to learn to drive. However, when that time came, I had a day I would never forget. I mistakenly asked my paranoid mom to take me out to practice. As we were driving down the road, the wind in my face, my hands gripping the wheel perfectly at ten and two o'clock, everything suddenly went very wrong.

"Ahhhhh. . . Watch out!" my mom screamed as she grabbed the steering wheel. My heart leaped and my knees buckled as I slammed on the breaks, nearly spinning out of control. As we pulled over to the side and stopped, I discovered the problem. Apparently a dog had crossed the street *one full mile* ahead. No, I'm not kidding. *One mile.* One simple rule as a passenger: Never grab the steering wheel! Needless to say, I never had my mom teach me again.

Funny thing is, we do this with God all the time. God *is* the driver of our lives, not the passenger. He is driving our lives down the road with absolute perfection and control, but when the ride gets unpredictable and scary, we panic and grab the wheel. The Bible says, "Give all your worries and cares to God, for he cares about you" (1 Peter 5:7).

Whatever causes you to stress, doubt, and worry, God wants you to give it to Him. He's in control. Have faith, and enjoy the ride.

GET REAL

Take a moment to list some things that cause stress and worry in your life. Write down the most pressing cares. Now give these to God, ask Him to give you peace, and try not to take them back.

Patience
Ramona Richards

Have you seen the bumper sticker that says, "Stuff Happens"? Life stuff—sometimes ugly—happens to everyone eventually. It tests our faith. That's just the way it is.

But God reminds us in James 1:3–4 that good can come out of this stuff: "For you know that when your faith is tested, your endurance has a chance to grow. So let it grow, for when your endurance is fully developed, you will be perfect and complete, needing nothing."

A friend of mine has a daughter, Susan, who's always getting into trouble. Diagnosed with ADHD, she runs like the wind and is skinny enough to slip through all kinds of narrow openings. She's continually falling out of trees and has broken twenty-one bones so far.

School became such a nightmare that my friend Daphne pulled Susan out and began homeschooling her. I asked Daphne, "How do you deal with this?"

Daphne responded, "I prayed for God to give me patience. Instead, He gave me Susan. Now I have patience. And the most creative daughter on the planet."

Whenever I'm upset about my problems, I remember Daphne. Our heavenly Father allows life stuff to happen in our lives so we can grow in our faith.

And, sometimes, we even learn patience.

GET REAL

God's love for us sometimes means that He pushes us to grow, to learn, to improve who we are. What are you going through right now? What are you learning besides patience?

Better Than a Smartphone
Steve Russo

I'm amazed at all the new smartphones released each month. Lots of people rush out to get the latest model immediately. They must have contracts for the next ten years!

What would happen if we treated the Bible like we do our smartphones? What would go down if we had to return home to get our Bible because we forgot it, or if we flipped through it several times a day to check for messages? What if we treated our Bible like we couldn't live without it, or if we used it in case of an emergency?

We don't realize the uniqueness of God's Word. No other book like it has ever been written. Billions of copies have been printed and sold. There's more ancient manuscript evidence to confirm the Bible than any ten pieces of classical literature.

The benefits of reading it are many and awesome. Here's just one example: "Your word is a lamp to guide my feet and a light for my path" (Psalm 119:105).

The Bible helps us know and understand God and ourselves. It also answers the questions we have about life.

One more thing—it's the coolest part of all. Unlike our smartphones, we don't ever have to worry about searching for service with our Bible. It's always connected to the Source—24-7.

GET REAL

How do you treat your Bible? Do you value it and see it as the most important app in your life? Make a commitment to read and study it each day.

When No One's Looking

Chuck Poe

Do you make the right choices when no one is looking? It's especially tough when things aren't going our way and we feel we deserve a break. We may think, *I could take this and no one will ever know what I've done.* However, something deep within us knows it's not right.

The Old Testament relates a story about four lepers—diseased individuals who were not permitted to live among the general population. So they remained at the city's gate. It gets worse. An attack on their city was imminent. A famine had hit hard. They were starving. So the lepers decided to surrender to the enemy in hopes of survival. The night before the lepers arrived at the enemy's camp, God caused the enemy to imagine the sounds of chariots, horses, and a great army. So the enemy soldiers left their camp and ran for their lives.

> *The men who had leprosy reached the edge of the camp, entered one of the tents and ate and drank. Then they took silver, gold and clothes, and went off and hid them. . . . Then they said to each other, "What we're doing is not right. This is a day of good news and we are keeping it to ourselves. . . . Let's go at once and report this to the royal palace."*
> (2 Kings 7:8–9 NIV)

Even though these rejects of society stumbled upon this great treasure, they could not keep the "good news" to themselves. They were convicted; then they chose to do the right thing.

GET REAL

Are you doing what is right—even when no one is looking?

Grateful Heart

Zoro

A big problem in our society—and even among Christians—is a lack of gratitude to God for all He has done for us. From the wonder of creation to the endless expressions of His love, it's obvious that God is far more than good. Unfortunately, too many fail to acknowledge this truth and take His amazing gifts for granted.

When we give in to envy and jealousy, desiring what others have, we lose a heart of gratitude. We end up in a place where we are never satisfied. Contentment and thankfulness are not feelings. They are choices made from a grateful heart.

First Timothy 6:6–8 says, "Yet true godliness with contentment is itself great wealth. After all, we brought nothing with us when we came into the world, and we can't take anything with us when we leave it. So if we have enough food and clothing, let us be content."

We please God by being happy with what we possess and having grateful hearts. Not only does God bless these attitudes, but they are contagious, spreading to those around us.

God's greatest gift is forgiveness of our sins and His promise of eternal life to those who surrender their lives to Jesus.

What's the condition of your heart?

GET REAL

One of the evidences of a grateful heart is a desire to thank God and those He has placed in your life to bless you. Whether they are parents, family members, teachers, mentors, or friends, it's very important that you demonstrate your gratitude through your actions. To whom should you express your gratefulness today?

Got Any Stolen Buckets?

Rusty Wright

My second year in college, I swiped a plastic bucket from behind the lectern in the psychology lecture hall. It had been there every day during the semester. "No one wants it," I convinced myself. "It deserves to be taken." I used it to wash my car.

Two years later I read a booklet about God's forgiveness. That bucket kept coming to mind. I not only needed to admit my theft to God. I needed to make restitution. Like Jesus said, "So if you are presenting a sacrifice at the altar in the Temple and you suddenly remember that someone has something against you, leave your sacrifice there at the altar. Go and be reconciled to that person. Then come and offer your sacrifice to God" (Matthew 5:23–24).

My plunder long since lost, I purchased a new bucket and carried it sheepishly across campus one afternoon. Finding no one in the psychology building to confess to, I left the bucket in a broom closet with a note of explanation. Maybe a janitor read it. My conscience was clear.

After hearing of this stolen bucket episode in a lecture, one friend wrote his former employer to confess all the items he had stolen and to offer restitution. "We all probably have some plastic buckets in our lives," observed another associate.

GET REAL

Got any plastic buckets in your life? Is there anything you need to do to make restitution or reconcile with someone you've wronged? Why not do it today? You'll probably sleep better tonight.

Yes, Lord
Susie Shellenberger

It's easy to say, "Yes, Lord," when skies are blue and we can feel the warmth of the sun. . .when our days are filled with fun phone calls, friends, praise music, and His presence so near.

But it's a little more difficult to say, "Yes, Lord," to gray skies, rain that won't go away, and thunder that smells of fear. Can we say, "Yes, Lord," to being alone? To tears and unfulfilled dreams? "Yes, Lord" when the music has stopped, and His presence can't be felt?

Anyone can say yes to Jesus when the race has been won, health is good, and laughter is easy. But God isn't looking for surface-level commitment. He is searching for those who will respond, "Yes, Lord," when the breakup happens, the bad report from the doctor comes, and laughter seems foreign. We need to have the attitude of the temple assistants when they wrote these words in Psalm 43:5 (TLB): "O my soul, why be so gloomy and discouraged? Trust in God! I shall again praise him for his wondrous help; he will make me smile again, *for he is my God!*"

Ask your Father in heaven to help you be someone who can praise Him on the mountaintops but also recognize that He's still in control even in the valleys of your life. Pray that God will help you to be thankful no matter what the circumstances of your life may be. Ask Him to enable you to stay grounded, solidified in an unshakable relationship with Him as Lord.

GET REAL

Are you in a valley or on a mountaintop in your life right now? Are you prepared spiritually for what you may experience next?

Seed, Soil, and You
Nicole O'Dell

The way we respond to people and situations in our lives can make a huge difference. It's about the way we choose to react. It's especially true spiritually.

Jesus used parables—stories—to teach life lessons. One time He used seeds and soil to illustrate the way people respond to the Bible. In biblical times farmers would plant seeds by walking through a field and tossing handfuls on the ground. This process is totally different from the way seeds are planted today, but it worked back then. Take a look at Luke 8:4–8:

> One day Jesus told a story in the form of a parable to a large crowd that had gathered from many towns to hear him: "A farmer went out to plant his seed. As he scattered it across his field, some seed fell on a footpath, where it was stepped on, and the birds ate it. Other seed fell among rocks. It began to grow, but the plant soon wilted and died for lack of moisture. Other seed fell among thorns that grew up with it and choked out the tender plants. Still other seed fell on fertile soil. This seed grew and produced a crop that was a hundred times as much as had been planted!"

When you read or hear God's Word, what type of soil best represents the way that you respond? Maybe you react differently depending on what message God is communicating to you. Our goal should be to respond like good soil as much as possible.

GET REAL

What is God specifically trying to teach you right now in your life? Ask God for help to change the way you're responding.

The Power of Love
Steve Russo

Babe Ruth was a baseball idol for many years. During one of the last games he ever played, he dropped the ball several times and struck out. Meanwhile, the opposing team scored five runs in just one inning. Leaving the game, the Babe hung his head and slowly walked off the field. He was greeted with a storm of boos by the crowd and angry people shaking their fists at him.

Then it happened! A young boy vaulted over the railing, running straight for Babe Ruth. With tears flowing down his cheeks, the little boy threw his arms around the great athlete. Babe Ruth reached down, gently picked him up, and hugged him. Then he took hold of the little boy's hand, and the two slowly walked toward the dugout.

Suddenly the booing stopped. Silence swept over the entire stadium. Then the crowd broke into huge, thunderous applause. Were they cheering Babe Ruth, whom they'd ridiculed only a moment before. . .or the little boy? Or were they simply caught up in the power of love?

Love has an amazing power. It can soothe a wounded spirit or heal a broken heart. Everyone needs to love and be loved. Jesus said, "Love your neighbor as yourself" (Mark 12:31). This can happen only when we love God and experience the power of His love in our lives.

Imagine how different our world would be if everyone experienced the power of God's love. Think about a high school campus caught up in the power of love. It starts with you and me.

GET REAL

Whose life is being changed by the power of Jesus' love overflowing in your life?

Un-favorite People
Melanie Stiles

It's easy to pray for my friends and family. But I also have a set of what I call "un-favorite" people who are tougher to pray for. These are the people I'm stuck with, such as certain teachers, friends of friends who are in my outer circle of acquaintances, and even some relatives. Are there any un-favorites in your life?

I have a boss at work who is one of my "un-favorites." I need the job, and the actual work isn't a problem. It's his attitude. His language borders on rude, and his voice carries a disrespectful tone most of the time.

I know we're all God's special creations, but this guy made praying tough. I finally realized that it was up to me to change *my* attitude if I wanted to keep the job. I focused on Romans 12:14: "Bless those who persecute you. Don't curse them; pray that God will bless them."

I decided to give it a try. It wasn't easy at first asking God to bless someone I was irritated with most of the time. But after a while, I noticed that he didn't grate on my nerves as much. I had expectations that God would change my boss's attitude. Did it happen? Nope. But I decided to keep praying anyway. I'm thankful that praying for my boss has helped to change my own attitude.

Do you need an adjustment in your attitude toward un-favorite people in your life?

GET REAL

Ask God to help you start praying for the difficult people in your life. Pray that He will bless them and change your attitude.

Talking about Me

Ramona Richards

We've all lost patience with people who are so stuck on themselves that every word out of their mouths is about them. What *they* did, where *they* went, who *they* know, how *they* won. By the end of the conversation, you're ready to do just about anything to get away from them.

But aren't we all a little bit like that? When we've done something good, aced a test, had a good tryout, been chosen for a part in the play, we're ready to brag a little.

There's nothing wrong with a little boasting and celebrating with good friends. But when the boasting doesn't stop, demanding that you be the center of attention all the time, then you have a problem. That's when it's not about what you've accomplished—it's about you.

But the truth is, it's *not* about me or you. Ever.

God's Word warns us against being self-centered. "How do you know what your life will be like tomorrow? Your life is like the morning fog—it's here a little while, then it's gone. What you ought to say is, 'If the Lord wants us to, we will live and do this or that.' Otherwise you are boasting about your own plans, and all such boasting is evil" (James 4:14–16).

Keep in mind that everything we have is a gift from God. Whatever we've achieved has happened because of what God has given us in the first place. So. . .

It's really all about Him.

GET REAL

Take some time by yourself today to thank God for what He has done in and through you. Make this practice a part of each day.

When You Least Expect It

Dale Robert Hicks

Neal and Gus became friends in kindergarten and were friends until high school graduation. Neal brought Gus to church and to youth group activities. The more he tried to talk about Jesus, the more Gus remained committed to being an atheist. One day, in his second semester at college, Gus called Neal. He told him that he wanted him to come to his baptism, because Neal had been the one to talk to him about Jesus all those years ago, and now he knew what Neal had been talking about.

The truth is, to Gus it never seemed like the time was right—and Neal didn't want to keep beating his head against the wall. Neal kept inviting and sharing when he could. No one was more surprised by that phone call than Neal.

Talking to others about Jesus isn't always easy. Then you read a verse like 2 Timothy 4:2: "Preach the word of God. Be prepared, whether the time is favorable or not. Patiently correct, rebuke, and encourage your people with good teaching." You think to yourself, *It's hard, it's scary, and it didn't work the last time.* Sometimes, seeing someone respond to Jesus takes years. But it's worth the wait. Don't give up.

GET REAL

When you talk to people about Jesus, a lot can happen, so you need to be prepared and patient. It may take them a long time to hear what you say, maybe even years. Ask God whom He wants you to talk to about Jesus today.

Being Selective
Mike Thune

In today's world we are presented with a huge buffet of options from which to choose. We can make choices concerning just about everything—which cell phone plan to purchase, which car to drive, which movie to go see this weekend, and so on. In many ways, having such a wide variety of options is pretty awesome. But our culture often tells us that we should respect and even celebrate *all* choices, including lifestyle and religious choices, and that we should consider them equal. Many of you are headed for college or may be taking college courses already. Some of your professors may try to convince you that you can choose to believe whatever you want and that no belief is true or false, or is any better than any other belief. They also may tell you that you shouldn't judge someone else's beliefs to be inferior to yours.

While scripture teaches that all *people* are created equally and are made in the image of God, it does not teach that all *ideas* or *beliefs* are equal. On the contrary, scripture tells us that some ideas are good, true, and worthy of acceptance, and that other ideas are bad, false, and worthy of rejection. First Thessalonians 5:21 says to "test everything that is said. Hold on to what is good." In other words, we need to be selective, using the Bible as a filter. Not every idea out there is true, and all ideas have consequences.

GET REAL

Do you find it easier to accept everything and "go along to get along"? How can you challenge yourself this week to pursue and hold fast to what is good?

The Impossible Throw
Nathan Finfrock

Have you ever thought of making the impossible possible? Think about it for a minute. Did the Wright brothers have doubts as they stared into the sky, dreaming of their first flight? What does Bear Grylls think as he begins his climb down the face of a two-hundred-foot cliff? One time as I stared at a giant rat from sixty feet away, I had thoughts like theirs (though my attempt wasn't nearly so impressive, of course). My friend had just handed me a rock and said, "I bet you can't hit that thing from here." Yes, it was an impossible throw, but I believed I could do it! I threw the rock, and as it left my hand, I knew it would find its target. Sure enough, the rock struck the rat square in the head. My friend and I stood in amazement at the feat I had just achieved.

Why do we believe we are unable to break out of the limitations other people set? Why do we refuse to believe in the miraculous? "I can do all things through Christ who strengthens me" (Philippians 4:13 NKJV). *All* things.

GET REAL

What dreams do you have that other people, or even your own mind, say are unattainable? Will you believe you can do all things through Christ, or will you live with imaginary boundaries of what is possible? Take the first step toward reaching an impossible goal today. Remember, with God there are no limits!

Greatest Sports Photo

Rich Thune

Sports photography has captured amazing moments of the thrill of victory *and* the agony of defeat. If you were given the task of selecting the best picture from among the outstanding photo ops of the twentieth century, which one would you choose? The picture of Michael Jordan making the winning shot in the NBA finals? Or would you pick a great moment in a Super Bowl, a World Series game, or a boxing match?

The editors of *Sports Illustrated* magazine set about to do just that. But their choice for the number-one sports picture of the twentieth century was none of the above. The winning shot was—get this—a football locker room minutes before a big game. "Huh?" you say. "What's the big deal about that?"

The winning picture didn't capture an awesome play, but the quiet and motionless focus of a football team, each player shining a flashlight into his soul and silently asking himself, "Do I have what it takes to win? Am I adequate for the job before me?" The writer of 2 Corinthians 3:5 answers these questions for us: "It is not that we think we are qualified to do anything on our own. Our qualification comes from God." Our only power and success come from the Lord.

GET REAL

Athletes or not, we all should be able to relate to that locker room moment of truth. We all face challenges that stretch us to the limit and remind us of our inadequacy. To whom do you turn for strength in tough situations?

Nobody Understands
Lesha Campbell

Nobody understands me—I mean *nobody*!

Ever heard these words. . .said these words. . .truly meant these words? I certainly have.

Life gets so hard so often that it seems it would be easier to give in to all the pressures and just forget it. Too much temptation to be with the wrong people, say the wrong words, be in the wrong place, take drugs or drink, have sex, or just do what I want without any consequences to my thoughts or actions. Leave the character building to someone else—someone stronger than me. After all, nobody understands how hard it is to be good and do the right thing in today's world. Things are so much harder now than they've ever been.

It's very difficult to live a life that honors God when so many seem to be happy doing just the opposite. Yes, there are times when "nobody understands" you.

But there's hope in the One who created us just the way we are—misunderstood by everybody, ourselves included. Check out Hebrews 4:14–15: "Since we have a great High Priest who has entered heaven, Jesus the Son of God, let us hold firmly to what we believe. This High Priest of ours understands our weaknesses, for he faced all of the same testings we do, yet he did not sin."

Jesus totally understands you—more than anyone else ever will.

GET REAL

You can talk with God about anything you are dealing with in your life. Take some time today to unload what's on your heart and mind that you haven't been able to share with anyone else.

Fire! Everybody Get Out!

Carson Pue

I fell asleep in class once with my elbows propped on my desk and my head resting in my hands. Not just "eyes closed, nodding off"—I was actually dreaming. My dream was of being in our house with a fire raging up the stairwell. Wakened by the urgency of this powerful dream, I stood up, shouting in class, "Fire! Fire! Everyone get out of the house!"

When I saw the teacher and everyone in the class staring at me, I was so embarrassed I wanted to melt. The teacher, noticing the terror in my eyes, calmly told me that everything was going to be all right; then she sent me to see the counselor to get "checked out." When I told him that I had been dreaming, he told me to get more sleep at night and to return to class.

As I walked down the beige-painted hallway back to the classroom, I felt I could not possibly show my face there again. I waited before turning the doorknob, and when I opened it—sure enough—the entire class was staring. I felt like such a nerd. Then the teacher gave me a big smile, and when I smiled back, guess what happened? The entire class burst out laughing, and several kids told me that was the funniest thing ever. They loved it, and for that day I was the coolest kid in class.

Had Jesus been in the class, would He have laughed? I think so. "The One who sits on his throne in heaven laughs" (Psalm 2:4 NIrV).

GET REAL

Find something to laugh about every day—even if you're by yourself.

Human and Divine

Ron Merrell

Think about Jesus for a minute. What comes to mind when you think about Him? Nice guy? Good teacher? Miracle worker? Powerful God? Friend? King?

Jesus' closest friend and disciple, John, had two powerful moments with Him: one focusing on His humanity, the other on His divinity. Both are important for us to get the full picture of who Jesus really is.

One scene has John leaned back against Jesus' chest after a meal. Imagine that! Jesus desired that His friends be so close to Him they could hear His heart beat! That's the type of guy Jesus was. If He walked into a room, He would be the first to pat people on the back, give hugs, or sit down and listen with a caring ear.

But fast-forward to the book of Revelation, and you find John seeing an overwhelming vision of his friend Jesus in all His divine glory! "His head and his hair were white like wool, as white as snow. And his eyes were like flames of fire. His feet were like polished bronze refined in a furnace, and his voice thundered like mighty ocean waves. He held seven stars in his right hand, and a sharp two-edged sword came from his mouth. And his face was like the sun in all its brilliance" (1:14–16). This view of Jesus puts John on his face before Him, trembling with fear.

GET REAL

Jesus is an approachable, close friend and the only true God of the universe. Does knowing this change the way you think about yourself and your lifestyle? What do you need to do differently?

Are You a Turn-off?

Chris Haidet

One of my favorite events of the year is watching the Super Bowl. The two best football teams square off against each other for the championship trophy. But it's more than just the game. I've grown to love the commercials in between. They're funny, creative, and, most of all, memorable. A good commercial makes you remember what's being advertised. I remember the great commercials for milk. . .*milk* of all things. They would show someone pounding down a peanut butter shortcake, all the while panicking because they have no milk. Good commercials make you long for the product and in some cases thirst for it.

But have you ever seen a bad one, the kind of commercial that makes you talk back to the TV in frustration as you look for the remote to turn it off? A commercial that actually makes you dislike or even hate the product?

The Bible says, "So whether you eat or drink, or whatever you do, do it all for the glory of God" (1 Corinthians 10:31). Remember, we are walking, talking commercials for God. Wherever we go, we are called to represent, to live a life that shows people the love of Christ. When people see you, do they see Jesus? Do your actions make people thirst for His love, or do they turn people off?

GET REAL

Think about your various groups of friends. Do you act differently with some than others? Would they think you are a good or bad commercial? Ask God to make you a reflection of Him and to give you courage to represent His love to others.

Sharing the Love
Ramona Richards

Frequently we see people show love to one another—and not just in a romantic way. For example, we see it in how people respond to local, national, and world crises. When our neighbors' house burns, we're there with blankets and food. When a flood wipes out a town, we show up to scrape off the mud and tear out drywall. When an earthquake destroys most of a country, people turn out from different parts of the globe to help clean up and rebuild.

Love one another. The command appears repeatedly in the Bible. "This is the message you have heard from the beginning: We should love one another" (1 John 3:11). This great commandment never changes. It's the kind of love that lives deep within us and shows up in what we do and say.

We use words as well as actions to show our love, offering encouragement and hope along with hot meals. We whisper support with our hugs, and sing songs of hope when words fail us.

We also love when life is normal, communicating our love in simple things like hanging out together just to have fun or helping a friend with a homework assignment.

Your corner of the world—at home, at school, and in your community—needs a touch of God's love. If you're a child of His, you have the privilege and responsibility to share it.

GET REAL

Do you know someone who needs to experience God's love through you today? Reach out to them and let them know someone cares.

Monsters

Doug Jones

Monsters. Ghost stories. Scary movies. All things we talk about around a campfire. You know why this is so much fun for us? Because deep down we know they aren't real and that we are completely safe. It has always been easy for me to portray creepy monsters on film, because at the end of the day, I get to unzip the rubber suit or wash off the makeup.

But what about those of us with real monsters in our lives? You won't find these people telling scary stories around the campfire, because they are living in fear of the monsters they must battle every day. Like the little girl in *Pan's Labyrinth*. You think she should be afraid of my Faun or Pale Man characters in the movie, but the real monster is her abusive, self-absorbed stepfather.

If this sounds familiar to you, here is the good news: Deuteronomy 28:7 (NIV) says, "The LORD will grant that the enemies who rise up against you will be defeated before you. They will come at you from one direction but flee from you in seven."

God has your back. "You, LORD, will keep the needy safe and will protect us forever from the wicked" (Psalm 12:7 NIV).

GET REAL

When one of your friends yells, "Boo!" and scares a scream out of you, take a minute after you've laughed to thank Jesus for making your world truly safe and monster-free.

Grow Up
Nicole O'Dell

Do you have a baby brother or sister? If so, then you know babies need a lot of care and attention. Someone has to carry them around, feed them, dress them, change their diapers—and give them hugs. As they grow up, things change gradually. They begin to crawl, then walk. Their food intake changes from milk to more solid food—but they still need hugs.

Growing spiritually involves a similar experience. Peter, an early Jesus follower, compares the two. "Like newborn babies, you must crave pure spiritual milk so that you will grow into a full experience of salvation. Cry out for this nourishment, now that you have had a taste of the Lord's kindness" (1 Peter 2:2–3).

People who have just surrendered their lives to Jesus, or those who haven't grown spiritually, are like newborns. They're fed from the milk—or basics—of scripture and should begin to have a desire to grow. The need for milk should be a sign that they are wanting more nourishment. They see their need for more of God's Word to grow in their relationship with Jesus. All of us start out as spiritual babies, but God never meant for us to stay that way. He wants us to grow up.

GET REAL

Are you developing an ever-increasing desire for God's Word? What specifically are you doing each day to grow up spiritually? Look for a simple plan that will help you grow in your biblical knowledge consistently.

Out of the Zone
Brian Sumner

Everyone has a comfort zone. It's a place that's safe and secure because we know what to expect there. It's usually a space where we're able to lie low, hide away, and stay under the radar. It's easy, comfortable. . .and stagnant, because we don't grow staying there.

God's best for us involves stepping out of the zone to a place that's not necessarily known or comfortable. The Bible relates several stories of people God used in awesome ways once they stepped out of the zone. For example, a young woman named Esther stood up to King Xerxes when he was being duped into wiping out the Jews.

She knew she would be risking her life if she approached the king without being summoned, so she told her cousin Mordecai, "Go and gather together all the Jews of Susa and fast for me. Do not eat or drink for three days, night or day. My maids and I will do the same. And then, though it is against the law, I will go in to see the king. If I must die, I must die" (Esther 4:16). She stepped out of the zone for the sake of others, and her actions saved a huge number of lives.

God also wants us to be willing to step out of our comfort zones so we can be used greatly by Him.

GET REAL

Are you willing to step out and be uncomfortable for the sake of those around you and God's kingdom? It's scary, but God doesn't ask you to go it alone. Ask Him to help you start today.

God Cares about the Details

Steve Russo

When God created the universe, His attention to detail was amazing. For example, think of the universe as an energy-efficient engine. The more efficient a system, the less energy that is lost within that system. A diesel engine has a mechanical efficiency rating of 40% loss, steam engines 12%, the human body just 1%, and the universe only 0.00000001%. Unbelievable! Our Creator's attention to detail shows up all around us.

Did you know that God numbered the hairs on each of our heads? Check out Matthew 10:29–31: "What is the price of two sparrows—one copper coin? But not a single sparrow can fall to the ground without your Father knowing it. And the very hairs on your head are all numbered. So don't be afraid; you are more valuable to God than a whole flock of sparrows."

At first you may be thinking, *Doesn't God have anything better to do than count the hairs on my head?* Or *I wonder if God knows how many hairs I lost in the shower this morning.*

Having our hairs numbered speaks volumes about how much God cares about us. Nothing escapes His attention. He is aware of everything we are experiencing, and He wants us to trust Him with the tough stuff of life.

We are so valuable that God sent His only Son to die for us on a cross so that we could have a right relationship with Him.

GET REAL

Because you are so valuable to God, you don't have to be afraid of any difficulties. What's going on in your life? Talk with God about it. He understands and wants to help you.

Heartache
Steve Russo

Early one morning my dad knocked on my bedroom door, came into my room, and sat down on the edge of my bed. "Son, I want you to know your mother and I are getting a divorce—we don't love each other anymore," he said. I was in shock. Instantly my stomach began to ache—it felt like it was tied in knots. My brother, sister, and I knew my parents had been fighting a lot, but we never thought it would end in divorce. I asked Dad if it was something my brother, sister, and I had done that caused them to split up. But he reassured me that it had nothing to do with us and everything to do with them. Not long after that my grandfather died—I'd never experienced this much heartache before. I didn't know who to turn to or what to do to make the pain go away. And I was angry with God. Why was He allowing all this stuff to happen to me?

Even though we may not understand why our parents split up or why someone we thought was our best friend dumped us, we can be sure of one thing—God will never let us down. He promises to always be there for us—no matter what happens. "I will never fail you. I will never abandon you" (Hebrews 13:5).

GET REAL

Nothing that occurs in your life takes God by surprise. He has a purpose for everything that happens. When your heart aches, lean on Him. Don't ask, "Why?" Ask, "What next?"

Discovering You

Steve Russo

Who are you? Not who do others think you are—but who is the real you? Who you are is determined by much more than what you have, what you do, or what you achieve. Your name, where you live, your school, or what you like doing are things about you. But you still haven't told me who you really are.

When you discover the real you, the way you think about life radically changes. Uncovering your identity makes you feel secure, important, and accepted. Then you can be the same person wherever you are—at home, at school—and whatever you're doing. Lots of people don't know how to find their identity, and even when they do, they don't want to believe it. They're afraid they have to be someone they don't want to be.

You become complete as a person and have meaning in your life when you realize that your true identity is found through a relationship with God. This happens when you decide to live your life for and like Jesus.

Only in Jesus can we find out who we really are. He's the One who put us together molecule by molecule. Check this out: "You made all the delicate, inner parts of my body and knit me together in my mother's womb. Thank you for making me so wonderfully complex! Your workmanship is marvelous—how well I know it" (Psalm 139:13–14).

This is huge! You and I are unique creations of God.

GET REAL

Since we are unique creations of God, we shouldn't treat ourselves or others with disrespect. Treat yourself and others with respect in what you say and do.

Why Doesn't God Answer My Prayers?

Steve Russo

After my Saturday-morning talk at a high school winter camp, a girl wanted to talk.

"I'm so mad at God," she said.

"Why?" I replied.

"Because He doesn't answer prayer anymore."

"When did He stop?" I asked.

"Last week I had a math test and asked God for help. I even gave Him options: having me sit beside the smartest person in class so I could see their answers or having the teacher give me the answer sheet when she passed out the tests. Or supernaturally implanting the answers into my brain. And He didn't do any of these things."

"I just have one question for you," I said. "Did you study for the test?"

"No," she responded, "but that has nothing to do with God not answering my prayers!"

Prayer is so misunderstood and underused. Sometimes we feel like God isn't even listening or answering our prayers.

There are several reasons God may not be answering our prayers. Maybe we don't really have a relationship with Him. Or maybe we have unconfessed sin in our lives. Or maybe it's not God's will—not in His plan and purpose for us.

It also might be that it's not God's time yet to answer a prayer. Check out David's words in Psalm 27:14: "Wait patiently for the LORD. Be brave and courageous. Yes, wait patiently for the LORD." Waiting is never easy, but it's always worth it.

GET REAL

Think about a recent unanswered prayer. Which reason fits your situation? What should you do about it?

Measuring a Year

Steve Russo

There are 525,600 minutes in a year. How do you measure a year? By the classes you're taking at school? The number of cheeseburgers or pizzas you've eaten? Parties? Dates? The amount of bank and bling you've built up? How do you evaluate a year of your life?

Time is the most valuable thing we possess. We've all been given an equal amount of minutes per year. What you accomplish in the next twelve months is up to you. So how will you spend your time? It's all about choices. How you choose to live today will determine how you live tomorrow.

As we think about measuring a year, there are two things to remember: the short amount of time we've been given in this life and the way that God measures time. Moses gives us awesome advice in Psalm 90:12: "Teach us to realize the brevity of life, so that we may grow in wisdom."

Every minute counts. Step out of your comfort zone and take a risk. Do it God's way, and make sure He gets the credit—then we know the results will be lasting!

We should be investing our energy in things that have eternal value. We don't have to look very far to find situations where God could use us to make a difference.

GET REAL

Take some time today to think about your future on this planet—however long that might be—and ask yourself, "What do I want to see happen in and through my life next year? Before I die? What small step can I take today toward achieving these goals?"

Campbell, Lesha
Days 5, 37, 72, 106, 140, 170, 206, 241, 301, 353

Lesha Campbell loves chocolate chip cookie dough, cake batter, and chips and salsa. She's a professional ventriloquist (for real) and has entertained audiences of over fifteen thousand—with puppets. Weird, huh? Lesha is also a certified MAC head! She even beat herself once in a talent show. . . . Hmmm. Visit her website at www.lesha.org.

Dunn, Patrick
Days 8, 27, 35, 54, 101

Patrick Dunn is a TV/radio producer at Focus on the Family, where he says he talks too much and confuses everyone. He writes the popular monthly column "The Way Guys See It" in SUSIE Magazine. Patrick loves football, likes cereal at any meal, and has the mysterious ability to communicate with squirrels. He lives in Colorado Springs with his wife, Sally, and son, Brendon.

Finfrock, Nathan
Days 64, 135, 198, 218, 234, 269, 293, 313, 333, 351

Nathan Finfrock is a professional recording artist and creative arts director. He likes training in mixed martial arts and watching a good UFC fight. His favorite things to do are traveling, scuba diving, and blowing up stuff. Check out www.nathanfinfrock.com.

Haidet, Chris
Days 7, 28, 44, 53, 65, 83, 94, 111, 121, 142, 156, 169, 189, 201, 223, 229, 246, 256, 276, 291, 305, 317, 323, 338, 356

Chris Haidet is an event producer, concert promoter, and wannabe pro bowler. His three favorite places to be are in an airplane traveling to a new destination, with his family at Disneyland, or in the front row of a metal concert, getting his ears melted.

Hicks, Dale Robert
Days 18, 29, 48, 62, 73, 85, 93, 105, 129, 146, 174, 191, 216, 232, 244, 253, 281, 302, 326, 349

Dale Robert Hicks is a teacher who makes his students laugh as much as they learn. He is a gamer who has mastered all the major game platforms but mostly plays the PS3. He is a fan of the Denver Broncos. His favorite candy bar is a Milky Way.

Jones, Doug
Days 22, 113, 164, 254, 358
Doug Jones is the actor who plays the heroic Silver Surfer in the Fantastic Four sequel; Abe Sapien in Hellboy and Hellboy II; the Faun, Pan, and the Pale Man in Pan's Labyrinth; Billy the Zombie in Hocus Pocus; and many more characters. He likes candy bars and puppies. Visit his website at www.thedougjonesexperience.com.

Klehn, Tracy
Days 76, 132, 193, 202, 209, 224, 271, 289, 297, 316
Tracy Klehn has been known to break out into full "dance party" mode in the most unusual of circumstances (while shopping, at the beach, at sporting events. . .). She has been an aerobics instructor for about a century, and she's also the "friendship expert" (seriously. . .she wrote the book!). Visit www.TracyKlehn.com.

Merrell, Ron
Days 6, 30, 43, 49, 67, 96, 115, 144, 165, 178, 184, 204, 222, 237, 261, 277, 292, 310, 327, 355
Ron Merrell is a storyteller and kinda-sorta standup comedian. He'd be happy if he could bodysurf, make people laugh, and get Starbucks every day. One time he accidently shoved his cat into the little pocket for pens on the front of his backpack. He'd be glad to tell you the story. Check out www.ronmerrell.com.

O'Dell, Nicole
Days 17, 24, 34, 47, 89, 92, 130, 196, 207, 228, 242, 252, 264, 274, 284, 300, 318, 335, 345, 359
Nicole O'Dell is the author of the popular Scenarios Interactive Fiction Series for Girls, a speaker to teens and parents, and the host of Teen Talk Radio. She has a passion for teenagers and is a mom of six—including triplets. Visit www.nicoleodell.com for more info. It's all about choices!

Poe, Chuck
Days 42, 81, 157, 233, 341
Chuck Poe is a student minister in the great state of Kentucky. His hobbies include hunting, fishing, and golf (which he is terrible at). He would love to play guitar, but he has a hard enough time playing an iPod.

Pue, Brenda

Days 39, 52, 77, 119, 149, 192, 212, 262, 287, 321

Brenda Pue loves hanging out with people, enjoys cooking, and is a licensed sailor. If Brenda can't find a word to describe something, she makes one up. She has only one word for chocolate. . .though many sumptuous adjectives. She loves dogs, cats, babies, and teenagers—not necessarily in that order! To learn more, go to www.arrowleadership.org.

Pue, Carson

Days 63, 110, 150, 182, 217, 238, 268, 303, 328, 354

Carson Pue is a party in a body. He travels the world, developing new potential, exploring possibilities, and sharing wisdom with leaders. Sailing on the Pacific Ocean restores him. His iTunes playlist is eclectic—from Neil Young, opera, U2, and '60s rock up to the latest indie recordings of screamo bands. Head to www.arrowleadership.org to learn more about Carson.

Ray, Danny

Days 23, 120, 172, 188, 203, 249, 267, 286, 312, 337

Danny Ray travels around the country and the world, sharing God's truth through illusions. He loves running, mountain biking, his superfun family, and making chocolate chip cookies disappear (which actually isn't an illusion). To see some of Danny's mind-boggling illusions, check out dannyray.tv.

Richards, Ramona

Days 10, 16, 25, 33, 45, 57, 68, 80, 95, 104, 114, 125, 136, 139, 173, 187, 199, 213, 221, 227, 236, 248, 258, 272, 288, 298, 311, 322, 332, 339, 348, 357

Ramona Richards, an award-winning writer, editor, and speaker, is the author of eight books, including Barbour's *Secrets of Confidence*. A frequent contributor to devotional collections, she is also the author of *A Moment with God for Single Parents*. Her latest novel, *House of Secrets* (April 2011), is available from Steeple Hill. An avid live music fan, Ramona loves her adopted hometown of Nashville, Tennessee.

Russo, Kati

Days 58, 127, 155, 307, 331

Kati Russo likes having girls' nights with her sister and her friends. She loves BBQ chicken pizza and chocolate; acting in plays; going to Los Angeles Lakers games; attending concerts; playing with her cat, Indy; and traveling. She hopes to visit Europe one day to meet her family in Italy. Visit her at www.utalkradio.com.

Russo, Steve

Days 1, 2, 3, 4, 15, 20, 26, 31, 36, 41, 46, 51, 55, 56, 61, 66, 69, 71, 78, 82, 87, 91, 97, 103, 107, 109, 112, 117, 123, 124, 128, 133, 137, 138, 143, 148, 151, 153, 158, 160, 161, 163, 168, 171, 176, 179, 180, 185, 186, 190, 195, 200, 205, 210, 215, 220, 225, 226, 230, 235, 240, 245, 250, 255, 260, 265, 270, 275, 278, 280, 285, 290, 294, 299, 304, 308, 309, 314, 319, 324, 325, 329, 334, 340, 346, 361, 362, 363, 364, 365
Steve Russo is a professional drummer, author, and speaker. He loves Italian food, Moose Tracks ice cream, and the Los Angeles Lakers. His favorite place to visit is Italy, but he also likes to hang out at the beach in northern California. Don't tell anyone—he was a tap dancer in elementary school.

Shellenberger, Susie

Days 12, 38, 90, 99, 122, 145, 183, 214, 239, 266, 279, 296, 330, 344
Susie Shellenberger loves playing Frisbee with her schnauzer, Obie. She has written forty-nine books, loves burnt hot dogs, and sometimes eats Honeycomb cereal for dinner. She loves all bright colors and is in awe of Skype. Visit her at www.susiemag.com.

Stiles, Melanie

Days 11, 21, 32, 40, 50, 60, 70, 79, 88, 98, 108, 116, 126, 134, 141, 152, 159, 167, 175, 181, 194, 208, 219, 231, 243, 251, 259, 263, 273, 283, 295, 306, 315, 320, 336, 347
Melanie Stiles has contributed nonfiction articles, anthology works, poetry, devotionals, and Christian development training to various publications and organizations. As an AACC Master Life Coach, Melanie uses her training and personal background to share life journeys with others through speaking and the written word. Learn more about Melanie at www.MelanieStiles.com.

Sumner, Brian

Days 75, 131, 177, 197, 257, 282, 360
Brian Sumner is a professional skateboarder hailing from the land of beans on toast, fish and chips, and a band with like-minded haircuts, the Beatles. Brian lives in Huntington Beach, California, where he continues to skate, loves to live, and has a fascination with knuckle balls. Visit him at www.briansumner.net.

Thune, Mike

Days 9, 102, 154, 247, 350
Mike Thune teaches philosophy in the Chicago area. In his spare time, he likes to hang out with his wife and two cats, fly small airplanes, and read books. Since his youth, he has been a Cubs fan—one of the greatest personal tests of patience and endurance.

Thune, Rich
Days 19, 84, 162, 211, 352

Rich Thune is a high school teacher in Southern California. He likes football, basketball, and baseball. He's never met an ice cream flavor he didn't like. Rich also likes (and loves) teenagers and considers himself lucky to be a part of their lives.

Wright, Rusty
Days 13, 59, 74, 86, 100, 118, 147, 166, 343

Rusty Wright is an award-winning author, lecturer, and syndicated columnist who has spoken on six continents to university students, professors, executives, diplomats, and professional athletes. He has appeared on TV talk shows in cities around the world and trains professionals in effective communication. Rusty's material has been used by mainstream newspapers across the United States and in any of fourteen languages by over five hundred websites. He holds a Bachelor of Science (psychology) degree from Duke University and a Master of Theology degree from Oxford University. For more information, go to www.RustyWright.com.

Zoro
Days 14, 342

Zoro is a world-renowned drummer, having toured with Lenny Kravitz, Bobby Brown, Frankie Valli, and scores more. He's a passionate ambassador for Christ and established Zoro International Ministries. His new global ministry helps young adults understand their God-given gifts, achieve success, and fulfill their divine assignments on earth. Curious? Head to www.zoroministries.org.

CONTACT INFORMAITION

Steve Russo
Real Answers
PO Box 1549
Ontario, California 91762

Phone: 909.466.7060
Fax: 909.466.7056
Text: GoLive to 411247

www.realanswers.com
www.steverusso.com
www.utalkradio.com
http://twitter.com/Steverusso1
http://www.facebook.com/steverussodrummer
http://www.myspace.com/steverusso1
http://www.youtube.com/steverussodrummer